COTTAGE
WATER
SYSTEMS

UPDATED EDITION

An Out-of-the-City Guide to Pumps, Plumbing,
Water Purification, and Privies

COTTAGE WATER SYSTEMS

AN OUT-OF-THE-CITY GUIDE TO PUMPS, PLUMBING, WATER PURIFICATION, AND PRIVIES

BY MAX BURNS

Cottage Life BOOKS

TORONTO, CANADA

The information in this book is accurate to the best of our knowledge. However, both nature and the tools and toys of humanity can present serious hazards to those who choose to confront or make use of either. So remember to mix in a healthy dose of common sense and good judgement when acting on any of the advice contained herein, when working with electricity near water, or when dealing with any of the many facets of cottage life in general. That way, chances are better the cottage will remain a place of fond memories – which is, after all, what it's all about.

© Copyright 1993, 1999 by Max Burns

Third printing
This edition updated 1999.

Cataloguing in Publication Data

Burns, Max, 1948–
Cottage water systems

Includes index.
ISBN 0-9696922-0-X

1. Water-supply, Rural.   2. Water – Purification.
3. Plumbing.   I. Title.

TD927.B87 1993   628'.7   C93-094407-0

Edited by Ann Vanderhoof
Design by Steve Manley, Overleaf Design Ltd.
Illustrations by Michael Esk
Additional illustrations by Patrick Corrigan

Printed and bound in Canada by
D. W. Friesen & Sons Ltd., Altona, Manitoba

Published by
Cottage Life Books
54 St. Patrick Street
Toronto, Ontario, Canada
M5T 1V1

Cottage Life Inc.
Box 1338
Ellicott Station
Buffalo, N.Y. U.S.A.
14205

Trade distribution by
Firefly Books
250 Sparks Avenue
Willowdale, Ontario, Canada
M2H 2S4
and
Firefly Books (U.S.)
Box 1338
Ellicott Station
Buffalo, N.Y. U.S.A.
14205

To Ann Vanderhoof,
for her unending encouragement and enthusiasm

CONTENTS

ILLUSTRATIONS

The reference material for illustrations in this book was drawn from brochures, products, and information bulletins provided by a number of companies, associations, and government sources in both Canada and the U.S. Thanks to Beatty Pumps, Bio-Let, Canada Cement LaFarge Ltd., Dow Chemical, Environment Ontario, F.E. Myers Company, Goulds Pumps Inc., GSW Pump Company, GSW Water Products Company, Heat-Line Corp., Jacuzzi, Philmac Valves and Fittings Inc., Polar Bear Water Distillers Mfg. Co. Ltd., Pumps & Softeners Limited, Research Products/Blankenship of Canada Ltd., Rintoul's Hand Pumps, Sun-Mar Corporation, Water Quality Association, Waterline Products Co. Ltd., Wedco.

OVERVIEW

The cottage, the world, and this book

THE PRACTICE OF TROOPING OFF TO THE cottage doesn't go back generations in my family, as it does in some cottage dynasties I know. My folks started making the trek about the time Dad bought his '49 Ford. Initially, it was to Treasure Island on the shores of Lake Ontario near Kingston. By the time Dad bought a '56 Ford, we'd moved westward and were now cottaging on the Bruce Peninsula, Lake Huron side. About two years after he traded the '56 in on a '58 Ford, we'd moved to Montreal, spending summers by Lake St. Louis or down in the Eastern Townships. By '65, we were back in Ontario but, despite his having bought another new Ford, Dad's interest in cottaging waned. Looking back now, I think he was more of a Ford man than a cottager. I was hooked, however, and I now live full-time in cottage country. You couldn't drag me away, even with a new Ford.

Historically, this thing we call a cottage, cabin, camp, or chalet has been a vacation home, at one time nothing more than a rustic building to keep most (or at least some) of the rain and bugs away whenever we weren't frolicking outside. For many, this minimalist vision of the cottage remains. Yet for others, the cottage has slowly edged towards becoming a second home, complete with most of the conveniences of life back in the city. What binds these apparent opposites together is the object – outdoor fun. The cottage is permission to break out of one's role in life, if just for the weekend. It is a place where good relations with neighbours and families are not only still possible, but also encouraged. It is also the closest connection many of us have to Mother Nature.

THE ADVANTAGES OF DOING IT YOURSELF

The most obvious connection to nature is via the cottage water system. This system is whatever means we use to obtain water and whatever means we use to expel it (including the water that has been run through the human digestive system) after use. It includes all manner of conventional cottage connections such as a water pump to an intake line, and a toilet to a septic tank – as well as more traditional alternatives such as a rain barrel and an outhouse.

The cottage water system is a private system; we are the owner/operators, totally responsible for all its strengths and failings. It can be a serious pain when it ceases to function – because as the owner/operators, it's our job to fix it.

Granted, there's genuine pleasure to be derived from do-it-yourself projects, particularly at the cottage where part of the fun is in the fixing. Repairs, construction work, landscaping – nothing seems beyond the cottage handyperson equipped with a $10 tool box (tools included).

The other neat thing about doing it yourself is the control it affords. You're not waiting for a tradesperson who might be out windsurfing because the wind's up, instead of fixing your broken pump or pipe. (Can't understand this lackadaisical lifestyle cottage country seems to foster.) By doing it yourself, you get the work done to your schedule – running water, no waiting. And, of course, the money you save ends up in your new-boat fund instead of the plumber's.

Even if we don't do the work ourselves, it sure saves money to know why it's being done a certain way. (Or maybe why it shouldn't be done a certain way.) Because when the tradesperson does find time to visit, nine times out of 10 we're standing over the poor guy, paying out umpteen dollars an hour for the privilege of interrupting to ask dumb questions.

So *Cottage Water Systems* is not just a how-to book, it's also a "why?" book. It has always been my belief that given the reasons why, folks are more likely to do the job right than if they're simply told how to go about some esoteric task. Knowledge converts the drudgery of work into understanding. Understanding puts you in control, which is where you should be as the owner/operator of your own water and sewage system.

Books on basic plumbing abound (some are even worth reading), but plumbing as it pertains to cottaging has been largely overlooked. What makes cottage plumbing different from that serving other rural residences is that cottages are used on a part-time basis, they're sometimes more remote and on more rugged terrain, and cottagers are willing to entertain alternative approaches to water and waste management. System oddities are often viewed by cottagers not as hardships, but as part of the cottage experience. *Cottage Water Systems* emphasizes those components and processes that pertain *specifically* to cottages, giving them links to mainstream plumbing.

THE ENVIRONMENTAL ARGUMENT

The most important link, however, remains that direct connection to Mother Nature. Regrettably, it hasn't always been a good one. In the introduction to *Bungalows, Camps and Mountain Houses*, a book first published in 1908, author William T. Comstock wrote, "Often the lake or stream which has been the most attractive feature of a site has been rendered noxious by the drainage from the dwellings on its shore. Whereas, this matter, if properly considered at the start, could have been so handled as to maintain the original purity of the adjacent waters." Writing styles may have changed since 1908 but the facts haven't – the connection between cottage and nature can be good or bad.

While it is true that agriculture and industry are the principal villains in the degradation of cottage water resources, cottagers themselves are certainly not innocent bystanders. But can one faulty septic system really ruin an entire lake?

Although I don't normally stoop to advancing the theories of economists, one member of this profession did have a good idea. During the '60s, Alfred Kahn came up with a concept he called the tyranny of small decisions. This catchy phrase describes the cumulative effect of a series of small decisions. For example, adding "just" the overflow from my septic system after a long weekend admittedly won't seriously pollute a large body of water. But add to that the effect of similar contributions from my neighbours and gradually the water becomes unfit to swim in, let alone drink. As every little bit helps, so too can it hurt, another reason to know the "whys" of our actions.

As part of the research for this book, I contacted 48 states, 10 provinces, and several federal agencies for information pertaining to regulations governing private water and sewage systems. (Alaska and the Canadian territories were left off the mailing list because they don't have enough summer; Hawaii, because it doesn't have enough winter.) The response was overwhelming, to the point that I might even take back some of those disparaging remarks I've made on occasion regarding the work ethics of government bureaucrats. Or at least say thanks.

JURISDICTIONAL OVERLOAD

The common theme to this amassed collection of regulatory paperwork is diversity of approaches and policies. I have on file about 60 different ways of "doing it right". In some jurisdictions a cottager is darn-near free to follow the whims of conscience, while in others it's easier to get a divorce than to put up an outhouse. (In my jurisdiction, friend Dave was recently threatened with divorce if he didn't soon provide a suitable indoor replacement for the outdoor loo.)

Out from under this mound of jurisdictional divergence of opinion come the obligatory caveats. Do not purchase any specialized piece of plumbing equipment or make any alterations to the cottage water system without getting prior approval regarding use and installation, preferably in writing. It may be necessary to get this approval from several government agencies and levels of government, such as those responsible for the environment; natural resources; conservation; public health; navigation of waterways; the welfare of fish; building, plumbing, and electrical codes; and local bylaws.

Hard to believe that many people could be interested in your family's toilet etiquette, but sometimes that's what it takes to flush out potential polluters. And to make this ball of red tape even stickier, you may discover that what's legal back home isn't legal at the cottage, and vice versa. So be patient; most bureaucrats are helpful to those appreciative of their efforts. (Gee, that's the second nice thing I've said about government bureaucrats in one day.)

GO FOR THE BEST

Cottage Water Systems generally aims for the highest common denominator, although the reader should keep in mind that even this goal is often based on the *minimum* standards of the more progressive jurisdictions. Minimum standards always yield minimum acceptable results for that area. The financial cost of exceeding those minimums is often negligible, even from my sedentary wallet's point of view, so go for the best you can buy. Less expensive is no bargain if it doesn't do an effective job.

Speaking of which, buy only from knowledgeable sources that specialize in (insert your current need here). This greatly increases the odds of getting a successful solution to your problem. Membership in relevant trade associations can be an indication of professional competence, but it's definitely no guarantee. Sometimes affiliation with a recognized association merely provides an honourable shield for shysters to hide behind. So get references from people capable of judging the particular skills or services of the company or person involved. After many years of dealing with retailers and tradespeople, a few (but certainly not all) with ethics that would embarrass the devil, I have developed this simple rule for character judgments: Never deal with anyone who talks faster than you can think. It's a rule that only fails me when I ignore it.

Some of the things discussed in *Cottage Water Systems* may contravene regulations in your cottage's locale. Unfortunately, with so many variations in the laws, this is unavoidable. So again: Read, and then check with the relevant authorities before taking any action.

It is my belief that the cottage experience, this unspoken permit to relax and enjoy the company of nature and neighbours, is a thing to protect and preserve. The goal of *Cottage Water Systems* is to enhance that experience through sensible approaches to water-system design and management. The rewards are reduced maintenance, greater understanding, and the preservation of a small part of the earth that we can be proud to pass on to the next generation. Some folks have a fancy name for that small piece of the earth, but we just call ours "the cottage".

2 SOURCES OF COTTAGE WATER

How to tap into the available options

Wishful thinking:
Forget the storybook well: Regardless of type, all wells must be capped and sealed to keep everything but water and air out.

DEMAND FOR WATER IS USUALLY LOWER AT the cottage than at the typical city home, or even most rural residences. Cottages usually have fewer appliances to feed, lawns to water, and cars to wash. People even tend to wash less while at the cottage. Sure, showers are often replaced by a swim, but there's also a more relaxed attitude towards hygiene – cottage air just doesn't seem to stick to the skin the way city air does. And, of course, the fact that most of us aren't at the cottage as much as we are at home reduces the demand even for drinking water. This is good environmental news because when we use less water, the earth in turn has to cope with less of our waste water. Reduced demand also leads to an interesting direct benefit: Cottagers can choose from a number of options when deciding where they're going to obtain their water – whether from a lake, river, rain collection, a spring, a variety of well types, or even by hauling it in.

Some of these water sources may not be on the menu of legal options for your cottage.

Regulations governing water sources vary widely, so check to ensure that your preference is acceptable to local authorities. Local laws may also determine whether cottagers can do any of the work themselves, some jurisdictions insisting that only licensed tradespeople work on water systems. Those restrictions aside, water sources considered even remotely within the grasp of an industrious do-it-yourselfer are labeled DIY in this chapter. Should you decide to tap into the water source yourself, most jurisdictions have information sheets and booklets that can make the job of conforming to local laws much easier. (Keep in mind that the object of these laws is not so much to prevent you from doing something wrong, as to guide you to doing it right.)

Scientists estimate that only about 3% of the earth's total water resources is both unsalted and available for human consumption. This pittance allotted to drinking, washing, and the myriad of other uses we have for fresh water comes from two sources: surface water and ground water. Surface water is what we see

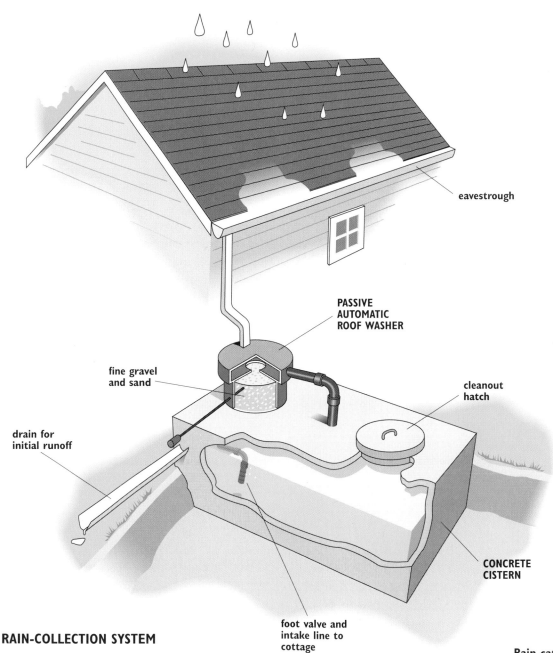

RAIN-COLLECTION SYSTEM

eavestrough

PASSIVE AUTOMATIC ROOF WASHER

fine gravel and sand

cleanout hatch

drain for initial runoff

CONCRETE CISTERN

foot valve and intake line to cottage

Rain catcher:
To collect the runoff from a roof, you can simply use standard eavestrough. However, the system should incorporate a roof washer to keep the initial dirty runoff out of the cistern.

– the lakes, rivers, ponds, streams, and wetlands that are so much an integral part of cottage country. Yet it accounts for a mere 3% of the meagre fresh-water quota, the remaining 97% being ground water. Ground water is the water housed beneath the earth's surface in unseen, underground reservoirs called aquifers. These aquifers feed our wells and springs, and help to replenish surface-water supplies.

SURFACE WATER (DIY)

Because of its exposure to both nature's and humanity's outpourings, surface water is easily polluted. Even in the remotest areas of cottage country, animals bathe and defecate in it, vegetable matter decomposes in and around it, and pollutants merge with it every time it rains. But this vulnerability isn't all bad news. Nature does tend to cleanse its surface waters, using the wind, sun, and earth to work at mitigating the damage through evaporation and filtration. Unfortunately, the cleansing process is often overwhelmed by the sheer quantities of contaminants surface water has to deal with. The only thing you can count on is that the constituents of surface water will vary. Consequently, *no* surface water should be considered potable without appropriate treatment. (We'll get to how to treat it in Chapter 6.)

Yet surface water should not be dismissed as a reasonable source of water for the cottage. After all, the majority of city water is treated surface water. And even without treatment, surface sources can still provide water for our nondrinking needs. Surface water is also tough to beat for handiness – for many cottagers, it's right out the front (or back) door. All that's needed is a bucket. With a bit of hose and a pump, we can even get it to flow into the cottage. Which explains why it's the traditional source of water in cottage country.

However, some cottagers do not have ready access to surface water. Others may want a system that's less likely to cause problems, especially when it comes to shutting down for the winter and starting up again in spring, or during winter use. But the principal motivator for seeking an alternative source for drinking water remains the concern over water quality, ground-water sources being less susceptible to contamination.

STORAGE SYSTEMS (DIY)
Usually cottage cisterns, reservoirs, and rain barrels are dependent on rainfall for supply. Because rain is basically surface water in transit, these water-storage systems form part of the surface-water repertoire. Therefore, many of the same potential pollution problems that affect lakes and rivers affect these catchment basins. Implicit in that similarity is the need for all such water to be treated before it can be considered safe to drink.

However, if the supply water is drawn from a well or hauled in, assuming the storage container is properly sealed, the risk of contamination is greatly reduced. Cottagers with low-yielding wells in particular will appreciate the

added reserve such a storage system provides.

To keep pollutants out, the storage container must be watertight. Its interior surface should be smooth and nonabsorbent to discourage various aqua-creeps (such as algae and pathogenic microorganisms) from collecting in cracks and crevices. Pay particular attention to the openings (for cleaning, filling, and draining), since bad or rough joints are probable stopovers, and sometimes breeding grounds, for the aqua-creeps. And any container should be easily accessible for cleaning.

Concrete, pargeted concrete block, steel, and plastic are all acceptable materials for water-storage tanks. Concrete-block tanks, and in most cases poured concrete ones as well, are constructed on site. Steel containers can also be custom fabricated to suit the needs of the cottager, or purchased ready-made. *Do not*, however, recycle steel drums for duty anywhere near water because of the high risk of residual toxic chemicals leaching into the water. (This warning applies whether the intention is to store water inside the drum or use the drum to support a floating dock.)

Plastic containers are sold ready-made, often marketed primarily as water-storage containers for livestock, and therefore are available at stores serving farming communities. Wooden rain barrels, the choice of romantics, regrettably make swell homes for microorganisms. So treat any water stored in wooden containers before drinking it – even if you've hauled the water in, rather than collected rain water off the roof.

The size of the container required depends both on the cottager's water needs and on how quickly the water can be replenished. Some jurisdictions require a minimum capacity of 19,000 L (5,000 US gal.) for water-storage containers serving full-time residences. Assuming your cottage isn't governed by such restrictions, you should be able to cope quite nicely on a 1,000 L–2,300 L (250 US gal.– 600 US gal.) tank if you use your cottage mainly on weekends and aren't disposed to city-style water consumption.

Regardless of container type or size, all outdoor water containers should be covered in order to keep out animals and their various droppings, not to mention the natural debris that seems bent on drifting into any container's open end. This closed-door attitude also discourages enterprising mosquitoes from converting your water supply into an insectile sex parlour. Outdoor drains and vents for water-storage containers should be noncorroding – brass or plastic, for instance – and screened to prevent nature's non-micro miscellanea, such as bugs and leaves, from getting into the stored water.

RAIN COLLECTION: HOW AND HOW MUCH?

The system used to collect the runoff from a roof and deliver it to a cistern is simply standard-issue eavestrough: The water flows into the trough and drains down the spout to whatever storage container rests below. Therefore, containers filled by rain water must have screened inlets to catch the big chunks. (Contrary to the popular nursery rhyme, inky-dinky spiders don't always climb back up the waterspout.)

In some jurisdictions, roof washers are mandatory. Roof washers are nifty gizmos that take advantage of initial rainfall to wash the roof clean of bird droppings and such before letting the water into the container. I'm not aware of any commercially available roof washers, so some jury-rigging will probably be necessary. There are basically two types. The simplest uses a manually operated diversion valve that directs runoff either into the container or away from it, depending on which way the valve is flipped. (Picture two doorways at the end of a hall, sharing one door, hinged between the doorways. When the door is opened for one doorway, it blocks entrance to the other, and vice versa.) Cottagers not so keen on venturing out into the rain to make the required adjustments can install passive automatic washers. These are self-draining sediment basins that soak up the initial dirty runoff. The basin is usually filled with sand and gravel, which prevent the water from rushing directly out the bottom drain. Once the basin is full of rain water, the overflow, by now (we hope) devoid of droppings, spills out the top of the basin and into the cistern.

How much water can you expect to collect from a cottage roof? Allowing for leakage, roof washing, and the like, 30 cm of rainfall yields about 19 L per 0.09 sq. m of roof area (12 in. yields 5 US gal. per sq. ft.). To get the figures for this formula, measure the cottage roof across the flat, *not* the pitch of the roof. Average annual rainfall statistics are available from local weather offices.

If you're using a pump to move water out of the storage container, place the pick-up point for the intake line about 30 cm (12 in.) above the container's floor to avoid sucking in settled debris. It's also a good idea to attach a float-activated shut-off switch to turn the pump off should demand exceed supply, thereby avoiding the ominous (and expensive) fragrance of fried pump.

Raised storage containers, such as water towers and reservoirs for hillside springs, can provide pressure for a cottage water system, eliminating the need for pressure tanks and perhaps even for a pump. Every 2.31 ft. up (measured from the tap to the water's surface) rewards us with 1 psi (pounds per square inch) of water pressure. In other words, a 30-ft. water tower would yield (30/2.31=) 13 psi, enough pressure to flush a toilet and wash with. But it makes for a pretty pathetic shower – although it's a shower nonetheless.

GROUND WATER

Ground water is the source of drinking water for about half the population of North America. When rain falls, the portion of water that doesn't evaporate or join surface sources seeps slowly downward through the earth to aquifers. Aquifers can be pockets of porous earth that hold water much as a sponge does, or cracks and underground caverns in rock. Aquifers can be isolated tankards, or they can extend for miles. When a pressure greater than atmospheric pressure is exerted on an aquifer by the geological formations resting above it, it is known as an artesian aquifer, the source of artesian springs and flowing (or artesian) wells.

Rain water is naturally soft and acidic. Be-

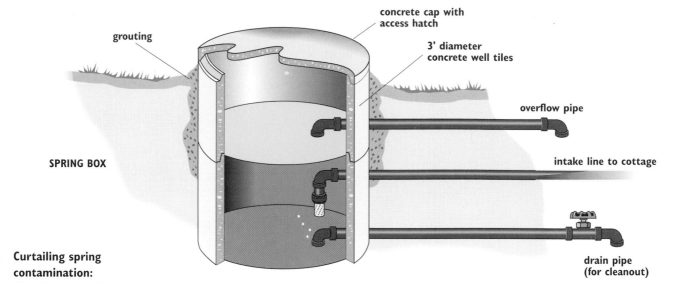

grouting

concrete cap with access hatch

3' diameter concrete well tiles

overflow pipe

intake line to cottage

SPRING BOX

drain pipe (for cleanout)

Curtailing spring contamination:

A spring box – which is essentially a cistern sitting at the spring mouth – protects the water from surface pollution. You can build one economically from well tiles.

cause of its corrosive personality, as it percolates through earth it absorbs soluble minerals from the rock and becomes harder. Simultaneously, microorganisms and many harmful chemicals accumulated during its progress are gradually left behind as the water continues to filter downward. This tendency for water to swap contaminants with the earth usually increases in proportion to the depths it must travel before hooking up with a suitable aquifer. It's this natural cleansing process and the relatively protected location of underground aquifers that makes ground water a safer and more consistent source of potable water than most surface-water sources.

However, being stuck underground, ground water does not benefit from any cleansing action the sun and wind might provide and, once polluted, it will likely remain that way for a very long time. How does it get polluted? Usually via some connection with the surface, such as a spring or a well.

1. SPRINGS (DIY)

When ground water flows naturally to the earth's surface, we call it a spring. Spring water has a reputation of being the cat's meow for purity but, in reality, it can be closer to some of the other things a cat emits. While it's true that water loses many of its worldly contaminants en route to finding an aquifer, if the return trip to the surface is unprotected, there's little to stop contaminants from re-

joining the flow. A well lining protects a well, but a spring has no such protection. Therefore, spring water almost invariably must be treated to make it safe for drinking.

There are two types of springs: gravity-fed springs, which are most often found flowing from a hillside; and artesian springs, which are fed by an aquifer under pressure. Artesian springs are less likely to stop running during dry spells and are less vulnerable to pollution (but not immune to it).

BUILDING A SPRING BOX

Contamination at the surface – for instance, from animals stopping by for a drink and maybe a few other things – can be curtailed by building a spring box. This "box" is essentially a cistern sitting at the mouth of the spring, fed by the spring rather than by surface water. It therefore shares many of the same construction criteria, although you'll want to check with local authorities regarding any additional restrictions in your cottage jurisdiction. Well tiles, 1 m (3 ft.) in diameter, make for an economical spring box, one reason I chose them to box the artesian spring at our cottage. Be forewarned, though, that these tiles are extremely heavy – even Waldo, my aged backhoe, had trouble lifting them into place. Those without backhoes should have a good cache of friends to call on come time to manoeuvre the tiles into place. (The main advantage of the backhoe, of course, is that it doesn't come with accompanying advice.)

A spring box needs a screened overflow – a pipe terminating away from the area surrounding the spring – to prevent soil erosion near the box. Ditches dug above the spring to divert surface runoff away from the area will also reduce the potential for pollution.

2. WELLS

For those without a handy spring, the only way to reach an aquifer is by way of a well. A well is a vertical shaft either dug, driven, jetted, bored, or drilled into the ground. The diameter is largely dependent on the choice of well type, while the depth is dependent on how deep the aquifer is and the volume of water that aquifer can produce, measured in litres or gallons per minute or hour. (Although, come to think of it, well depth could also be related to the payments on the well driller's new boat.)

The protected environment of a well keeps animals away from the water and boaters away from the intake line. Depending on the terrain, drawing your water from a well could also allow you to bury the entire intake line. This luxury eliminates many of the more labour-intensive jobs that tend to dominate opening and closing routines for the majority of cottagers who draw their water from lakes and rivers. It also ends worries over whether the ice will tear the intake line apart should you decide against such labour.

Yet by far the greatest advantage a well has over surface-water sources is the potential for consistent water quality – whatever is in the water today is likely going to be in there tomorrow as well. This makes treating the water much easier – if indeed treatment is required at all.

Decided disadvantages to wells are the labour and costs involved in construction. And even after having spent the time and money, there's no guarantee that you will find water, or that the aquifer will have sufficient yield, or be potable. However, there are indicators which at least give us hints as to the location, quantity, and quality of nature's buried treasure.

HOW TO LOCATE WATER

Geological and ground-water surveys are available from government sources for many areas of North America. Using the surveys, government geologists or persons similarly inclined can provide a scientific opinion as to whether there might be ground water in the area of your cottage, and at what depth. Neighbouring wells are sometimes better indicators, particularly of water quality, as are local well drillers who may be familiar with conditions in your area.

Keep in mind, however, that wells may be where the expression "There are no guarantees in life" originated. The well driller that friend and neighbour Dave chose to drill a new well had just finished two wells a bit south of us. The two are not more than 90 m (300 ft.) apart. The first measures a little more than 60 m (200 ft.) deep, the second a tad over 30 m (100 ft.). Dave ended up with a hole drilled 88 m (290 ft.) down into bedrock before a suitable aquifer was found. All three wells have plenty of water, and the quality is first-rate. About the same distance from Dave's deep, swell well sits my artesian spring, 2 m (6 ft.) deep, again with no shortage on the supply side, although the quality can be inconsistent. And across the road from the two of us, another neighbour recently dug a new well and hit plenty of good water about 9 m (30 ft.) down. Such is the often-unpredictable nature of aquifers.

DOWSING OR DIVINING: WATER WITH A STICK

One ancient method of locating that elusive aquifer is witching, also known as dowsing, divining, or a bunch of hooey-balooey. There's no basis in science for this practice, but since the same could be said for a lot of things humanity embraces as fact, it's worth considering. The witch (dowse or divining rod) is a Y-shaped implement about 30 cm (12 in.) long at the bottom of the Y, the two upper branches each being about 40 cm (16 in.) long, although the measurements aren't set in stone. Neither is the rest of the hocus-pocus. The rod can be anything from a willow branch to

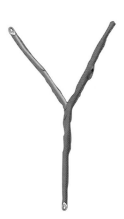

Divining style: *Traditionalists use a willow branch, while others choose metal coat hangers to help them find water.*

rusty coat hangers (I'm not sure if the rust is essential), and there are as many methods of holding it as there are crooked politicians.

When I was considering a new well, I called on neighbour Jürgen because he claimed to have once witched and found water. Jürgen's also a traditionalist. He insists the rod be cut from a suitable tree growing in the area to be witched, and is particular about the manner in which the witch is held: With forearms bent at the elbows and held out in front, hands palmside up, you clasp the forks of the Y, the end of the Y pointing outward and slightly upward in front of you. Then you walk around the yard with this backwards slingshot in your hand, hoping no one who hasn't read the above paragraphs will stop and ask what the heck it is you're doing.

Jürgen and I headed off in different directions, not wanting the findings of one witcher to influence the other. About a half hour into our choreographed tramp about the yard, the end of the puny Y-shaped stick I was holding suddenly pulled at my arms, pointing to the ground with alarming force. The intensity of this hyperactive stick was such that I strained muscles trying to hold onto it. I was dumbfounded, unable to do anything but laugh as some of the red in my neck found a more appropriate home in my face.

Jürgen came over and, without knowing the location of my find, confirmed the results with his witch. So we fired up Waldo, the backhoe, and went digging. Voilà, water. The only thing missing was the scientific explanation, not to mention a cottage within easy

SUGGESTED MINIMUM SETBACKS AND CLEARANCES FOR WELLS

(check with local authorities for approval)

NOTE: Double any setbacks from pollution sources that are located uphill from the well.

Septic system absorption area
    —Dug, bored, or driven well ....45 m (150 ft.)
    —Drilled well with watertight casing 6 m (20 ft.) deep ....30 m (100 ft.)
Septic or holding tank ....15 m (50 ft.)
Vault privy ....15 m (50 ft.)
Pit privy or grey water system
    —Dug or driven well ....30 m (100 ft.)
    —Drilled well with watertight casing 6 m (20 ft.) deep ....15 m (50 ft.)
Sewer line (gravity) or building foundation drain ....15 m (50 ft.)
Surface water, including cistern, pool, or hot tub ....7.5 m (25 ft.)
Property line, building, or driveway ....3 m (10 ft.)
Barn, building housing animals ....15 m (50 ft.)
Manure-storage site, automobile scrap yard, or road-salt storage area ......75 m (250 ft.)
Abandoned well ....60 m (200 ft.)
Closed-loop ground-source heating pipe ....22.5 m (75 ft.)
Sewage lagoon or treatment plant, sanitary landfill site ....300 m (1000 ft.)
Hazardous wastes site ....360 m (1200 ft.)
Cemetery (either human or pet) ....15 m (50 ft.)

ADDITIONAL SETBACKS FOR SPRINGS
Human activity (including habitation) from spring used as drinking-water source:
    —downhill from spring ....15 m (50 ft.)
    —laterally from spring ....30 m (100 ft.)
    —uphill from spring ....60 m (200 ft.)

reach of this new-found source of water. But I can't fault the witching for that.

Custom has it that not all of us are capable of witching. Certainly, during the witching spree at our cottage, neither my wife nor my son noticed any unusual behaviour exhibited by their carefully chosen sticks. As Chief Dan George said in the movie *Little Big Man*, "Sometimes the magic works; sometimes it doesn't."

DUG WELLS (DIY)

Digging holes in the ground to find aquifers goes back millennia (definitely long before the backhoe was invented, in any event). A typical dug well is not very deep – about 6 m (20 ft.), and rarely more than 9 m (30 ft.). But it has a large girth – it's usually about 1 m (3 ft.) in diameter, and occasionally up to 2 m (6 ft.); about the same proportions as my friend Bruce, actually. And, in common with Bruce, this large diameter allows for more storage, an advantage at least for the well, especially if the yield of the aquifer is low.

It's possible (where not prohibited by law) for a cottager to dig a well using the shovel-and-blisters method. My grandfather did, and I'm proud of him for it. But strenuous bouts of manual labour are not in keeping with the true spirit of the cottage (that's the rationale I use, at least). And besides, it's an awful lot of work to go through on the off-chance you might hit water. I know one group of weekend diggers who managed to get 2 m (6 ft.) down before they hit dry bedrock. Digging a well by hand only makes sense if the cottage is remote and not accessible to heavy equipment. And only if you know somebody who can witch.

LINING A DUG WELL

In common with clouds, every well must have a lining – basically a tube that runs between the water and the surrounding earth. The reasons for this are threefold: to prevent the earth from caving back in on the hole; to create a reservoir to gather and hold the water; and to prevent pollutants from infiltrating that reservoir. Concrete well tiles have pushed aside stone as the preferred well-lining material for

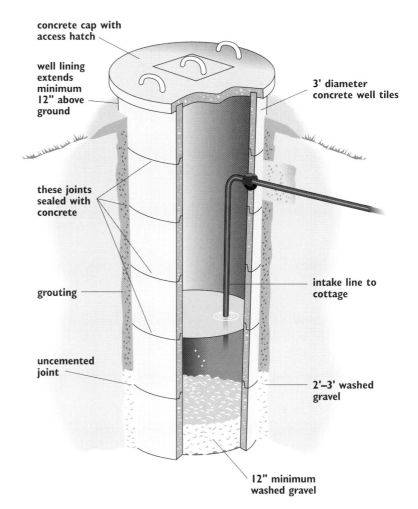

concrete cap with access hatch

well lining extends minimum 12" above ground

these joints sealed with concrete

grouting

uncemented joint

3' diameter concrete well tiles

intake line to cottage

2'–3' washed gravel

12" minimum washed gravel

DUG OR BORED WELL

both dug and bored wells. Concrete tiles are faster to install than laying stone and do a much better job of keeping contaminants out of the well. The 1-m (3-ft.) diameter by about 0.76 m (2½ ft.) high concrete tile is almost universal now because it provides a good-sized reservoir and enough room for a human to climb down a ladder and service a foot valve if necessary. The sections of tile are grooved along the perimeters to facilitate a loose kind of fit (production tolerances being a little slack). Galvanized metal pipes should not be used for well lining because even slightly acidic water can cause the lead in the galvanizing to leach out into the water.

Whatever the material, the well lining should extend 30 cm (12 in.) at the very minimum above the surface of the ground, and all joints within 2.5 m (8 ft.) of the surface must be sealed with grouting. (See below.) Dump

Dig it:
Dug wells are relatively economical to build but also shallow – which means they are prone to leaving you short of water during dry spells. Concrete well tiles, capped with a circular concrete slab, help provide a good-sized reservoir.

about 30 cm (12 in.) of washed gravel into the bottom of the well and 60 cm–90 cm (2 ft.–3 ft.) into the annular space (the space between the outside of the well lining and the hole) to restrict the transfer of sand and other fine particles into the well.

The annular space between this gravel and the surface must then be sealed to solve the problem of contaminants seeping through it. Some jurisdictions require that the annular space be at least 6 cm (2 in.) in width around the well lining, and that it be drilled, bored, or dug to at least 3 m (10 ft.) below the surface. The hole must be filled with a grouting such as "neat" cement. Neat cement is more sloppy than neat, being the standard 43-kg (94-lb.) bag of Portland cement mixed with 17 L–25 L (4½ US gal.–6½ US gal.) of water. Other acceptable groutings include concrete, quick-setting cement, and Bentonite clay mixed with water.

Because it sets quickly underwater, we used quick-setting cement to seal the tiles and intake-line hole in our spring box. Since you have only five minutes to get the stuff into place, it's not a relaxed sort of medium to work with, but the frantic pace does mean the job gets done faster, leaving more time to stand back and admire your enterprise.

Even if laws in your cottage jurisdiction don't require it, it just doesn't make sense not to properly seal the annular space around a well.

THE SHOVEL VS. THE BACKHOE

Whether you're digging with a backhoe or garden hoe, cave-ins can be a problem in loose soil such as sand, especially as the hole begins to fill with water. In this respect, hand digging has one advantage over any mechanized means. The problem with doing it by machine is that the entire hole must be dug before installing the well tiles, which means constantly removing earth as the sides cave in. Anyone who has played in beach sand knows this from experience, and also knows that the hole always ends up being much larger than originally called for – unless we use a pail, which is what we do in a sense when we dig by

hand. When the hole is hand dug to about 1 m (3 ft.) deep, the first tile is set in place. (Plenty of friends and a home-made tripod hoist will be required.) Using a short-handled shovel, continue to remove earth from both the well hole itself and from under the perimeter of the tile. The scooped earth is loaded into a bucket, which is then hoisted out of the hole on a rope by a topside helper. Gravity lowers the tiles at a speed directly in proportion to how much soil the digger can remove from under the bottom tile, additional tiles being added to the top as the lower tiles slip downward.

The well tiles hold back the earth like a pail set into a hole at the beach, so there's no chance of a cave-in. But, jeez, it's a lot of work, not to mention a mite claustrophobic as you struggle to manoeuvre a shovel and the bulk of one human around in a hole that's 1 m (3 ft.) in diameter and maybe 3 m (10 ft.) or more deep.

CAPPING A DUG WELL

Historically, a dug well remained open at the top so a bucket could be lowered on a rope to haul up the water. This open concept became a romantic focal point in many a movie, the loving couple leaning over the edge to see their giddy passion reflected in the water below. More likely than not, a penny was tossed in to accompany a wish.

However, with the blindfolds of romance removed, humanity was able to reflect on the menagerie of microorganisms, bird droppings, unlucky squirrels, dead leaves, and your-guess-is-as-good-as-mine that also made the descent into the drinking-water supply. (Gadzooks! Is it possible we have inadvertently stumbled across the true origin of the term "lovesick"?) Any well, regardless of type, must be capped and sealed to prevent all but water and air from entering its confines, the capping occurring after the necessary plumbing is installed in the well. A dug well lined with concrete tiles is capped with a circular concrete slab, whose outer edges are grooved to slip over the upper well tile.

A variation on capping a dug well is the

buried-slab method. The same slab as above is placed over the tiles, but at a depth of at least 3 m (10 ft.) down; the slab is cemented to the upper tile. Secured and sealed to the slab is a section of 6-in. diameter well casing long enough to extend through the slab and poke at least 30 cm (12 in.) above ground level. A pitless adapter (see below) can now be installed, the smaller well casing capped, and the well backfilled to within 30 cm (12 in.) of the top of the casing. With the top sealed in this manner, any surface water that reaches the well will be filtered through that layer of earth first, removing some contaminants.

DUMMY WELLS

An interesting marriage of surface water and dug well is the dummy well. A dug well is constructed about 1.5 m–3 m (5 ft.–10 ft.) back from the water's edge. As the surface water seeps through to the well, the soil between the two acts as a filter, removing some contaminants and thus reducing the amount of treatment required (or possibly eliminating the need for treatment entirely – have the water tested to be sure). This method also takes a lot of the guesswork out of where to dig for water.

Dummy wells may not be legal in your cottage jurisdiction, so check with all the requisite authorities, including any that may regulate alterations to the shoreline.

DRIVEN AND JETTED WELLS (DIY)

Driven wells – sometimes referred to as sand points – are constructed by pounding long sections of pipe into the ground. The usual pipe material is steel, normally 2 in.–3 in. in diameter, and sometimes perforated. At the end is a driving point, usually a forged-steel affair wrapped around a cone-shaped brass strainer. The depth of driven wells is typically about the same as that of dug wells. Driven wells work best in sandy conditions. In soil containing more gravel, a variation of the driven well called the jetted well is often used. A blast of high-pressure water is forced out the lower end of the pipe, the pipe being fed down as the earth is eroded away by this powerful jet of

water. Driven and jetted wells are not feasible when boulders or solid-rock formations are encountered.

The small diameter and restricted depth of driven and jetted wells makes for limited storage capacity. Where the practice is permitted, this disadvantage can be partially offset by linking two or more such wells together, thereby increasing their yield (as well as the cost, work, and risk of contamination).

Dug, driven, and jetted wells are all relatively economical to build. Because they are also shallow, all three are susceptible to water shortages during dry periods, although this may not be a problem for cottagers with limited water needs. However, because of their proximity to the surface, contamination of the aquifer, and therefore the well, is of greater concern. Such wells are better protected than surface water or springs, but they are no match for deep wells when it comes to consistent water quality. The deeper the well, the greater the opportunity the water has to be filtered by the earth before it joins the aquifer.

BORED WELLS

While the term "bored well" could describe anyone within earshot of a politician, in this context it refers to a well constructed using what is essentially a huge hole saw. A boring rig turns the boring bucket – picture an upside-down barrel with cutting blades on its leading edge – which is raised and emptied as it fills with earth. The soil must be stable so the hole won't cave in (which rules out sand) and free of boulders and solid rock.

The hole a boring rig makes averages about 0.6 m–1 m (2 ft.–3 ft.) in diameter, and is rarely over 15 m (50 ft.) deep. As with a dug well, storage capacity is high. The choice for well-lining material is the same as for dug wells, as are the requirements for sealing, capping, and placement of the gravel filter medium.

Boring a well involves more labour than drilling a well, and the equipment for boring is just as costly as that for drilling. Since the bored well suffers many of the same problems as the much-less-expensive-to-construct dug well (questionable supply, vulnerability to pollution), most well contractors have forsaken the boring rig for the drilling rig.

DRILLED WELLS

A drilled well is a hole, usually 4 in.–6 in. in diameter, drilled into the earth until a suitable aquifer is found. More often than not, this occurs at around 30 m–90 m (100 ft.–300 ft.), but it could be more than 300 m (1,000 ft.). The use of diamond-tipped drill bits, usually air or water cooled, means that not even the Precambrian rock of the Canadian Shield is immune to being punctured in the quest for water. Although small in diameter, a drilled well can offer reasonable reserve capacity because of its depth.

The well casing, or lining, of a drilled well is usually made of steel, but plastic can also be used (preferable if the water is acidic, since plastic doesn't corrode as steel does). A minimum of 7.5 m (25 ft.) of casing should be installed into the hole, and the casing should extend at least 30 cm (12 in.) above the surface. When a well is drilled into solid rock, the above minimums for the casing are usually sufficient. There is one notable exception to this rule – when the rock is limestone. Limestone is laced with countless cracks and crevices, interconnecting like city streets twisted by an earthquake (or maybe designed by a traffic consultant). Each crack in the rock becomes a thoroughfare for microorganisms and a variety of surface contaminants, such as pesticides and petrochemicals. Therefore, any well lining in limestone should extend at least 12 m (40 ft.) into the rock, and the annular space sealed for the well's entire length or to a depth of 15 m (50 ft.), whichever is less.

The casing might also need to extend beyond these minimums if there is risk of a cave-in, as there is when drilling through loose fill.

Steel casings are either welded or screwed together, while plastic casing sections are joined with a nontoxic glue. The casing must be capped with a watertight seal, some jurisdictions also insisting that it have a lock on it. The cap must also be vented (and the vent screened) to allow air in and out as the water level inside fluctuates. Because of its greater storage capacity, a 6-in. casing is a better choice than the slightly less-expensive 4-in. variety. When the aquifer resides in sand or loose gravel, a well screen is attached to the bottom of the casing to prevent the fine-grained particles from sneaking into the system and playing havoc with the pump and plumbing. The screen is made of perforated stainless steel or some other suitable noncorrosive material, the size of its pores being determined by the size of the particulate that needs filtering out.

Because a drilled well usually reaches much deeper aquifers than other types of wells, it is the least likely to run dry or become polluted.

DEVELOPING A WELL

The purpose of developing, or conditioning, a well is to remove any initial turbidity stirred up by construction, and to ensure that the pores in the well screen or the cracks in the rock through which the aquifer flows are not plugged by construction debris. If you have ever used a plunger to unplug a drain, you're already familiar with the basic principles of well development. Air or water is surged back and forth, dislodging any fine particles, either into the aquifer away from the screen, or into the well itself. Then the well is pumped until the excess turbidity is removed. Developing is followed by disinfecting (using superchlorination, see Chapter 6) and then testing. (See Chapter 5.)

POLLUTED WELLS

Once it has been disinfected, how likely is it that a well will become polluted? A survey of well-water quality conducted by the US Environmental Protection Agency showed that 37% of the wells tested were contaminated by coliform bacteria. (See Chapter 5.) How do wells become polluted? The probable causes listed in the survey were: well casings or linings that are insufficient or substandard, letting surface water into the well; annular spaces not adequately sealed, allowing surface water to seep down the outside of the well lining into the aquifer; and well pits admitting contaminants. (Well pits are recesses in the ground at the top of the well, their original purpose being to provide frost-free access to the connection point of well and pipe.) California's *Well Water Standards* booklet adds four more likely causes to this list: wells located too close to pollution sources (abandoned wells being included as one of the sources); the polluting of one aquifer by another, the two aquifers joined by the well; surface water seeping into the well around the poorly sealed base of a top-mounted pump; and wells being used accidentally or otherwise for the dumping of wastes.

SOLVING THE POLLUTION PROBLEM

The first problem is a result of skimping on well-lining material, either in quantity or in quality. Any well constructed to current codes applicable in any province or state within North America will not suffer from this predicament. The second problem is solved by adequately sealing the annular space, as described on p. 22.

Since the arrival of the pitless adapter, well pits are no longer necessary, and in fact are no longer legal, for most new wells. The pitless adapter is an assembled pipe fitting that, as its name implies, allows elimination of the well pit. At some point below the frost line (the depth below which the ground does not freeze), a small hole a tad bigger than the pitless adapter's inlet is made in the well lining, using either a hole saw or a cutting torch. The pitless adapter is installed through the hole. In most cases, a rubber-like gasket is sandwiched between the adapter and the well casing, although sometimes the adapter is welded in place. Inside the well, another part of the adapter holds the drop pipe – the section of pipe running down into the well. (If a submersible pump is installed, it is attached to the end of this drop pipe.) The inner piece of the adapter slides into the part of the adapter already joined to the casing. An O-ring seal makes the fitting watertight, while allowing for the drop pipe to be lifted out for servicing. The intake line to the cottage is connected to the adapter on the outside of the well, and the hole around the adapter is backfilled. Cottagers with an existing well pit can add an extension to the top of the well lining, install a pitless adapter, and then fill the pit in with grouting.

LOCATION, LOCATION, LOCATION

There is no excuse for locating a new well too close to pollution sources. Use the setbacks listed on p. 20 as guides, keeping in mind that they are minimums – increasing any of them increases the safety factor. Whenever possible, locate wells uphill from pollution sources, and slope the surrounding earth away from the well to encourage surface water to drain in that direction.

Stopping the transfer of contaminants from one aquifer into another is accomplished by sealing the section of annular space that links the two aquifers – mandatory in many jurisdictions and a darn good idea in the others. As for wastes in the well, the solution is simple – don't put them there. Don't work on the outboard motor near the well, or change the oil in the lawn mower, or discard wash water, or fertilize the grass, or tie up the dog. In essence, anything you dump on the ground near the well could end up in your drinking water.

ABANDONED WELLS (DIY)

Any well that is no longer in use should be sealed. It's the law in most jurisdictions. This provision is not just to keep animals and people from falling in. Abandoned wells are prime candidates for pollution, and once an aquifer is polluted it can seep into neighbouring aquifers, contaminating any wells within its underground reach. The correct way to abandon a well, also known as the destruction of a well, is to fill the well hole with the same grouting material described above for sealing the annular space. The grouting should be applied through a hose or pipe extending to the bottom of the well, so that you're filling the hole from the bottom up, thereby preventing the formation of air pockets. This can be a tricky task; if you have any reservations about tackling it yourself, or are not permitted to do so in the jurisdiction in which your cottage is located, call in a licensed well contractor experienced in well destruction.

3 PUMP AND CIRCUMSTANCE

How to put together a pump system that works

Grandma's pump:
*The traditional
alternative to
more complicated
electric pumps
can still do the trick.*

THE THEORY OF PUMP OPERATION

IF THE COTTAGE WERE DOWNHILL FROM THE water source, getting water in would be simple: Open the tap (or window) and let gravity do the rest. However, life is never simple. The obvious complicating factor is that cottages are rarely downhill from the nearest water (leaks in the roof aside, of course). So to get water from down there to up here, we need a pump.

A pump is just a method of imparting motion to water by mechanical means. As a pump begins to move water, a low-pressure area develops on the intake side of the pump. Meanwhile, atmospheric pressure bears down on the surface of the water source at a force proportional to the weight of air sitting above the source. It's the force of this weight that pushes the water up to the pump. No matter how powerful the pump, it can never cause water to flow to it faster or in greater quantities than atmospheric pressure is able to push it there.

This illustrates the First Principle of Cottage Plumbing, which states that water cannot be pulled, it can only be pushed – atmospheric pressure pushing it to the pump; the pump pushing it to the kitchen tap.

HOW HIGH CAN YOU PUSH WATER?

At sea level, atmospheric pressure works out to about 14.7 pounds per square inch (psi). Because one pound of pressure will push water straight up 2.31 ft., in theory atmospheric pressure could push a column of water up 34 ft., assuming a complete frictionless vacuum were hovering above it. But there isn't. Due to mechanical and frictional losses, the pump can only manage to lower the pressure, not get rid of it. So the very best we can expect is 25 ft. of lift, and that's when the pump is mounted directly over the water source. When the pump is offset from the source – as most cottage systems are – don't count on more than 22 ft. of lift.

Obviously, not all cottages sit at sea level. As we move inland to higher ground, the weight of air above us diminishes. The resulting loss of pressure leads to less lift, about 1 ft. less for every 1,000-ft. increase in altitude. So a cabin located in the Beartooth Range, Wyoming, 8,000 feet above sea level (just a rock slide east of Yellowstone National Park), would have an approximate maximum lift of about 14 ft. for an offset pump.

While the atmosphere can only flex 14.7 psi worth of pressure at best to push water around, even a centrifugal pump can muster as much as 150 psi at the push of a button. So let the pump do as much of the work as possible. The easiest way to do this is to locate the pump as close to the water source as possible. (See Prime Real Estate, p. 35.)

Which brings us to the Second Principle of Cottage Plumbing: Nothing achieves 100% efficiency, mainly because of losses due to friction. Many cottagers experience this phenomenon first hand each time younger members of the family are conscripted to do the dishes. Less visible yet potentially more irritating is head loss. Head loss is not what you threaten the kids with, but rather the friction generated between moving water and the surrounding pipe wall. This loss varies with temperature, pipe size, pipe material, type of fittings (such as elbows and in-line valves), volume of water being transported through the pipe, and pipe length. Head loss increases as distance, volume, and number of fittings become greater. It applies to both lift and discharge heads (see box at right), and horizontal runs, head loss reducing the theoretical potential of all three. Lift and head loss determine the maximum allowable offset for pumps.

If it weren't for head loss, a pump operating at 50 psi could push water 115 feet up and move water horizontally forever. You can often compensate for head loss, at least in part, by increasing pipe diameter. But installing oversize pipe will overwork the pump too. Pipe should always be of the correct diameter for the distance and pump involved. Consult your pump manual or plumbing-supply shop for the particulars on your pump.

Besides knowing the total lift and total head of your site, another helpful measure of performance is a pump's capacity to move water, rated in litres per minute (L/min) or US gallons per minute (US gpm). The pump must be able to handle peak demands, like those busy hours around breakfast and early evening. Most cottagers can get by with a pump capacity of about 20 L/min (5 US gpm), those without showers and such requiring even less. But if you've got a thirsty cottage, with multiple washrooms, a dishwasher, hot tub, and the like, seek out a reputable plumbing store or plumber with all the necessary charts and figures to calculate the correct size for your pump.

TYPES OF PUMPS

What follows is a description of the types of pumps most suitable for cottage use. Capacities within classifications will vary, as do prices, the two usually being related.

Some jurisdictions have very stringent rules governing pumps and their installation (such as Wisconsin, where only licensed installers are allowed to put in a pump), while others

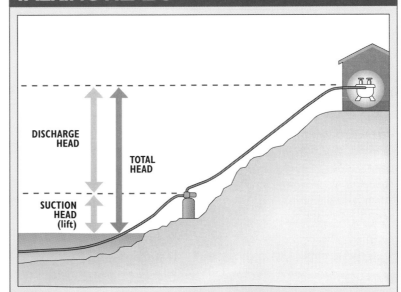

TALKING HEADS

The vertical distance from the surface of the water source at its lowest point up to the inlet of the pump is known as lift or suction head. The distance from the pump to its highest point of delivery is the discharge head. The sum of the two is known as the total head.

Suction head + Discharge head = Total head

don't seem to care who the heck does it or how. Check with your local authorities before they check with you.

HAND PUMPS: THE LOW-TECH OPTION

The traditional hand pump (or cistern pump as it is also known) is a positive-displacement pump. It draws one batch of water into the pump at a time, displacing existing water inside the pump with incoming water, the water being pushed out in small batches rather than in a continuous flow. It's also a bit of mechanical history – one of the few props seen in better westerns everywhere that is still made today.

The big advantage of the traditional hand pump is simplicity, which invariably translates into low cost ($50–$135) and reliability. And, of course, the electric company doesn't have its hand out every time you want a glass of water, making it the pump of choice for most cottages lacking electricity. My in-laws had a hand pump drawing from the well at their first cottage. The pump fed a 45-L (12-US gal.) tank sitting atop a water tower. The tank was set at cottage roof height, thus providing pressure for the kitchen tap and a low-volume-flush indoor loo. The system worked surprisingly well, the only real lack being a blow-me-down high-pressure shower.

Only a few manufacturers are still making traditional hand pumps, a reflection of their declining popularity (which in turn increases prices). No question, the hand pump comes up wanting when asked to supply sufficient on-demand pressure to operate all the plumbing luxuries that have evolved into necessities, such as automatic dishwashers and showers; cottagers willing to forsake such modern conveniences for the simpler life should be reminded that the hand pump is hand-powered. Just imagine – a form of exercise that doesn't involve official uniforms and dedicated sports equipment.

The handle of the hand pump is connected via a rod to a piston that moves up and down inside the cylindrical pump body. A circular piece of leather attached to the piston makes a sliding seal between the piston and the cylinder. When the handle is pushed down,

the piston is raised, creating a low-pressure area behind it. This lifts a flapper valve (a small hinged lid not unlike a toilet seat in concept) at the bottom of the cylinder, allowing water to flow into the cylinder. As the handle is raised, the piston is forced back down and the lower flapper valve falls shut, while the water forces a second flapper on the top of the piston open. The water flows through this second flapper valve past the piston, but remains in the cylinder.

Astute readers will note that we're now back where we started – almost. The big difference is that the next time we push the handle down, as the piston rises (the upper flapper held in closed position by the water above), the water now on top of the piston is pushed out the pump spout as a new batch of water is drawn in below. This cycle is repeated for as long as the handle is pumped. (Attach a campaigning politician's right hand to the pump handle and you'll have a constant supply of water, at least until the election is over.)

Like other positive-displacement pumps, the traditional hand pump doesn't need a foot valve to keep the water from running out the bottom of the intake line or a check valve to keep the water from running out the bottom of the pump (the flapper valves acting as the latter). And it won't lose prime if a little air gets in the system. Usually, a cup or two of water poured in the top of a hand pump is all the

JUST ADD WATER AND STIR

A self-priming pump is one that can draw water up an empty suction line. Most so-called self-priming units – the hand pump, for instance – can only do this following an initial prime, and for such a pump to remain self-priming, some water must remain in the pump housing (the quantity depends on the design of the pump). So when brochures or folks in the business talk about self-priming, what they usually mean is self-*re*priming. Pumps that are truly self-priming (like a diaphragm pump, for example), meaning that they can draw in water without any initial prime, will be referred to here-in as true self-priming.

priming it needs as long as the lower flapper valve remains wet and supple enough to seal efficiently. This valve will eventually let the water inside sneak past, drying the flapper enough to require repriming of the pump. How long it takes for this to happen depends on the make and condition of the pump, but it might go on working fine all summer. Flapper valves and piston seals can wear over time (usually from long periods of remaining dry), so leave a few bucks in the will for your grandchildren to replace them.

For deep-well applications (that is, lifts greater than 25 feet), special hand pumps are available; the piston and cylinder are remotely located near the bottom of the well, connected to the handle with a long rod. Then, atmospheric pressure only has to push the water into the submerged end of the pump, the pump pushing the water up from there. Because the rod between the handle and piston must be almost vertical, this type of pump doesn't lend itself to high-lift lakeside applications. It also taxes the pumper more, and costs at least twice that of a standard hand pump.

PISTON PUMPS: FOR THE INCURABLE TINKERER

The piston pump (also known in some circles as the reciprocating pump) is essentially a motorized version of the traditional hand pump, at least from the standpoint of how the water is drawn in. Good for lifts up to 25 ft., it's simple to prime – remove the priming plug (located on top of the water box), fill the water box with water, and start the pump. When the water pours out the plug hole, stop the pump and replace the plug. Then turn the pump back on and if it works, you're done. If not, repeat the procedure. However, Max's Amazing Easy Prime is a more expedient and sure-fire method of priming, and it works with all types of powered pumps (with the exception of the submersible pump, which is self-priming). See Chapter 11 for details.

While the capacity of a jet pump (see p. 32) is controlled to a great extent through the design of its internal bits, the ultimate limit on available pressure is regulated by nature. There are natural restrictions placed on the speed of water, which in turn limits the potential pressure a jet pump can generate, the jet pump's efficiency (and therefore discharge head) diminishing as pressure rises. A positive displacement pump, such as the piston pump, is not dependent on the speed of water to build pressure, so any decrease in discharge head is restricted to frictional losses only. This is an advantage that is only truly realized when high discharge heads are encountered and the water just keeps flowing. Or pulsating, actually, the water being delivered in tiny, rapid-fire batches.

The piston pump is complex and more costly (about $400–$800) than the more popular centrifugal pump, and a little noisier. But it's a glorious thing to watch in action, with crankshaft, connecting rod, piston, and valves chugging away – a pump for the incurable tinkerer. There are oil levels and belt tension to check, oil to change – if you're really lucky, you might even have to repack the stuffing boxes. Those keen on such things will be rewarded with a reliable pump. Those who lack an interest in preventative tinkering will be better served by a jet pump.

Inside the piston pump, the flow of water is controlled by valve rubbers which perform the same function as the hand pump's flapper valves. Instead of displacing a single cylinder of water as the hand pump does, this pump's piston fills and empties two chambers as it reciprocates through each cycle. Like the hand pump, it requires neither a foot valve nor a check valve (although it will reprime more readily with a foot valve); the twin lower valve rubbers stop water from draining out of the water box. The water box must be full of water for the valve rubbers to work, but after its initial prime, the pump can tolerate a fair amount of air without losing prime. This makes it a good choice for low yield-wells (like sand points) and springs. But fine sand can wear out the valves and seals.

To protect inquisitive fingers, a piston pump should be installed with the pulleys against the wall or equipped with a belt guard.

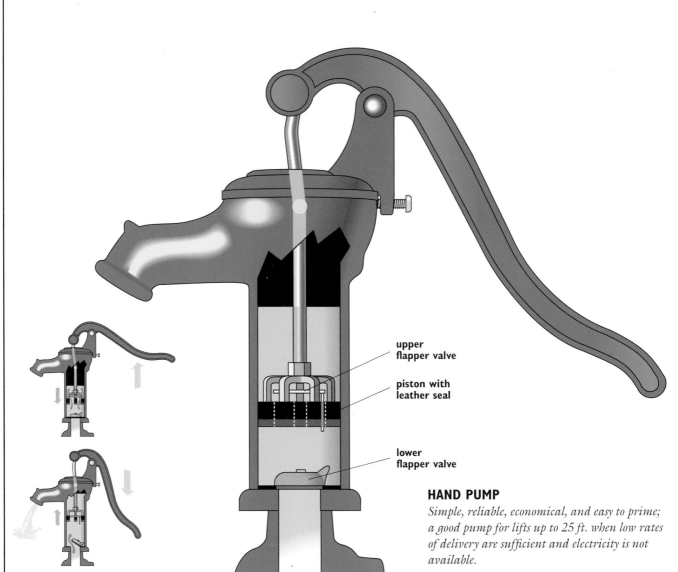

upper
flapper valve

piston with
leather seal

lower
flapper valve

HAND PUMP

Simple, reliable, economical, and easy to prime;
a good pump for lifts up to 25 ft. when low rates
of delivery are sufficient and electricity is not
available.

What happens in a hand pump:

When the handle is pushed down, the piston is raised, and a flapper valve lifts, allowing water to flow in. When the handle is raised, the piston is forced back down, and the valve shuts. A second valve on top of the piston is forced open, and the water flows through this valve and past the piston but remains in the cylinder. When the handle is pushed down again, as the piston rises, the water is pushed out the spout.

If the motor on a piston pump should ever fail, one can be salvaged from a cast-off washing machine or similar device, a luxury not shared with other types of pumps. This flexibility allows for the installation of a more powerful motor to increase pump capacity, as long as the electrical circuitry is up to handling the increased loads.

Piston pumps consume less electricity than comparable centrifugal pumps at start-up, and are therefore better suited to drawing power from a portable generator, a potential advantage for remote sites. And of course with the generator roaring away, it's unlikely anyone would notice the piston pump's slightly higher noise level compared to the centrifugal pump.

CENTRIFUGAL PUMPS: HIGH-VOLUME DELIVERY

The centrifugal pump belongs to a class of pumps known as dynamic (or kinetic) pumps. The centrifugal pump spins an impeller within its housing (or case), thereby accelerating the flow of incoming water. (An impeller moves water, as opposed to a propeller which moves the object to which it is attached – such as a boat – through water.) As the speed of any liquid increases, its pressure drops, creating a low-pressure area behind it. At the same time, the spinning impeller discharges the accelerating water into either a volute (similar in shape to the shell of a snail) or a diffuser (a compacted version of the volute), both of which slow the flow as it progresses

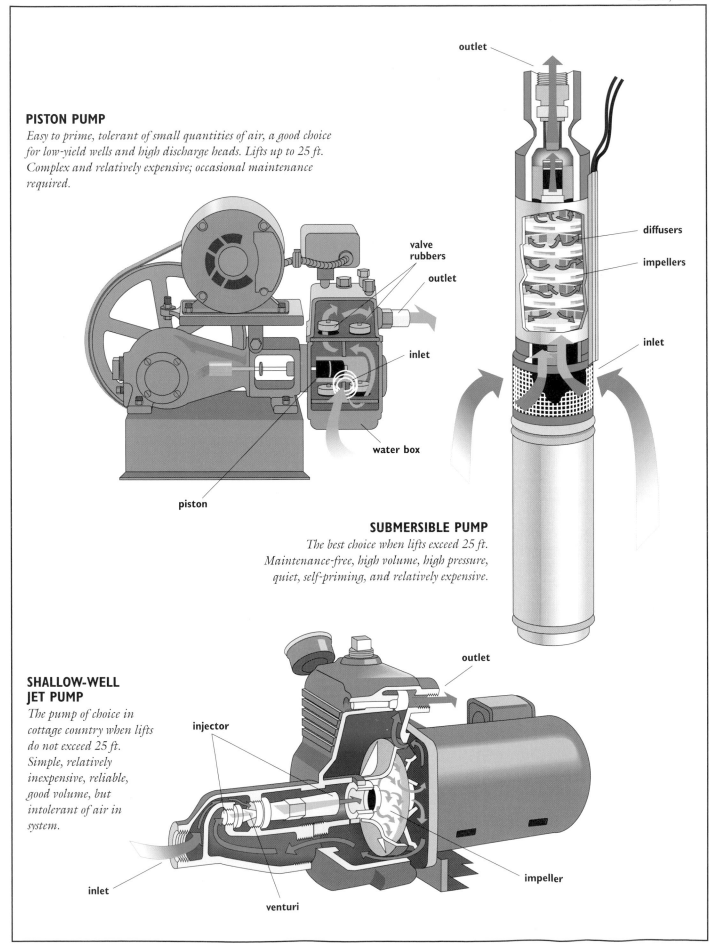

PISTON PUMP

Easy to prime, tolerant of small quantities of air, a good choice for low-yield wells and high discharge heads. Lifts up to 25 ft. Complex and relatively expensive; occasional maintenance required.

valve rubbers

outlet

inlet

water box

piston

SUBMERSIBLE PUMP

The best choice when lifts exceed 25 ft. Maintenance-free, high volume, high pressure, quiet, self-priming, and relatively expensive.

outlet

diffusers

impellers

inlet

SHALLOW-WELL JET PUMP

The pump of choice in cottage country when lifts do not exceed 25 ft. Simple, relatively inexpensive, reliable, good volume, but intolerant of air in system.

injector

outlet

inlet

venturi

impeller

through an ever-widening passageway. As the speed of the moving liquid decreases, its pressure increases. In the confines of a pump, where frictional losses are minimal, the resultant pressure is what we count on to deliver the water to the kitchen tap. Daniel Bernoulli, king of the fluid frontier and avid cottager (by my guess), discovered this relationship between velocity and water pressure more than 300 years ago.

The capacity of a centrifugal pump is controlled by a balanced partnership of motor, impeller, and diffuser (or volute). A manufacturer must match all three to work together, as a centrifugal pump functions best when it's operating at full capacity. It delivers water in a smooth, steady stream, and doesn't like variations in either the pressure or the volume of the incoming water. It's also intolerant of air; any break in the water around the impeller, including even air bubbles, can lead to loss of prime. And without water to lubricate and cool the mechanical seal (the seal located where the impeller shaft enters the pump casing), the seal will quickly burn out. Sand, gravel, and sediment can wear the impeller, the volute or diffuser, and the mechanical seal, although this pump is not as sensitive to such debris as the piston pump.

Most permutations of the basic centrifugal pump likely to turn up at the cottage are self-priming after the initial prime, as long as water remains in the pump casing and intake line. A foot valve or a check valve just before the pump is a must. The pump is simple, inexpensive for a motor-driven pump ($200–$600), not as noisy as the piston pump, reliable, and low on maintenance – not a good pump for avid tinkerers. The basic centrifugal pump is best suited to moving water in high volumes, rather than at high pressure, and as such will most likely be found around the cottage in the form of a portable gas-powered pump (used either to fill reservoirs or for potential fire-fighting duties) or as a sewage pump. (See Chapter 7.) However, there are variations of the centrifugal pump designed specifically for filling the needs of a pressurized water system, such as the one at the cottage.

JET PUMPS: CENTRIFUGAL PUMPS WITH A BONUS

The jet pump is a type of centrifugal pump with an important bonus – an injector (sometimes referred to as an ejector). The injector sits in the path of the incoming water. As water is drawn into the pump by the action of the impeller, a portion of the water that might otherwise be destined for some cottage plumbing fixture is recirculated back through the injector. Inside the injector is a venturi (a narrow tube through which the water is forced). Much as a river picks up speed as its banks converge, any water passing through the injector will also accelerate. It is this sudden increase in speed that establishes the low-pressure area required for atmospheric pressure to push the source water up to the injector. This incoming source water joins the fast-flowing, pressurized recirculating water to squeeze through the venturi. The speed of the water then slows as it flows out through an ever widening cone-shaped passage. As velocity diminishes, pressure increases, much in the same manner as when water leaves the fast flow around the impeller for the diffuser (which also explains why many manufacturers refer to the entire venturi tube as a diffuser).

Jacuzzi lays claim to being the first pump manufacturer to implement this clever application of Bernoulli's observations. Obviously, Dan (as Bernoulli's friends called him) must have had a real cantankerous pump to have figured out all this stuff about the flow of cottage liquids. In essence, what the jet pump is doing is exchanging a portion of potential output (in the form of energy lost in recirculating the water through the injector) for an additional boost in pressure on the lift side of the impeller. How does this improve pumping? It depends on the location of the injector.

SHALLOW-WELL JET PUMPS: NOT JUST FOR WELLS

Like the piston pump, a shallow-well jet pump is designed to lift water up to the cottage from any source that is less than 25 ft. below the pump, such as a shallow well (surprise) or a lake. It is by far the most common pump across cottage country. The shallow-well jet pump has its injector built right into (or attached directly to) the pump casing immediately before the impeller. The injector acts like a supercharger, increasing the pressure of the water being fed to the impeller, which in turn increases it again.

The shallow-well jet is relatively inexpensive ($230–$450), a simple variation of the basic centrifugal design, and if working within its design limitations, delivers a good supply of water. Most jet pumps will quickly lose prime if air gets into the line, so they are not the best choice for low-yield wells like sand points. Loss of prime can also result from such perennial favourites as leaks in the suction line or foot-valve failure – but whatever the cause, the pump's impeller will soon be spinning in air. And this is not just a problem for cottagers caught in the shower. Just as with a centrifugal pump, the mechanical seal on a jet pump (the seal located where the impeller shaft enters the pump casing) will quickly burn out without water to lubricate and cool it.

Sand, gravel, and sediment can block the injector and wear the impeller, diffuser, and mechanical seal, although the jet pump is not as sensitive to such debris as the piston pump. And as long as the water box doesn't run dry, the jet pump tends to be more reliable than the piston pump, and about as maintenance free as any non-submersible pump can get.

The fastest way to prime a shallow-well jet pump is to ignore manufacturer's instructions (pull the priming cap, pour water in, turn the impeller by hand to rid it of any air bubbles, replace the cap, start the pump, and repeat as required) and reach for fast-acting Max's Amazing Easy Prime (Chapter 11).

DEEP-WELL JET PUMPS: FOR THAT EXTRA LIFT

Unfortunately, water is not always available within a 25-ft. lift from the pump. One solution to this dilemma is the deep-well jet pump. If you fight your way through the cobwebs in a cottage crawl space or pump house and happen to stumble across a deep-well jet pump, you wouldn't notice much of a difference from its shallow-well cousin. What differs most between the two is something you can't see: A deep-well jet pump's injector is submerged in, or positioned close to, the water source.

When water is being drawn from a lake, a river, or a well of 4-in. diameter or greater, the deep-well jet pump system employs two pipes running between the injector and the pump – one for the incoming water (the delivery or suction line) and the other for the water being recirculated back to the injector in its remote location (the pressure or return line). At this end (if it's submerged you won't see it), the two pipes join at the injector in a Y-shaped housing. The leg of this Y points down and incorporates a foot valve. The pump forces the recirculated water down the pressure line to one arm of the Y, where it makes a 180° turn to head up the other arm of the Y back towards the pump. At the turn, it passes through the venturi, creating a low-pressure area about as close to the end of the delivery line as you can get. Atmospheric pressure acting on the source water pushes the water through the foot valve into the remote injector (technically, suction head only encompasses this distance between the foot valve and injector venturi), where it joins the recirculated water, passing through the venturi and, presto, velocity decreases and pressure increases (just as it would with a shallow-well system). The water sent down the pressure line, through the injector, and subsequently back up the delivery line is being motivated by pump pressure, which is considerably greater than what your local atmosphere can muster. This is the force that carries the incoming water back up to the pump, which explains why the vertical rise of a deep-well jet can exceed the 25 ft. maximum of any shallow-well pump.

In fact, by using the pressure it produces at the pump to deliver source water to itself, a deep-well jet pump can lift water as high as 120 ft. But as lift increases, the quantity of water recirculated down to the injector must also increase, which reduces pressure on the discharge side of the pump. When the lift reaches about 60 ft., the water decides it's easier to head for the kitchen tap than to deal with these long-distance push-ups. Robbed of sufficient pressurized water, the injector can't do its job and the flow stops. To keep enough water travelling back down to the injector, a control cock valve is added to the discharge side of the pump, between the pump and the pressure tank. Its purpose is to create sufficient back pressure to force the required quantity of water back down to the injector. (It's sort of like an attendant standing outside the parking lot closest to the restaurant you're headed for, waving most of the cars by but letting the occasional one in as space becomes available. If you don't get in, you drive around the block again, building up pressure.) Because so much of the pump's water, and therefore pressure, is used just to get the water to the tap, deep-well jet pumps are not the hot setup for killer showers when lifts exceed 60 ft.

For low-yield wells, a 9-m (30-ft.) tailpipe is added to the leg of the injector. This simple gizmo gradually decreases the amount of water being pumped as the level of the well drops, preventing the water line from dropping below the foot valve and therefore losing prime.

Wells less than 4 in. in diameter but greater than 2 in. can use an inner pipe injector (or packer jet) that uses the space between the delivery line and the well casing as a pressure line, the working principles being the same as the standard double line. Many older drilled wells have 2-in. casings. For driven wells like sand points, where the lift is greater than 25 ft., there is no other option if you want an electric pump. (The well liner is too small in diameter to house a submersible pump.)

The deep-well jet pump is a real nuisance to prime and is not self repriming. Both pipes must be kept full of water for the pump to work, and both must be manually filled as part of the priming procedure. Check your manual for the details specific to your preference in brand and clear the area of children and other innocents. A foot valve is essential for all deep-well jet pumps.

When the pump is offset from the water source by more than 40 ft., calculations for head loss for this dual pipe system get a little weird but, fortunately, each pump manufacturer supplies charts to make choosing the right pipes almost easy. Installation, however, is another matter. A deep-well jet pump system starts at around $500, the price rising in proportion to the lift and horizontal run required. Because of the difficulty in priming a deep-well jet pump, its expense, and the minimal pres-

PREVENTION IS WORTH A POUND OF BURNT-OUT PUMPS

Goulds Pumps Incorporated has a neat solution to the problem of lost prime on its J and G series of shallow-well jet pumps; a diaphragm that divides the water box. The diaphragm is a stiff piece of rubber-like material with two quarter-sized holes towards the top. The water enters the impeller side of the diaphragm through the injector, and exits back into the discharge side through the two upper holes. As only the water above those holes is being pumped out, if we're not bringing any additional water in, the water won't rise above that level. It's a bit like the overflow drain on the bathtub – the water pours in, spilling out the overflow when it rises to that level. Water always remains in the tub until somebody pulls the plug. What does this mean to cottagers?

The company claims that if the pump loses its prime – from a leaky foot valve or hole in the line,

for instance – the diaphragm keeps the impeller and the seal in water. The only way to rid the water box entirely of water is to remove the drain plugs. Just like a tub. The impeller just splashes around in its own bath, it and the seal staying lubricated and cool for up to 36 hours, at least according to the admittedly biased manufacturer. Personally, I don't have the resources to sit around waiting for a pump to burn up, just to see how long it takes. However, what I have witnessed is how well the Goulds pump will self-reprime without having to add any water, and that is neat. Company representatives even boast that a cottage system having a 1-in. line, a 15-ft. vertical lift, and 100 ft. of offset between the water source and pump, will start pumping water in about four minutes after filling the water box with about 1 L (1 US qt.) of water.

sure it yields when the lift is greater than 60 ft., this permutation of the centrifugal pump is quickly being replaced by the submersible pump.

SUBMERSIBLE PUMPS: THE UNDERWATER WONDERS

For about the same amount of money as you would spend on a deep-well jet pump, you can get a submersible pump. Because the entire pump is immersed in water, a submersible never needs priming. Tucked away in the well or lake, submersibles contribute nothing in the way of noise to the cottage environment. Better-quality submersibles are designed to handle suspended sand and turbid water without suffering severe wear. (The sand will still wear away at seals and impellers, but it takes much longer for the parts to fail, at least in theory.) Submersibles are essentially maintenance free, have a long life expectancy, and are capable of pumping high volumes of water.

Undoubtedly, the submersible pump is the best pump to use when lifts exceed 25 ft. Because the pump attaches to the submerged end of the delivery line, all the water is being delivered to the cottage with the full force of the pump. In other words, the pump is pushing the water the entire way to the kitchen tap – atmospheric pressure only has to push the water into the spinning impellers. Suction head is therefore negligible; discharge head equals total head (that certainly takes the figuring out of it), and the total head can be quite substantial – more than 1,000 ft. for some models.

The submersible pump is a multi-stage centrifugal pump, which means it has a series of impellers and diffusers stacked together, each additional stage benefiting from, and adding to, the previous impeller's work. Physically, it's about a 2 ft.–4 ft. long tube, 4 in.–6 in. in diameter, a hot-dogular shape that allows it to be lowered down a standard drilled well casing if need be.

While surface-mounted pumps rely on air circulation for cooling, the submersible depends on the flow of water being drawn past the motor. When the flow-rate drops below the manufacturer's specifications, the motor can overheat and burn out. In a drilled well, this is not usually a concern since the water drawn into the pump must squeeze between the pump body and the well casing, the speed of flow past the motor therefore increasing (just as the speed of water flow increases as it passes through the venturi in a jet pump injector). However, in a large body of water,

PRIME REAL ESTATE

Obviously, it's tough to beat submersible pumps when it comes to minimizing the distance to the water source, but landlubber pumps can certainly benefit from being moved to waterfront real estate, like boathouses or pump houses. The object is to take maximum advantage of that meagre potential 14.7 psi of atmospheric pressure. Because such a move reduces suction-head loss, the water arrives at the pump closer to the initial pressure push atmospheric pressure gave it. This results in faster start-ups and less wear on the pump, and the water arrives at its final destination under more pressure.

Aside from improving pump efficiency, relocation puts the noise outside the cottage. A pump house should be weather-proof, adequately vented, and insulated if winter use is planned. With insulation appropriate for your particular cottage climate, the pump house can be kept above the freezing mark by leaving a single 60-watt light bulb on inside. (This gives the mice something to read by.) Insulation will also subdue pump noise.

The structure should be above the high-water mark or flood plane (if possible), and if pack ice is likely to overflow the shoreline in the spring, set back far enough to escape damage. It's also nice to have enough room to move around and service the pump. Although some jurisdictions forbid the use of pump houses for anything else but housing the pump (wonder where they got the name?), it's not a bad place to store life jackets, canoe paddles, and similar cottage accoutrements.

And regardless of locale, pumps should always be securely anchored in place. A bouncing or moving pump puts a strain on the joints connecting the water lines to it, which is a bit like putting the welcome mat out for leaks.

even though the quantities of water are great, the speed of the water passing by the motor is much reduced. Also, in surface sources such as lakes and rivers, the temperature of the water can get quite warm during the summer months. The solution is to install a flow-inducer sleeve over the pump (picture a family-size bean can being slipped over a smaller one), duplicating the water-flow characteristics of the smaller-diameter well casing. Manufacturers consider this sleeve a must in these situations (although many installers don't agree).

If a submersible is placed in a dug well, because of the limited demands placed on the pump during typical cottage use, the flow-inducer sleeve is considered unnecessary. The sleeve is usually made from a stainless-steel tube or a piece of 4-in. ABS or PVC plastic pipe, the discharge end plugged with a well cap to accommodate the discharge pipe and electrical lines. At the intake end, a stainless-steel screen will keep out the creepy-crawlies, minnows, and frogs. In addition to helping keep the motor cool by speeding up the flow of water past it, the sleeve will also protect the motor from getting bumped by rocks, boats, swimmers, and the large fish that got away.

Electrically speaking, there are three types of submersibles: the three-wire 230V, three-wire 115V, and two-wire 115V. If the pump is more than 90 m (300 ft.) from the main electrical panel, a 230V circuit is pretty well a must due to electrical losses in the wire (similar in concept to head loss in water pipes). And, all other things being equal, a 115V motor does not run as efficiently as a similar 230V motor and therefore will (at least in theory) cost a little more to operate and wear a little quicker. Whether a cottager will notice the difference is debatable. (Gosh knows I've debated it long enough with several experts, and that's as close to a definitive answer I can get on this planet.)

That said, the less-common two-wire 115V submersible is the way for the do-it-yourselfer to go because it's much easier to install. This is especially true of submersibles installed in lakes or rivers, when a GFI (Class A ground fault interrupter) is required. The GFI, which monitors the flow of electricity and shuts the power off if any leakage is detected, protects swimmers from the ever-unpopular death by electrical shock should some adventurous electrons decide it's time for a little water recreation (such as when a wire is severed or frayed). A run-of-the-mill 115V GFI outdoor outlet can be located at the water's edge, which is a darn sight easier and less expensive to install than wiring the main electrical panel for a 10 milliamp 230V GFI, a task I would have serious reservations about suggesting the average cottage handyperson tackle. With good instructions (which your plumbing-supply store should supply), the 115V pump could even be installed by a lawyer. Well, maybe it's not that simple, but you get the idea.

Regardless of voltage, a submersible pump is the most problem-free of all motorized pumps, the most efficient, and the most likely to bowl you over in the shower. Like deep-well jet pumps, submersibles tend to increase in price in direct proportion to lifts.

YOU GET WHAT YOU PAY FOR: THE SAD ECONOMIC REALITIES OF QUALITY PUMPS

Regrettably, the pump most likely to give you the most years of trouble-free service is probably one of the more expensive models. The sad fact is, higher-quality materials usually cost more.

In a jet pump, look for what is called a double-ball-bearing motor, meaning the motor's shaft rides in ball bearings at each end. Cheaper pumps usually have a sleeve bearing at one end of the motor with a ball bearing at the other. Ball bearings reduce friction, which usually translates into longer life. If the motor's shaft is stainless steel instead of cold-rolled steel, so much the better.

Dampness is a piston or jet pump's nemesis. These motors rely on air for cooling. Humidity in the air gets into the motor and corrodes the inner workings. Submersibles, although immersed in water, don't have this problem since the motor must be sealed to keep moisture out. Water is also a more efficient means of cooling than air, so submersibles tend to run cooler too. Next to moisture, heat is the big enemy of electrical components. Like the flow of water through pipes, the flow of electrons through wire creates friction, which in turn generates heat. Because heat destroys the insulated coatings of wire and the wire itself, all things electric go into self-destruct mode as soon as you turn them on. How quickly this happens depends on many things, including the choice of material for wire.

Most less-expensive pumps use aluminum for the inner workings. Aluminum heats up very quickly. More-expensive pumps often use copper for the areas of greatest load (and therefore greatest potential heat build-up), reserving the less-expensive aluminum for lesser duties. Because copper wire conducts electricity more efficiently, it runs much cooler, so copper wire is less apt to be at the cause of motor failure.

Big bolts are another nice feature to look for – and one you can actually see without having to ask a salesperson. They're especially nice in places that come in contact with water, such as when they protrude into the water box of a jet or piston pump. Small bolts and nuts don't afford sufficient leverage for undoing when rusted in place after 10 years of faithfully serving the cottage. Should you ever feel disposed to take your pump apart in order to replace a seal or whatever, you won't take much notice of hefty bolts. However, your attention will quickly be focused on lesser bolts and nuts that snap or strip as you try to fix the pump down in the claustrophobic crawl space when the sun is shining outside for the first time this week and you can hear the neighbours out water-skiing, laughing... Mind the tongue, they can probably hear you too.

There are genuine differences in pump quality, most of which even the uninformed can ferret out by asking questions and looking beyond the price tag. Cheaper pumps will work, and may last a lifetime. Me, I'm not much of a gambler. I bought a good pump with a well-known reputation for quality.

BLOWIN' IN THE WIND: WIND-DRIVEN PUMPS

One pumping system that I haven't yet owned but most certainly will, for it has captivated me since childhood (which works out to a fair number of years), is the windmill. Admittedly, the main motivator is romance, although once you are past the fright of the initial cost, you can justify the choice by its negligible operating expenses. But who needs to justify the tranquil beauty of a windmill's blades spinning slothfully through a gentle breeze as they toss the glow of a setting sun all over the lake and yard?

While it can be argued (quite successfully) that the windmill is an impractical mechanism for romantics when it comes to the production of electricity, for cottages without electricity, a wind-powered pump makes sense. Mostly, it relates to storage. Electricity is difficult and expensive to store. Water is easy and economical to store.

Even in a stiff breeze, don't expect a windmill to deliver water like a submersible pump. Traditional windmill pumps are positive-displacement pumps, basically hand pumps powered by wind, with delivery to match. With tower, blades, pump, and all related goodies suitable for a 15-m (50-ft.) drilled well, a traditional windmill will cost about $4,000–5,000. And it must be mounted directly above the water source, limiting it to well applications. Such a unit will deliver about 6.5 L/min (1.7 US gpm) in a 20 kph (12 mph) breeze. If the breeze holds, you can expect 400 L in an hour. At 5 kph, you'll get 4 L–8 L an hour. At wind speeds below that, most windmill pumps won't start. The windmill should be about 5 m (16 ft.) above any objects within 125 m (400 ft.) of the tower.

For those not bent on tradition, there is a more modern and less-expensive alternative, suitable for dug wells and surface-water applications that require an offset power source. This windmill operates a diaphragm pump (see next page for basic operating theory), which in turn pumps air into a reciprocal water pump – a submerged tubular chamber with a float valve towards the top. As the water enters the chamber, the float valve rises, closing off the intake. The wind-driven diaphragm pump forces air through a long hose down into the chamber, pushing the water out and up the intake line to the cottage. When the water level in the chamber drops to a predetermined level, another valve releases the air (and therefore the pressure) out of the chamber and the upper float valve drops, letting another bunch of water in; the water in the tube rises, forcing the float valve shut, and the process starts all over again. Because this windmill is designed to fill watering troughs for farm animals, it will run in extremely light winds (3 kph–4 kph), delivering just a shade less water than the above-mentioned traditional windmill. All this and spinning blades for less than $1,000.

Both types of windmills are true self-priming pumps, and are unaffected by dry operation. You can leave either to operate on its own, filling the reservoir as long as there's water to pump, and should the well (or lake) run dry, the blades just keep spinning around aimlessly with no harm done, ready for the well to replenish itself. Ideal for low-yield situations.

Like the hand pump, windmills are not for serious consumers of water. The size of the reservoir required must take into consideration the family's needs, peak demands, average wind speeds for your cottage area, and windless days. And, just in case the wind doesn't cooperate at all, it's a good idea to have a backup pumping system. Like the hand-operated diaphragm pump.

THE HAND-OPERATED DIAPHRAGM PUMP: THE NO-PRIME PRIMING PUMP

The hand-operated diaphragm pump is a positive-displacement pump, but instead of using a piston in a cylinder, it takes advantage of the flexible nature of a thin rubber-like membrane – the diaphragm. When raised, the handle of the pump lifts the diaphragm, increasing the volume of the pumping chamber to establish the required low-pressure area. This in turn pulls open a small flapper valve on the intake side while pulling another shut against the pump body on the delivery side (much like the traditional hand pump's flappers, only smaller). When the handle is lowered, the downward thrust of the diaphragm pushes the intake valve shut while forcing the pump's contents out the discharge flapper. The pump works in or out of water, and will pump air or water, which means no priming required, thank you very much – a true self-primer and swell cottage accessory.

EQUAL TIME FOR PERSONAL PREJUDICES DEPARTMENT

Yes, there are other brands of hand-operated diaphragm pumps on the market, but I really like the Guzzler. Although we used a Guzzler to supply our cottage for several months while we were between pumps (recreational activities taking precedence over work at the cottage you know), this pump's main purpose in life is to assist in the priming of jet and piston pumps. (See Chapter 11.) But it will also pump out a sailboat after the big storm (or dunking), supply water during power outages, replace a traditional hand pump, fill a cistern or water tower (it has a 9-m or 30-ft. potential discharge head) or, with a simple nozzle attachment, shoot water over 9 m (30 ft.) horizontally or 5 m (16 ft.) straight up, making it a dandy device for emergency fire fighting or dousing the neighbour's noisy kids and their portable stereo. You can even hook it up backwards and push the water out of a line for winter storage. All this and more without using a watt of electricity.

The plastic-bodied Guzzler is small and light (550 grams, 1¼ lbs.), and it sells for about $50–$60, depending on whether you count your pay cheque in US or Canadian dollars.

BUCKETS OF ALTERNATIVE ADVICE

Our cottage property has two residential buildings on it, the original cottage and an eternally-in-progress year-round home. When the decision was made to build the latter, we decided to move full time into the former because of the obvious convenience of living in close proximity to the construction site. During the ensuing months, work and play eased into a conceptual marriage, not always in perfect harmony, but usually acting as one.

The cottage has no indoor plumbing. Rain barrels exceed wash-water demand in the spring and fall, with drinking water and supplemental wash water drawn from an artesian spring. The spring lies about 60 m (200 ft.) beyond the outhouse, tucked in behind a 9-m (30-ft.) high outcropping of bedrock. Even when the official outhouse thermometer dares to touch the minus 40 mark, the water in the spring still flows. There is a peculiar and undefinable pleasure derived from going to get water at these times, the silence of winter broken only by the sound of snowflakes murmuring under the soft sweep of snowshoes, each step dragging work and play closer to a shared definition.

Our first winter was the season of no pump and a temporary spring box. We slid the top aside and scooped out a bucket of cold, spring water. The buckets we used (humanity having long ago discovered that it is far easier to carry two heavy buckets than to struggle with the imbalanced – albeit lighter – load of one) were plastic food-grade 10-L (2.6-US gal.) pails that first saw duty as peanut butter containers at the local bulk-food store. The lids snap on tight, preventing the water from spilling out and things from getting in during transit. Back at the cottage, the water got decanted into either glass jars (drinking water) or a large plastic water container blessed with a tap (supplemental wash water). Whenever the thermometer stayed on the warm side of the freezing mark, we stepped out the back door and dipped a pot into the rain barrel for washing water.

Had we been aware from the outset that this routine would stretch out for nearly three years, no question we would have taken a pass, thank you very much. However, having experienced it, it really wasn't that bad. Honest. Hauling your own water makes you aware of how much gets used, and how little you actually need. You become part of the system, not just a detached, unquenchable consumer.

Even cottagers with electricity shouldn't dismiss hauling water from a lake, river, or well without considering whether its merits can mesh with the owners' lifestyle. A bucket patrol eliminates the cost and maintenance of pumps and pressurized plumbing. Humans can be quicker to coax (or threaten) into service each spring, don't need to be drained for the winter and, even when not in their prime, are still able to move water. It's a proven, time-honoured tradition. It's also a bit of work, and makes a wintertime hot shower all but impossible. So we got a pump for the new house.

But when we finally get around to constructing a log cabin back in the woods (project #5,397), there won't be a pump in sight. Although, maybe a windmill...

4 HOOKING UP THE SYSTEM

How to keep your pipe dreams from turning into plumbing nightmares

System setup:
Most problems related to maintaining the pump's prime have their roots in the intake line: If the pump can't draw water in, it can't pump it out.

COTTAGE PLUMBING IS A PARTNERSHIP OF opposites: the supply system and the waste system. The supply system consists of two subsystems – the incoming system and the inside-the-cottage pressure system – while the waste system is everything on the exit side of the plumbing, even if it's pressurized (as it is with a sewage pump, for instance). For water to complete the loop from earth to cottage and back to earth, each component of the water system must be doing its part. Failure at any point can threaten not only the frivolous stuff such as having a shower and flushing the loo, but also the essentials, such as producing ice cubes for the lemonade.

A typical supply system could include (not necessarily in this order) a strainer, foot valve, intake line, check valve, pump, line out of the pump, sediment filter, pressure tank or reservoir, and water-treatment device, followed by the usual maze of indoor plumbing we have come either to ignore or to despise. Since the mechanics of piecing pipe together are covered in countless other books (see Chapter 13 for recommended reading), such basics will be left to those journals. Instead, the focus of this chapter is on the idiosyncrasies of the cottage water system, most of which are overlooked in general how-to books.

THE INTAKE LINE

Atmospheric pressure doesn't only exist at the end of an intake line, pushing the water up the pipe; it exerts the same pressure along the total length of pipe. The majority of problems related to maintaining the pump's prime can be traced to the intake line running between the water source and the pump. When this line depends on the low pressure established in the pump to draw water through it (as opposed to the water being pushed through the pipe, as it is with a submersible pump), it is also referred to as a suction line. If it's easier for atmospheric pressure to sneak in through a crack or poorly sealed joint than to push the water up the length of a suction line, it will. If that leak resides above the wa-

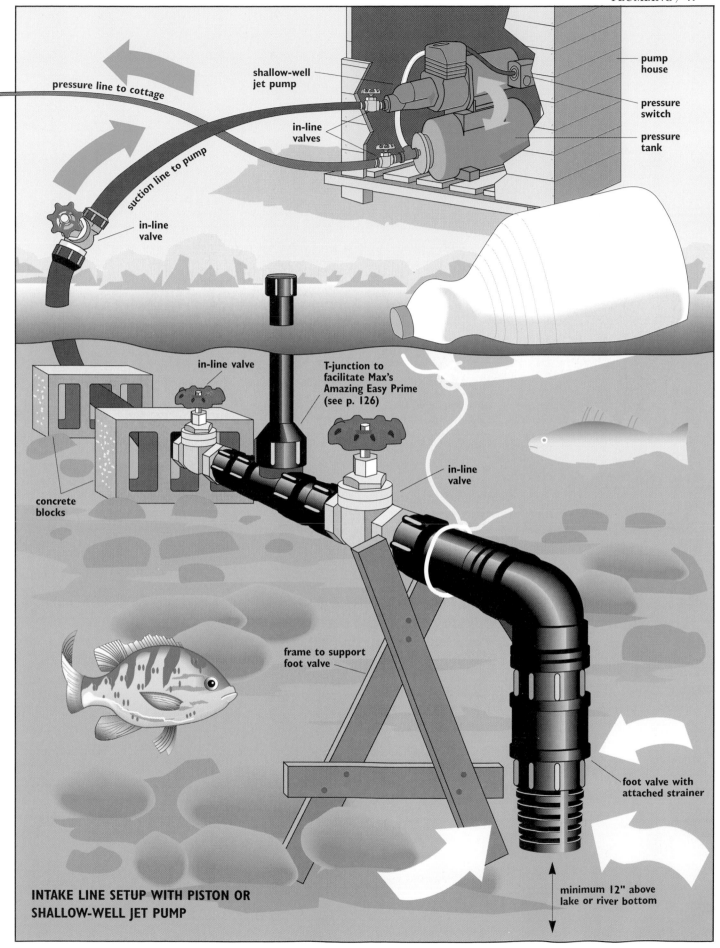

pressure line to cottage

shallow-well jet pump

in-line valves

pump house

pressure switch

pressure tank

suction line to pump

in-line valve

in-line valve

T-junction to facilitate Max's Amazing Easy Prime (see p. 126)

in-line valve

concrete blocks

frame to support foot valve

foot valve with attached strainer

minimum 12" above lake or river bottom

INTAKE LINE SETUP WITH PISTON OR SHALLOW-WELL JET PUMP

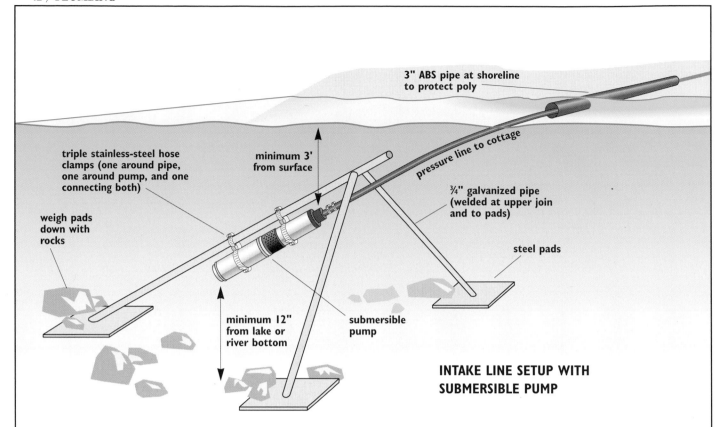

triple stainless-steel hose
clamps (one around pipe,
one around pump, and one
connecting both)

3" ABS pipe at shoreline
to protect poly

minimum 3'
from surface

pressure line to cottage

¾" galvanized pipe
(welded at upper join
and to pads)

weigh pads
down with
rocks

steel pads

minimum 12"
from lake or
river bottom

submersible
pump

**INTAKE LINE SETUP WITH
SUBMERSIBLE PUMP**

Line management:
*Choose poly pipe with
a 100-psi rating or
higher to make your
intake line more
damage-resistant.
It also makes sense to
run it through an
outer protective sleeve
at water's edge.*

ter line, atmospheric pressure will push air into the cracks, and it's so long, prime.

The line from the water source to the cottage can be on the surface, underground, or some combination of the two. Underground runs tend to be more expensive and more reliable. Surface installations are relatively inexpensive, more problematic and, unless you own your own backhoe, better suited to the do-it-yourselfer. Traditionally, intake lines were best installed on a continuous, gradual upward slope from source to cottage, with no dips or flat spots along the way, to ease priming and draining. However, modern pump technology and hand-operated diaphragm pumps – which can be used to fill the line with water for priming and force air through for draining – have nearly eliminated this requirement. Yet a slope – about a 2-cm drop per metre of horizontal run, or ¼ in. per foot, *minimum* (see Chapter 12 for winter use variances) – is still a worthy goal to aim for. While it is possible to force the water out of a roller-coasteresque line at season's end, why use elbow grease when gravity will do the job? For shallow-well pumps operating without foot valves (more on these valves later), a self-draining line remains a must.

If the suction line terminates in surface water, an economical way to keep the pipe secured and submerged, and not floating or drifting aimlessly about like a teenager on a Saturday night, is to run the line through a concrete building block every metre (3 ft.) or so. (Hmm, maybe that might work for teenagers too....)

CHOOSING AND INSTALLING AN INTAKE LINE

Black polyethylene pipe (PE, or poly to its friends) has become *de rigueur* for cottage intake lines, all but replacing corrosion-prone metal pipe. In fact, if your water is the least bit acidic, you should never use galvanized metal for pipes or fittings.

In Canada, look for the CSA approval stamp on the side of poly pipe, and in the US, the ANSI, ASTM, or NSF stamps, although approvals from all of these testing organizations are increasingly becoming accepted on either side of the border. Poly is also graded by its maximum-allowable pressure rating. The higher-rated pipe has thicker walls

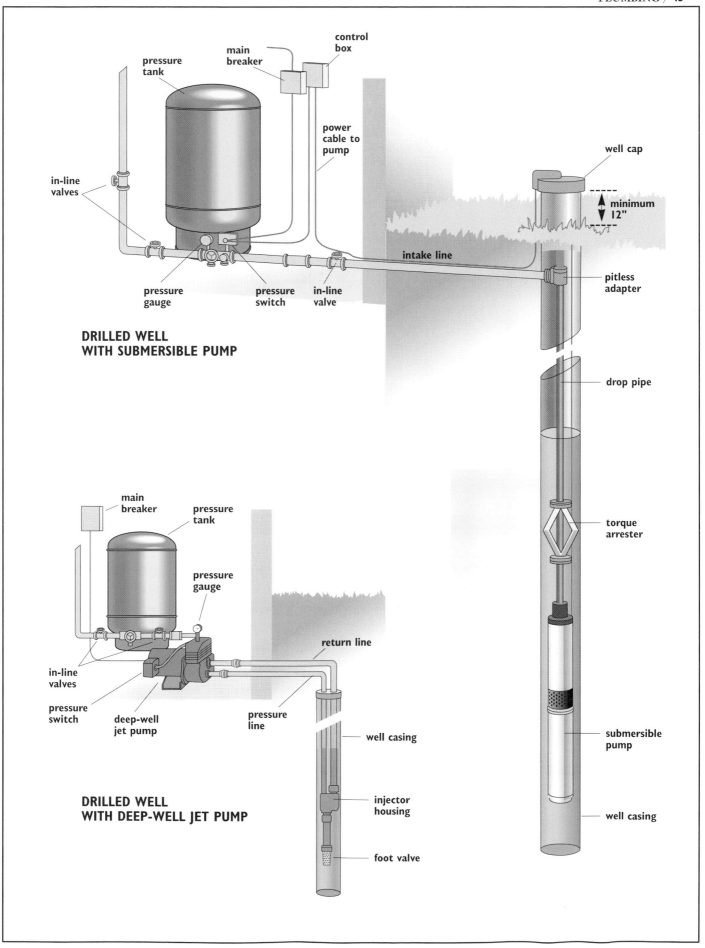

pressure
tank

main
breaker

control
box

power
cable to
pump

well cap

minimum
12"

in-line
valves

intake line

pitless
adapter

pressure
gauge

pressure
switch

in-line
valve

**DRILLED WELL
WITH SUBMERSIBLE PUMP**

drop pipe

torque
arrester

main
breaker

pressure
tank

pressure
gauge

return line

in-line
valves

pressure
switch

deep-well
jet pump

pressure
line

well casing

submersible
pump

injector
housing

**DRILLED WELL
WITH DEEP-WELL JET PUMP**

foot valve

well casing

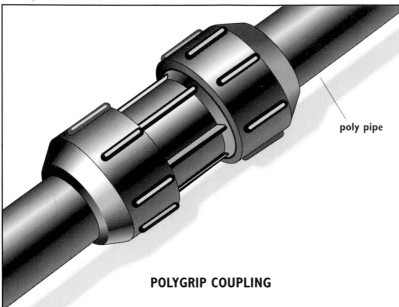

POLYGRIP COUPLING

poly pipe

Joint action:
*You can join poly pipes
using a barbed
coupling and hose
clamps (below). Using
two clamps for each
end makes the joint
less likely to leak. Or
you can switch to
PolyGrip compression
fittings (above), which
make connecting and
disconnecting as easy
as turning a nut.*

and is therefore a little more difficult to handle, but it is substantially tougher, and subsequently more resistant to damage. Go with a
100-psi rating or higher. Some jurisdictions,
such as Wisconsin, won't permit anything less
than 150-psi poly for suction lines, while others exempt owner-occupied, single-family
dwellings on private water systems (which describes most cottages) from the plumbing
code entirely. While lax laws may open the
door to low-grade (or utility-grade) poly, don't
be tempted – the savings are simply not worth
the aggravation. The more often you stress a
pipe to its design limits, the sooner it will fail
and transfer that stress to you. As a cottage is
supposed to be a stress-reduced environment,
buy only quality pipe and fixtures. In most

cases, an approved, 100-psi, 1 in.–1½–in.
diameter intake line will do the job.

Whether you run the intake line above
ground or below, a dandy way to protect it is
to run it inside an outer protective shell, like 4-
in. diameter corrugated plastic drain pipe.
This sleeve is inexpensive, curves easily around
90° bends, keeps the sun off the inner pipe
(sunlight degrades plastics), and stops the poly
and joints from chafing against rocks and such.
If the line is buried underground, the sleeve
prevents rocks or sand from caving in around
the pipe. This means you can pull the poly
out of the sleeve should repairs be required,
and then feed the pipe back in without having
to dig up the whole mess. (None of this applies where regulations call for concentric pip-
ing, where the buried suction line is enclosed
in a larger pipe filled with water pressurized by
the cottage system.)

The trick to getting poly through corrugated drain pipe is to cram a large caster into
the end of the poly, securing it in place with
tape and a self-tapping screw. The caster encourages the leading lip of the poly to roll
over the corrugations instead of getting hung
up on each and every ridge. Feeding the poly
into the sleeve is best accomplished with two
teams – one pushing the poly, the other dragging the sleeve over top. (Up our way, we're
trying to get this popular activity recognized
as an official Olympic sport. Or at least part of
the fall fair.)

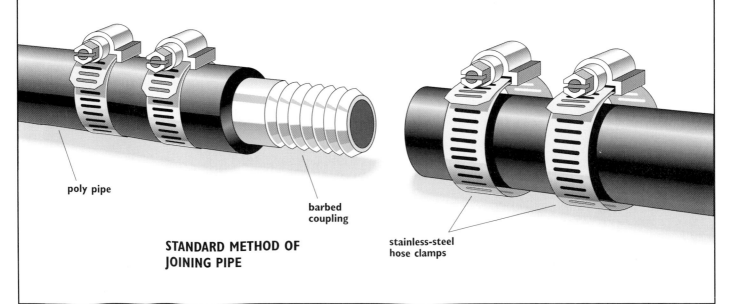

poly pipe

barbed
coupling

**STANDARD METHOD OF
JOINING PIPE**

stainless-steel
hose clamps

Since joints are the most probable points of potential leaks, ideally the intake line should be one continuous pipe, with connections only at each end. Admittedly, this can be difficult to achieve with overland lines that need to be rolled up for winter storage, but the fewer joints, the better.

HOW TO JOIN INTAKE LINES

The traditional method of joining poly to pump or poly to poly is to use a barbed coupling (threaded on one end when it's connecting poly to a pump, barbed on both when it's connecting poly to poly). A barbed coupling works like a fishhook or an arrowhead – it slides in (with a bit of work) but has slanted rings whose edges grip the inside of the pipe when you try to pull it out. In addition to this coupling, you will need two stainless-steel worm-drive joint clamps for each barbed end of the coupling. They're called worm-drive because the screw sort of crawls along a row of slits cut into the clamp, but they're often sold simply as hose clamps. You can get away with one clamp on each end of the coupling, but doubling up makes the joint much less likely to leak, and the extra expense is minimal. Slip the slack clamps onto the pipe first, then slide the pipe over the coupling. Pouring hot water over the end of the pipe prior to this makes the plastic more pliable and easier to force onto the coupling. (A hair dryer will also do the trick if hot water is not available.) Tighten the clamps, and you're done. (Always test the joint for leaks before burying or installing in an outer sleeve.)

REPAIRING LEAKS IN THE INTAKE LINE

Whenever barbed couplings are removed from the pipe (such as when storing the pipe for winter), the poly has a tendency to crack. Leaks can also result from the pipe being stepped on or run over, or simply from old age. Whatever the cause, cracks or splits in poly have to be cut out (a hacksaw works best for this task) and a new piece spliced in using the above joining techniques. If a leak finds you short on extra pipe and couplings and long on visiting relatives, temporary repairs can be made to small splits by wrapping them first in tape (duct tape works best), then a section of inner tube (perhaps liberated from the bicycle of the kid who ran over the pipe?) or similar squishy substance, and then securing the patch in place with a few hose clamps. Spare hose clamps, like bandages and snacks, are cottage essentials.

Or you could switch to PolyGrip. No, not the substance of similar name designed to hold dentures in place, but PolyGrip compression fittings for plastic pipe. Made in Australia, these wonders are similar in principle to the compression fittings found on the air tools a mechanic overtightens things with, except that instead of snapping hoses together, you simply turn a nut. Joints that are likely to be disconnected at the end of each season, such as those at the foot valve and pump ends of the pipe, become a breeze to put together and take apart, a one-minute job so simple a politician could do it without even having to establish a committee to study the matter first. And leaks from cracked pipe at these connections are virtually eliminated.

PolyGrip fittings are approved for use in most jurisdictions and are stronger than the pipe they join to. They are more expensive than traditional clamps and couplings, but ever so much nicer, and come in an endless array of shapes and sizes to suit most cottage needs, including foot valves and in-line ball valves. Repairs can even be done underwater, in the winter, or both if you're seriously masochistic. Cut out the cracked section, attach the PolyGrip fittings to the two ends, and screw them together, no gluing or heating required. That's the good news. The bad news is that PolyGrip fittings can be difficult to find. Nag your local plumbing supplier, for they are available and worth their premium price.

WHAT'S ON THE INTAKE LINE

THE STRAINER: POSITION IT PROPERLY

At the submerged end of the intake line is (or should be) a strainer. The strainer's purpose is to prevent pebbles and other debris from getting into the water line, all of which can destroy valves and pump seals, not to mention the texture such stuff adds to your drinking water. Sometimes the strainer is part of the foot valve or, in the case of the submersible, integrated into the pump. Never use a strainer with holes smaller or larger than what's recommended by the pump's manufacturer.

While the strainer should be kept below the water's surface at all times so the pump does not take to sucking air, it should not be left to rest on the bottom. In wells, the strainer's position is usually determined by the depth of the line and type of pump. But whether it's submerged in a well or surface water, keep the strainer a minimum of 30 cm (12 in.) above the bottom and 1 m (3 ft.) below the surface. For surface-water applications, the distance from shore is dictated by the water's depth (keeping in mind any change in water level over the summer), the location of the dock (with its associated boat droppings and sweaty-swimmer slime), and ease of installation and maintenance.

If the bottom of the lake or river is covered in stones, placing the strainer within a larger basket or crib will protect it from damage and clogging. You can purchase ready-made foot-valve protectors that do a very fine job of keeping aqua-trash out. Another solution is to secure the strainer and intake line to a simple, easy to build platform or A-frame structure, the frame anchored in place with rocks. If the bottom is soft mud, the strainer can be suspended from a buoy to keep it from ingesting the muck.

FOOT VALVES AND CHECK VALVES: HOW THEY WORK AND WHY THEY SOMETIMES DON'T

Immediately up from the strainer, and usually attached to it, is the foot valve, a type of check valve whose name is derived from its location (at the foot of the system) and its function (a valve being a device to control flow – in this case, the flow of water; a check valve permits the water to flow in one direction only). Specifically, the purpose of the foot valve is to keep the intake line full of water, ready for the next time the pump is called to

action. Check valves located elsewhere along the line, usually just a bit before the pump (or in the case of a submersible, just after the pump), are known simply as check valves.

In the case of a foot valve or any check valve that precedes the pump, when the pump starts up, the low pressure it creates will open the valve and the water flows up the intake line. When the pump stops, a spring shuts the valve, assisted by the weight of water held in the line above it. If a valve fails, the water drains back into the lake or well. Then the pump sucks on a pipe full of air, the cottage taps burping and gurgling like mischievous kids belting back a bottle of ginger ale. When a check valve follows the pump (as is the case with a submersible pump, for instance), the valve is opened by water pressure, the spring and water above the valve closing it when the pressure relents (as when the submersible pump shuts off).

More often than not, check-valve failure is caused by dirt lodged between the valve and the valve seat (against which the valve closes), or an improper seal at the joint where the line meets the valve. In either case, the water above it sneaks by. To test a foot valve,

KEEPING WATER IN LINE

An in-line valve is a tap without a spout, its purpose being to isolate the various sections of the supply system. This makes for faster, less troublesome repair, as you won't have to drain and then reprime the entire system after tending to a localized problem. In fact, in many cases, in-line valves permit continued use of the system while a localized repair is taking place. Use only gate valves or ball valves for this task; the less-expensive conventional types, also known as globe valves, restrict flow even when fully open. This is particularly important on intake lines because any restriction reduces the potential lift. By peering through a gate or ball valve as you open it, you'll be able to see the gate lifting or the ball turning; when these valves are fully open, nothing obstructs the view. In contrast, you won't be able to see much through an open conventional in-line valve.

Good places for in-line valves are at the foot valve, on both the intake and output sides of the pump, at the pressure tank, and before any fixture, such as the toilet or kitchen sink.

the line must be hoisted out of the water. Regular check valves are usually above the surface and accessible. Inspect for seepage around the joint, looking carefully for cracks in the pipe where it meets the valve.

If there are no apparent leaks at the joint, remove the valve from the line. Hold the valve upright and pour water in the top (with the strainer removed if it's a foot valve). No water should pour out the bottom. If it does, you've got a leak. Invert the mechanism, and while holding the valve open, pour clean water through to flush it out. Use an old toothbrush or the end of your finger to clean the surfaces where the valve and valve seat meet. Hold it upright and check for leaks again. If the cleaning did not work, then either the spring, the seat, or the valve itself is kaput, and it's time for a new valve.

One of the best things you can do for a check valve is the one most often ignored – keep the valve as close as possible to the position it was designed to operate in. For example, in surface-water applications, foot valves are often installed in the horizontal position. However, if the valve is propped up vertically, or at least at a 45° angle, the water column inside the pipe above it can then help close the valve. This results in less wear on the spring. Also, dirt will be more inclined to fall through the valve rather than get hung up on the valve seat. Speaking of dirt, even the lowly strainer attached to the foot valve will be less likely to clog if it's kept vertical. And while submersible pumps and injectors on deep-well jet pumps can work fine lying on their sides, the foot valves and most check valves attached to them cannot. But not all check valves are designed to operate vertically. In-line check valves, such as the one you might install on the intake line immediately preceding a jet pump, usually operate best in the horizontal position. (The same goes for a few cottagers I know.)

LIGHTNING ARRESTERS: A BRIGHT IDEA WITH SUBMERSIBLE PUMPS

The submersible pump requires a peripheral piece of plumbing paraphernalia. Because submersibles are both at the end of the line, elec-

trically speaking, and sitting in water, they are theoretically more susceptible to damage from lightning than surface-mounted pumps. They are also expensive to replace should lightning strike. Therefore, lightning arresters should be installed at the control box (if mounted separately from the pump) and the spot where the incoming electrical lines enter the cottage. If the pump sits in a well, install another one at the well head (the top of the well). In addition to the arresters, the system should be grounded using at least two 3-m (10-ft.) grounding rods driven vertically into the ground, 3 m (10 ft.) apart, the top of each at least 30 cm (12 in.) below the earth's surface.

Aside from the advantages the two-wire 115V submersible offers the do-it-yourselfer (see Chapter 3), the plumbing-supply store of preference in the village immediately south of me suggests there may be one more reason to go the two-wire route. Over the years, the folks in the shop have noticed the owners of three-wire pumps coming in for replacement control boxes (at a cost of about $50–$70 a pop) because the boxes were getting hit by lightning. The two-wire 115V submersibles, meanwhile, didn't appear to be getting hit at all. Keep in mind that this is an observation in a small area of cottage country, not a survey conducted using recognized statistical methods. Still, the two-wire pumps seem to have saved the shop's customers a few bucks on post-storm repairs.

THE INSIDE STORY ON PRESSURE LINES

The advent of the submersible pump has somewhat confused the issue of where an intake line ends and the pressure line begins. To limit the confusion, it is hereby declared that the term "pressure lines" will include everything from the pressure tank on, although some of the theory will certainly apply to a pressurized intake line (such as the intake line between a submersible pump and the cottage).

In relation to atmospheric pressure, pressure lines have the opposite problem to suction

PRESSURE TACTICS: THE THEORY BEHIND THE SYSTEM

Pressure is defined as force per unit area. In other words, when atmospheric pressure at sea level is rated at 14.7 psi, there are 14.7 pounds of air weighing down on every square inch of our head and shoulders as you stand looking out over the ocean, contemplating the meaning of life. With this kind of burden to bear, is it any wonder more people prefer to take their towels to the beach and lie down rather than philosophize?

Fortunately, it wasn't always so. In fact, during the 17th century, a true gentleman's first priority was not the trolling of beaches for ladies working on their tans. No, indeed. It was instead, at least by all indications, the pursuit of a pressurized water system for the cottage.

For example, Robert Boyle, an English philosopher, chemist, and father of the modern pressure tank, discovered that pressure varies inversely with volume – an observation now known as Boyle's Law. And about the same time, Blaise Pascal, noted French mathematician, physicist, and part-time plumber, observed that the pressure applied to a fluid at rest is transmitted equally in all directions.

Meanwhile, back at our present-day cottage, things get even more complicated. We have just filled a bucket at the kitchen sink, the tap is turned off, but the pump is still running. Why? It's replenishing the pressure tank. A pressure tank is known as a hydropneumatic device, meaning that it involves the combined action of water and air. According to Boyle, as water is pumped into the tank, any air held in the tank will compress, increasing in pressure as it decreases in volume. When the pressure reaches a predetermined level (usually 40 psi or 50 psi), a pressure-sensitive switch turns off the pump. The system is now fully pressurized, waiting for our next demand for water.

This is where Pascal's observations come in. The water sitting in the cottage pressure lines is attempting, with equal force, to break out of every square inch of pipe, tap, or joint. If there's a leak or weak spot, it will find it. If we turn the tap on, the water will pour out. It has no choice because (back to you, Boyle) it's being pushed out by the compressed air in the pressure tank. And as the water exits the tank, the air inside expands, decreasing in pressure. When the pressure switch senses that the pressure has reached its predetermined minimum, (usually 20 psi to 30 psi), a signal is sent to the pump to start up and begin supplying water to the system and the tank again.

Why do we need the air? Why not simply compress the water? Water won't compress, but air will. And because air compresses, its presence in the pressure tank also acts as a shock absorber, reducing the shock of sudden cut-offs to the plumbing system (such as quickly turning off a tap).

Pascal's perceptions also mean that a pipe stamped with a specific pressure rating, such as 100 psi, is designed to tolerate a force equal to that rating, being exerted from within, over every square inch of its interior surface. When new. But time and abuse from nature and humanity take their toll. As the pipe weakens, its designated pressure rating drops, which is why it's better to install pipe rated substantially higher than the theoretical maximum pressure you plan to subject it to.

And you thought you left that atmosphere of pressure back at the city.

---

lines – the pressure inside is greater than that outside. While air pressure outside remains 14.7 psi at sea level, the pressure inside usually ranges from 20 to 50 psi, but it can be substantially higher for short bursts when a tap is suddenly shut off. And, opposite again to a suction line, these pressure differentials are at their peak when the water inside the pipe is at a standstill, not when it's flowing (an open tap providing a release for the pressure). So the water sitting in the cottage pressure lines is under continual pressure to get the heck out of there, anyway it can. This is great news if you are about to have a shower, but not nearly as welcome if the water has just found an unauthorized escape route.

Because a leak creates a constant demand, leaks on the delivery side overwork the pump. However, you can always console yourself with the fact that as the life expectancy of your pump diminishes, you are at least contributing more to the local electrical power company coffers. If you don't find this consoling, you'll have to fix the leak.

CHOOSING PIPE FOR THE PRESSURE LINES

The word "plumbing" is derived from the Latin *plumbum*, meaning "lead". From Roman times right up to the middle of the 20th century, lead was considered the material of choice for pipes, primarily because it's watertight and reasonably malleable. However, since the discovery that lead is toxic to humans, and that it leaches out of the pipes into our drinking water, lead pipes are no longer embraced with such enthusiasm. Even the small amounts contained in the soldered joints of copper pipes and fixtures can be a problem. In fact, in most jurisdictions, the use of lead is forbidden anywhere in potable water lines.

Fortunately, non-lead solders are now available, as are a growing variety of pipe materials. Depending on acceptance by local plumbing codes, you can choose between copper, galvanized steel, CPVC (chlorinated polyvinyl chloride), or PB (polybutylene) for interior pressure lines. CPVC is not the same stuff as PVC (polyvinyl chloride), the latter good only for cold-water pressure lines and waste lines, not hot-water lines. All are available in ½ in.–¾ in. diameters, the size of pipe most often used for cottage pressure lines. (ABS is suitable only for waste lines.)

In general, plastic pipe is a better choice for the do-it-yourselfer. First, the skill levels required to glue pieces of it together are much lower than those required to make watertight soldered joints. That said, there are solderless, non-glue fittings and connectors for both copper and plastic that make assembling a pressurized plumbing system a snap. Literally. Watertight joints every time; no fumes; and much less work – how could you lose? When you get out your wallet to pay for them, actually. The catch is the cost – about three to four times more than comparable copper or plastic glue-type fittings. Still, for small repair jobs, they are worth considering simply because of the ease and speed of installation.

Plastic also tends to corrode less than metal alternatives, leaching less into the water while remaining unobstructed from build-up of internal scale.

Another advantage to plastic is that, like lead, it's malleable. CVPC will move a little, but PB bends like a vacuum-cleaner hose, the minimum allowable radius of the curve being approximately 12 times the pipe's diameter. In other words, a ½-in. PB pipe could be curved around a 6-in. radius. This allows you to make long swooping curves from one point to another with no joints or fittings required. There's also an economical non-glue system of joining PB pressure lines that is unique to this type of pipe – the crimped copper fitting. Copper elbows, Ts, and such slip into the ends of PB pipe and are then crimped in place with a special tool (which can usually be rented at the plumbing-supply outlet from which you purchased the pipe). Again, no muss, no fuss, and not much expense. This is a partic-

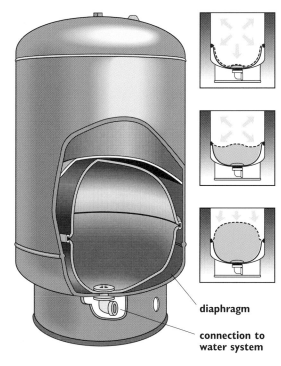

Diaphragm pressure tank:
1. Tank empty; pump starts up and begins to fill diaphragm.

2. As diaphragm fills, air above it is compressed.

3. When air is compressed to amount determined by pressure switch, pump shuts off, leaving diaphragm full of water under pressure, ready to pour out of tap.

diaphragm

connection to water system

ularly nice system if you're plumbing the entire cottage or an addition. PB will sag, however, so it demands more frequent support (with plastic clamps or by running it through cottage framing members) than rigid pipe, such as CVPC or copper; you'll need to support it about every 75 cm (30 in.). It will also stretch and contract, so an extra 3 mm (⅛ in.) per 30 cm (12 in.) of PB pipe must be added to the length of each run to accommodate longitudinal fluctuations.

All plastic pipe must be protected from heat sources, such as heating ducts and recessed lighting, and from possible punctures, such as those caused by driving nails into the wall to hang pictures of offspring proudly displaying fish caught with their new rods.

Continues after Troubleshooting Chart, p. 53

TROUBLESHOOTING GUIDE

PROBLEM	PROBABLE CAUSE AND REMEDY
PUMP FAILS TO REPRIME AFTER INITIAL PRIME	**Initial prime was inadequate** *(remove priming plug and look for water)*: Repeat the priming procedure. (Max's Amazing Easy Prime precludes the possibility of this problem.) **Mechanical seal leaks:** Replace the seal. **Air leak in intake line:** Check for cracks in the pipe and for loose clamps and leaking joints. **Strainer clogged:** Clean. **Foot valve is defective:** Clean or replace as necessary. **Suction head too great:** Place the pump closer to the water source. (See Chapter 3.) **Piston pump pooped:** Should the motor run yet no water spew forth and all the above faults have been discounted, the piston leather, valves, or valve seats could be worn. Consult the owner's manual and your toolbox, or *TV Guide* and a plumber. Also, check belt tension. If you are lucky, the simple tightening of a loose belt may be all that is needed. Again, consult the manual for correct amount of free play. **Control cock valve on deep-well jet pump not adjusted correctly:** Check manual and adjust valve for sufficient back pressure to operate remote injector. **Water leak on inner pipe injector (packer jet of deep-well pump):** Leak can be between packer assembly and well casing or between defective well casing and surrounding soil (the latter more likely on an older drilled well). Call a plumber.
CAN'T FIND PUMP MANUAL	**Manual not at cottage:** Look again, check the house back in the city, or order a new one. Whatever type of pump you have, the manual is a must.
REDUCED DISCHARGE RATE OR NO DELIVERY	**Strainer clogged:** Clean. **Foot valve is defective:** Clean or replace as necessary. **Air leak in intake line:** Check for cracks in the pipe and for loose clamps and leaking joints. **Incorrect pipe size:** Change pipe for appropriate diameter. If your system employs any steel piping, it could be corroded, thereby restricting flow. This might be an opportune time to switch to plastic pipe. **Impeller is excessively worn:** Replace the impeller. **Leather worn on piston pump:** Replace the leather. **Valves not seating properly on piston pump:** Clean or replace. **Suction or discharge head is too high:** Change pump position to correct. If total head is too high, or you're unable to reduce combination of suction head and head loss, a deep-well type of pump may be required. **Debris is lodged in the impeller:** Clean out the impeller. **Pipes are frozen:** Thaw pipes. (See Chapter 12.)
PUMP DISCHARGES SMALL AMOUNT OF WATER, THEN FAILS	**Air is trapped in the pump or line:** Reprime. **Suction head is too great:** Place the pump closer to the water source. **Intake line is too long or the diameter of pipe too small:** Place the pump closer to the water source and/or increase pipe size.

PROBLEM	PROBABLE CAUSE AND REMEDY
PUMP DISCHARGES FULL STREAM, THEN FAILS	**Obstruction in strainer, foot valve, intake line, or impeller:** Check and clean.
	Air leak in intake line: Repair.
	Water level is dropping below the intake *(sometimes this can happen during heavy wave action or if lake level drops substantially during the course of a season):* Lower the intake (foot valve).
PUMP MOTOR DOES NOT RUN	**Switch is not on:** Turn on the switch, then fabricate an appropriate and confused technical excuse for the pump's failure so as to avoid potential ridicule from friends and family. ("Yeah, uh, a problem with the electron-flow gate. Noticed it right away, of course, but it took a while to reactivate. Boy, you really gotta know what you're doing with those things. Did I ever tell you about the time Father and I....").
	Fuse blown or breaker tripped: Replace the fuse or reset breaker. If it happens again, call an electrician. (They are usually cheaper than a plumber.) The overload protector on a three-wire submersible can sometimes trip if the control box becomes hot to the touch from exposure to some external heat source, like direct sunlight. Make a sun-shade for the box (a small roof does the trick) or move the box away from the heat source. Overload protectors on jet and piston pump motors can also trip if the motor overheats, the most probable cause being insufficient ventilation. Give it some air.
	Loose or disconnected wires at the motor: Turn the power off at the main panel and reconnect the loose wires.
	Pressure switch contacts are dirty: Turn the power off, remove the pressure switch cover, and clean the contacts with clean white paper or very fine emery cloth or, if they are badly corroded, with a fingernail file. (Actually, the plumber's or electrician's business card will usually serve quite nicely for this task.)
	Impeller is jammed *(called a "bound pump" on a submersible):* Clean out the impeller and eliminate source of debris. Always run any pump serving a new well until the water clears, to avoid leaving any initial sludge sitting in the impeller(s).
	Stuffing box on piston pump adjusted too tight: Now don't you wish you could tell your friends you had a problem like that? Slacken the adjusting nut.
	Defective motor: Trade wallet for new motor or pump.
PUMP DOES NOT SHUT OFF	**Pressure switch contacts are stuck in the "on" position:** Turn the power off, remove the pressure switch cover, and clean the contacts with clean white paper or very fine emery cloth or, if they are badly corroded, with a fingernail file.
	Taps left on or toilet running: Turn the tap off, or fiddle with the levers and chains inside the toilet tank until it seals properly. (If this problem recurs, you will need to replace the offending bits in the tank.)
	Foot valve, strainer, or submersible pump screen blocked: Clean and check for source of debris. Relocation of the strainer, etc., may be necessary to achieve sufficient clearance from the bottom of the water source.
	Check valve stuck closed: Clean or replace.
	Major leak in cottage plumbing or pipes: Issue life jackets and repair leak.

Continued on next page

TROUBLESHOOTING GUIDE *(continued)*

PROBLEM	PROBABLE CAUSE AND REMEDY
PUMP DOES NOT SHUT OFF *(continued)*	**Water level dropped either below end of intake line or far enough that suction head exceeds the maximum allowable lift** *(a maximum of 25 ft. at sea level, for example)*: Lower intake line in water source, move pump closer to source, restrict pump capacity to match low yield (e.g.: install tail pipe on deep well jet pump, larger pulley on piston pump motor), purchase smaller pump. **Pump worn:** Replace leathers on piston pump; impeller on centrifugal, jet, or submersible; or replace pump. **Pump shaft broken on submersible or the coupling that joins motor to pump is loose:** Replace defective parts or entire pump (whichever depletes the new-boat fund the least). **Control box on submersible defective:** Call a plumber or replace the box (again, whichever depletes the new-boat fund the least).
PUMP RUNS FREQUENTLY WHEN NO APPARENT DEMAND FOR WATER *(Motor will be excessively hot)*	*See possible causes under "Pump Does Not Shut Off".* **Pressure tank waterlogged:** See tank manual for correct procedure on checking air-volume control or snifter valve. Clean or replace control or valve, and drain and recharge tank. (Consult your manual.)
EXCESS PUMP NOISE	**Pump moving on mounts:** Secure pump in place on adequate footings. **Motor bearings worn:** Replace bearings or motor. **Water level low** *(air getting into line)*: Lower intake line (may require moving pump closer to source). **Foot valve or strainer partially obstructed:** Clean. **Intake line too restrictive:** Move pump closer to source and/or install larger diameter pipe. **Low oil level in piston pump crankcase:** Top up with appropriate grade of oil. (See manual.) **Piston pump pulleys loose:** Turn power off and tighten set screws on pulleys. **Piston pump belt too loose or too tight:** Turn power off and adjust belt.
EVERYTHING SEEMS TO WORK FINE	**Something must be wrong:** Relax and you're done for. What was that noise? Better check the pump. No, maybe it's the foot valve. Better lie down on the dock and listen for the foot valve. This could take time.

LAYING OUT THE PRESSURE LINES

Regardless of choice of materials, the entire pressurized system should follow a gradual slope to a central drain point or, if this isn't possible, to a couple of points. Usually, this is required by the plumbing code, although it has been my experience that it's a rule rarely adhered to. The reason for the slant is to facilitate draining of the system at season's end. Even if you don't partake in this annual ritual, an easily drained system takes some of the aggravation out of doing repairs and modifications. Use the same 2-cm drop per metre of horizontal run (¼ in. per foot) minimum, as suggested for the intake line.

The best place for the central drain is at the lowest spot – most often found next to the pump or pressure tank. Connect a hose to the tap to let it run outside. If your cottage water system doesn't have a drain tap at its lowest point, install one.

THE PURPOSE OF THE PRESSURE TANK

Indoor plumbing is a distribution system that provides water on demand. We open a tap, and water pours out. What sorcery is at the root of this flow? Gravity is one answer. If the water source or storage container is higher than the tap, the water will flow out every time the tap is opened. At the cottage, a well or spring at the top of a hill can provide sufficient pressure to keep the indoor system full of water, ready to pour out. So too can a water tower. Water towers are, in fact, used by many municipalities to maintain water pressure. My in-laws' first cottage made use of one too, although obviously on a much-smaller scale.

Unfortunately, few cottages can boast a well or spring located on a convenient hill out back. And water towers can be expensive to construct. (The pressure is controlled by volume and height, meaning you need a large container stuck high in the air if you're a fan of the high-pressure shower.) A tower is also susceptible to freezing and general wear and tear from the weather. And you still require a pump to lift the water up to the tower to maximize pressure. If power is available to operate a pump, then it's tough to beat the pressure tank for convenience.

The pressure tank serves a dual function in the cottage water system: It provides a modicum of storage so that the pump does not have to operate every time water is demanded; and it maintains pressure throughout the system when the pump is not operating. (See Pressure Tactics, p. 48.) The amount of water that can be drained from a tank before the pressure switch asks the pump to start up again is known as its drawdown, or sometimes draw-off. (More on this below.) Ideally, the drawdown should not empty the tank, but keep a small reserve for power outages. Your local plumbing supplier will be able to help you size the tank to your requirements, but if in doubt, bigger is better, since the pump then has to work less frequently.

There are two basic types of pressure tanks: the conventional galvanized steel tank and the bladder or diaphragm tank. In the galvanized tank, the air and water contained within are in direct contact with each other. Water, being the almost-universal solvent, absorbs air molecules, a process that increases in direct proportion to increases in pressure. Slowly, the amount of air available to compress diminishes, decreasing the drawdown. (For the explanation of why, see Pressure Tactics, p. 48.) The smaller the drawdown, the more often the pump cycles, a situation usually well documented in your electric bill. Not so visible is the added wear on the pump. When a tank's drawdown is reduced in this manner, the tank is referred to as being waterlogged.

To combat this phenomenon, a floating disc is sometimes inserted between the water and air to discourage their incessant mingling. This disc works about as well as a drunk chaperon at a teen dance. A better method is to simply acknowledge the problem and keep adding air. By using an air-volume control, or air-charger, air is automatically injected into the tank as needed each time the pump turns on. The charger incorporates a neat little valve known as a snifter. The snifter, which is usually spring mounted, is drawn open or shut by pressure differentials between the water adjacent to the valve and the surrounding air. These differentials are at their extremes when the pump starts or stops. When the snifter opens, the control sucks in a wee blast of air. When the snifter closes, the water pressure in the line pushes the air into the tank.

Iron tends to oxidize when exposed to the air in a conventional pressure tank. If there is enough iron in the water, it will turn the water brown even before it makes its way to the tap.

A bladder or diaphragm tank solves all of the above problems by separating the water from the air. The water is contained within a flexible sealed bag (or bladder), or behind a flexible membrane (or diaphragm) bonded to the inside of the tank. The bladder type is slightly more efficient, but in either case, the air and water don't mix so there is no loss of drawdown. As a result, no air-volume control is needed (one less thing to break), and any iron present won't oxidize and discolour the water until it's out of the tap and into the soup, and who's to know by then? Bladder and diaphragm tanks are more expensive than conventional galvanized tanks, which explains why galvanized tanks are still on the market.

Either tank may be sold as a package with a top-mounted jet pump, making for a compact unit well suited to the often cramped quarters of cottage crawl spaces and pump houses.

THE PRESSURE SWITCH: HOW TO KEEP IT WORKING

Attached to the pump, the pressure tank, or the line between the two is a small rectangular box about 6 cm x 6 cm x 9 cm (2½ in. x 2½ in. x 3 in.). Usually, it's grey with a squared "D" embossed on the top. This is the pressure switch. A flexible diaphragm inside senses pressure changes in the system, opening or closing a set of contact points to turn the pump off or on in response to those changes. The switch is preset at the factory to maintain pressure between 20 psi to 40 psi, or 30 psi to 50 psi.

Over time, the contacts in the switch can become corroded and pitted, particularly if the switch is situated in a damp area (such as

the ubiquitous cottage crawl space or pump house), causing the points to stick and the pump to remain on. With the power to the pump and switch turned off, remove the small nut on top of the switch cover to expose the inner workings. The four contact points are easily identified. Force them open with your hand or a screwdriver, then carefully clean the contacts with clean, white paper (such as the plumber's business card) or fine emery cloth or, if they're badly corroded, with a fingernail file. Blow the filings away (the contacts will close by themselves), put the cover back on, and turn on the electricity. If the pump still misbehaves, the switch may need replacing. (Don't throw away that business card yet.)

GETTING INTO HOT WATER

Hot water at the cottage is one of those things you can do without, but wouldn't it be nice to have a hot bath at the end of a damp, cool day? The problem is, hot-water tanks are expensive to operate; in most cases, they're the single greatest consumer of energy inside the cottage. Enter the so-called space-saver hot-water tank. These are small tanks, ranging from 25 L–115 L (7 US gal.–30 US gal.), the larger of which will handle most cottage needs (not including such heavy hot-water users as dishwashers, automatic washers, and whirlpool tubs). They offer a few important advantages to cottagers. The tanks fit into small places, such as under the kitchen counter; and because there's less water to heat, recovery time is faster and operating costs are lower. As a bonus, most of the small tanks are available in 115V format, making wiring a less-intimidating experience.

Tankless, on-demand hot-water heaters are also available; they take up very little space and, because they only heat the water as you need it, they use less electricity than conventional tanks. However, as these units are at least double the cost of a small hot-water tank, and in most cases one unit is needed for every hot-water outlet, each wired into its own dedicated 230V circuit, it's hard to justify the initial expense. Initial expense is also the downfall of most active-solar hot-water systems – justifiable in high-demand situations such as back home in Consumerville, but tough to rationalize at an occasional-use cottage.

For cottagers with limited hot-water demands, or no access to electricity or propane, there are passive-solar hot-water heaters available that take advantage of a principle known as thermosiphon. A series of connected tubes sits on the roof of the cottage, facing south. As the water is warmed by the sun, the heated water rises within the tubes, drawing up cold water from a storage tank, this incoming water forcing the hotter water down to that same tank. The water keeps circulating, gathering heat until a tap is opened. Or at least it does as long as the sun is out. The system produces limited quantities of warm water and is subject to freezing if used (or left full) during cold spells, but it's simple and cheap, and well within the grasp of an industrious do-it-yourselfer.

There are also solar hot-water bags on the market: black plastic bags that warm the water inside when the sun is shining. During the summer months, we use a black plastic garbage pail at our cottage for the same purpose. Set beside an outside sink, the pail is filled with run-off from the roof each time it rains. It's not the hot setup for a bath because of the black flies (bites in other places are bad enough, thanks just the same), but it works reasonably well for before-dinner wash-ups as long as you aren't too particular about temperature.

THE WASTE SYSTEM

Plumbed waste systems for cottages differ from conventional city systems only once they venture beyond the cottage walls. As in the city, the road to effective drainage is all downhill – a 1 cm–2 cm drop per metre of horizontal run, or ⅛ in.–¼ in. per foot, to be exact. Surprisingly, increasing the slope of the waste pipes does not reward you with better drainage; it actually hinders the flow. It has to do with the dynamics of dung, which needs a certain amount of water in order to move

through the pipes. Steeper slopes let the liquids run out but leave the solids hanging. Of course, there are times when cottage design or topography dictates that the line must drop at a greater angle, in which case it should be set at no less than 45°.

As with the supply system, plastic is the material of choice for cottage waste lines, usually ABS (acrylonitrile butadiene styrene) for the inside and PVC for the lines outside. (Check with local authorities for approval.) Main waste lines are usually 4 in. in diameter, while secondary feed lines and vent stacks can range from 1½ in. to 4 in. To aid drainage and provide the fumes with an easy exit to the great outdoors, vent pipes for every fixture are essential. Often, these vents are connected to the central stack that vents the main sewage line.

The methods of treating cottage wastes are varied, and in some cases very cottage-specific. Given the importance of doing it right, four full chapters (Chapters 7–10) are dedicated to the discussion of dung and grey water disposal.

5 CHECKING YOUR WATER QUALITY

What could be lurking in your lake or well?

Testing the waters:
A bacteriological test looks for evidence of coliforms – which means there's reason to believe pathogenic (disease-causing) bacteria, protozoa, and viruses are also present.

THE GLASS OF WATER I HOLD IN MY HAND at this moment has come from our artesian spring; a shallow-well jet pump delivered the water to the kitchen tap. A few tiny grains of sand rest on the bottom of the glass, but the water is essentially clear. It is also cold, and tastes better than anything that ever poured out of a city tap. It has flavour – we drink it for pleasure, not just to quench thirst. But is it safe to drink?

It must be. I mean, look at the stuff – what nasty substances could possibly lurk in water so transparently pure?

Actually, plenty. H_2O is the consummate capricious companion, a flirtatious molecule that has intimate relations with just about everything it meets. It's as close as you can get to the universal solvent, the secret ingredient that makes hot chocolate or coffee drinkable, and the excuse to leave the dishes "to soak". In fact, if nature were forced to print a list of ingredients on the side of each glass of water, as required for most other food products, its length could easily surpass that of the list adorning the family's preferred junk food. And it's quite conceivable such a list would vary from glass to glass over a few days, weeks, or months, even if all were drawn from the same lake or well.

But is this bad? We don't want perfectly pure water because H_2O on its own has no taste. What we want is good tasting, healthful *drinking* water. Deciding what constitutes that, and how to achieve it, is another matter. In both cases, we soon discover that when it comes to water, science is far from exact. The problem is that we are dealing with two major variables: humanity and water. Susceptibility to contaminants differs for every individual and for every body of water. And even if we were able to eliminate the variables, science is still undecided as to how little of a given substance it takes to harm an individual, a fact reflected in the wide variance in official water-quality standards throughout North America.

But to put these potential hazards into perspective, the most dangerous aspect of water for cottagers is that people drown in it. Statistically, we are much more likely to succumb to this tragedy than to any that might result from drinking the water. With this in mind, let's look at the list of constituents most likely to pour out of a cottage tap.

MICROORGANISMS

Contrary to popular belief, the majority of microorganisms are not harmful to humanity. In fact, their existence is essential to life. Unfortunately, however, a small group has given the rest of the micros a bad name. These disease-causing critters are referred to as pathogens.

Most waterborne pathogens are between homes, having recently vacated the intestine of some warm-blooded animal in search of another. Any time faecal material from pets, wild animals, or humans gets into the water (directly or via dysfunctional or improperly located municipal sewage systems, septic systems, or outhouses), you can bet a full case of Pepto that pathogens are probably present. There are three groups of potentially pathogenic microorganisms that can turn up in cottage-country water: bacteria, protozoa, and viruses.

BACTERIA

Bacteria are microscopic, single-celled organisms, weighing in at about one-trillionth of a gram each. Without bacteria, we wouldn't have yoghurt, or vinegar for the fries, or cheese for the burger. On the pathogenic side of things, dysentery is the most likely bacterial ailment to afflict us via the water. But the majority of bacteria only take a serious interest in things that are dead, and who's to complain at that point?

PROTOZOA

Protozoa are also microscopic, single-celled organisms, only slightly larger than and one step up the evolutionary ladder from bacteria (the difference having to do with where each parks its DNA). Two examples of pathogenic protozoa with water wings are *Giardia*, the courier of giardiasis, better known as beaver

fever, and *Entamoeba*. Either can double your annual budget for toilet paper in a few weeks.

CYSTS

Cysts, the tanks of the microorganism army, are essentially bacteria or protozoa with armour plating, an outer coating that protects these microbes against hostile attacks (by disinfectants or cold temperatures, for instance). *Giardia* is the most prevalent waterborne pathogenic cyst in North America, the protozoa becoming encysted (that is, donning their armour) just before leaving home-sweet-intestine, and losing it again once inside their next host.

VIRUSES

Although many biologists suggest that, technically speaking, viruses are not organisms, viruses are still considered to be microorganisms. The confusion lies in their cell structure: Viruses don't have any which, according to some scientists, classifies them as nonliving. Scientific debates aside, viruses are smaller than bacteria and are parasitic, dependent on their host cells for life and propagation. (Sound a bit like lawyers, don't they?) The hosts can be bacteria, plants, or animals. In water there are more viruses than there are all forms of bacteria combined. Although not all viruses are

BEAVERS VICTIMS OF BAD PRESS

The beaver gets a bad rap for beaver fever, aka giardiasis. Yes, this toothy rodent can spread the disease, but so can many other animals, including deer, moose, and Homo sapiens. In fact, it's quite probable that the beaver acquired the pathogen by drinking waters contaminated by the faeces of humanity before depositing the bug back into the water. Statistically, you are more likely to contract giardiasis from soiled diapers at a daycare centre than you are from your cottage drinking water. (Even the most diligent of liability lawyers would have a hard time pinning that one on the beaver.)

Of course, this doesn't mean you shouldn't be worried about contracting giardiasis at the cottage, but quit blaming the beaver, eh? Maybe we should rename the disease Diaper Delirium.

harmful to humans, pathogenic viruses are responsible for many of humanity's diseases, including infectious hepatitis.

Billions of microorganisms can be lurking in a single glass of water. And it only takes a very small percentage of this crowd – the pathogenic group – to make you very sick. (It's difficult to quantify how few pathogens are required to make you sick and how sick you may become; it depends on the individual immune system and its ability to fight off the pathogens.) So if we can't see them, how do we know if the pathogens are present? We get the water tested.

TESTING THE WATERS

A bacteriological test looks for the presence of coliforms, which are aerobic bacteria (ones needing oxygen to survive) that are, or resemble, a particular bacterial species found in the intestines of warm-blooded animals. The genuine ones of intestinal origin are known as faecal coliforms; the lookalike pretenders are just plain coliforms usually giving vegetable matter as their previous address. But coliforms – faecal or otherwise – aren't the bad guys. Some help us control our body's water balance and, unless you boil your salads, you're likely downing a bunch of them with each mouthful of fresh veggies. So what's the big hoo-ha about coliforms?

Coliforms are known to hang around with a bad crowd – pathogens. Pathogens don't live long out on their own and, relative to coliforms, there aren't very many of them. These two factors make pathogens difficult and expensive to detect. So we take the easy way out and look for the biggest gang of microorganisms pathogens are most likely to hang around with – coliforms.

Coliforms are known as indicators; evidence of them in your water means there is good reason to believe there is faecal contamination, which usually means that pathogenic bacteria, protozoa, and viruses are also present, encysted or otherwise. Evidence of *any* faecal coliforms means the water has recently been contaminated by intestinal waste (the life expectancy of faecal coliforms being very short outside the intestine), definitely not a harbinger of good news for drinking water.

Should a zero count show up on your bacteriological test, the sample of water tested is considered to be free of pathogens. This is great news, but please don't con yourself into thinking it's a guarantee of safe drinking water. It's only one sample. Lakes and rivers, the surface-water sources from which most cottagers draw their water, are easily contaminated. Therefore, the coliform count can vary by the hour and from one spot to another a few feet away – which is why you should *never* drink surface water unless it's treated first. Some ground-water sources, such as shallow wells and springs, are also susceptible to such variances in water quality. And it is theoretically conceivable that microorganism activity has been curtailed by some other disagreeable substance in the water.

NONPATHOGENIC, BUT STILL A NUISANCE

Two nuisance microorganisms that aren't associated with coliforms are iron bacteria and manganese bacteria. These bacteria show up only in water containing iron or manganese, getting their energy by oxidizing one or the other mineral. Just as the oxidization of the metal on the family car leads to rust, this same process occurring with water-dissolved iron and manganese causes the water to turn reddish-brown, sometimes leaving an unsightly brown slime on plumbing fixtures. It takes only small amounts of either mineral to support the bacteria, allowing them to besmirch your sink or toilet bowl. And, as a bonus from nature, they often are accompanied by sulphate-reducing bacteria which bestow the charming fragrance of rotten eggs on your water (although hydrogen-sulphide gas from vegetable matter composting in the water is the usual culprit responsible for this unpleasant odour). Neither iron nor manganese bacteria are a health threat, but both cause staining and make for a sickly-looking glass of water.

TANNIC ACID

Another nuisance contaminant is tannic acid, also known as tannin. Tannin is present throughout the plant world. (It occurs naturally in coffee and tea, for instance.) Because it resists decomposition, it is a very good preservative, one of its better-known uses being the preservation of leather (hence, the leather-treatment process known as tanning).

Tannin in drinking water usually comes from composting vegetable matter, and is most likely to appear in springs and wells bordering swampy areas or surrounded by coniferous trees. (Part of the reason the needles of coniferous trees are slow to decompose is that they contain tannic acid.) As this acid is secreted into the soil, the tannin leaches into ground-water sources. Like iron bacteria and manganese bacteria, it colours the water, stains fixtures, and ruins the aesthetic quality of drinks. It also interferes with the absorption of iron, both in iron-removal filtration systems and in our bodies (although the scientific consensus is that its impact on our bodies is trivial).

MINERALS

Because of water's aforementioned propensity for palling around with just about any old molecule, all sorts of minerals can become dissolved in it. Some (like cadmium, lead, and mercury) are extremely toxic and, when passed through the food chain, can accumulate in the body, building up over time. Others are necessary and beneficial to life – in the right quantities. For example, we all need a certain amount of iron to assist in transporting oxygen via our bloodstream. But excess amounts of iron in our water can give it a metallic taste and stain plumbing fixtures, making it appear that nobody ever cleans the bowl. ("Honest, Mom, I did it just yesterday.")

HARD VS. SOFT WATER

Two other minerals, calcium and magnesium, determine water's relative hardness. These two minerals dissolve in water in the form of carbonates; the more calcium carbonate and/or magnesium carbonate compounds, the harder the water. Hard water can cause encrustations in pipes, kettles, and water heaters. While excessively hard water can taste nasty, many people prefer the taste of moderately hard water. Soft water is usually nicer to wash in, although extremely soft water doesn't do a very good job of rinsing soap and dirt residue from the skin.

Appearance, taste, and smell are all good indicators of the presence of minerals in the water, but the only way to know which ones are there for sure – and therefore how to remove them, or even whether they need to be removed – is to have the water tested. (See below.)

ACIDIC VS. ALKALINE

There is also an indirect relation between the hardness/softness and the alkalinity/acidity of water. Carbonates tend to increase its alkalinity. Since fewer carbonates occur naturally in soft water, its potential to become acidic is increased.

Surface water and ground water taken from shallow wells tend to be slightly acidic to neutral, and also soft; ground water taken from deep, drilled wells, because of its exposure to

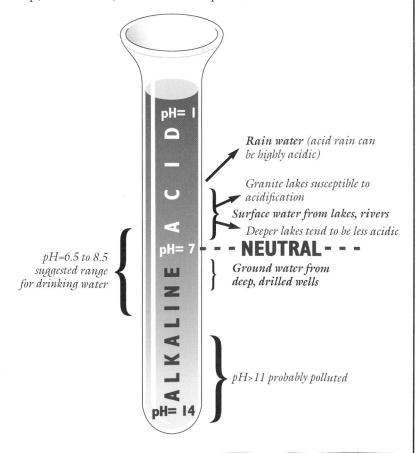

pH= 1

A C I D

pH= 7 - - - **NEUTRAL** - - -

A L K A L I N E

pH= 14

pH=6.5 to 8.5 suggested range for drinking water

Rain water (acid rain can be highly acidic)

Granite lakes susceptible to acidification

Surface water from lakes, rivers
Deeper lakes tend to be less acidic

Ground water from deep, drilled wells

pH>11 probably polluted

various minerals, is usually alkaline and hard. Rainwater is naturally soft and somewhat acidic, but it can become severely acidic depending on the pollutants in the air (hence acid rain), which can in turn affect the acidity of surface water. Deeper lakes, because they have a greater volume of water relative to their surface area than shallow lakes, are less vulnerable to pH changes from acid rain, and therefore tend to be less acidic. Lakes and rivers that reside in areas where much of the rock is granite, such as those along the heavily cottaged Canadian Shield, are more susceptible to acidification. That's because granite does not dissolve in the same manner as softer rock, such as limestone, so in this part of cottage country little of the acid from air and composting vegetable matter is neutralized.

The relative acidity of water is measured using the pH scale, which tells us how much acid is contained in a water sample relative to the amount of alkali. The scale is numbered from 1 to 14. A pH of 7 is considered neutral (that is, the acidity and the alkalinity are in balance and cancel one another out); below 7, acidic; and above 7, alkaline (also referred to as basic). For instance, the bile sloshing about in our stomachs, which has to be very acidic in order to break down all the oddities we drop into it, has a pH level of around 2. Sometimes, like after a serious cottage pig-out, stomach pH will drop even lower. Fortunately, checking in at around 10 are a number of alkaline antacids we can take to counteract the corrosive effects of increased stomach acidity.

The suggested pH range for drinking water is between 6.5 and 8.5. Water that is more acidic can corrode plumbing systems. This is not simply a problem related to system longevity; significant amounts of lead and copper have been measured in tap water that has spent the night sitting in metal pipes. Water often sits in the plumbing system of a cottage for much longer periods; if the water is acidic enough to corrode the plumbing, then the potential for higher concentrations of toxic metals in the water is also increased.

At the other end of the pH scale, the problem presented by overly alkaline water, as with hard water, is mostly one of aesthetics and taste, although a pH level over 11 indicates the water is probably polluted as well – usually by caustic effluents released by industry. (Levels that high rarely occur naturally.)

In response to evidence of acid rain affecting water quality, some governments have begun to categorize the lakes within their jurisdictions by the lake's relative sensitivity to acidification. This is a measure of the body of water's potential to become acidic (or more acidic), rather than its actual pH level. To determine the pH level of your water, be it a lake, river, well, or spring, the water must be tested.

PASSING ON THE SALT

Salt (sodium chloride) wins the mineral-popularity contest, ending up in more places in greater amounts than any other mineral. (My friend Paul regularly reaffirms the validity of this statement every time he orders a batch of fries.) Too much sodium chloride renders water undrinkable, the salt acting as a dehydrant in our system.

Two potential problem areas are water sources adjacent to busy highways on which large quantities of salt are used to melt snow and ice, and ground-water supplies along coastal regions where sea water seeps into an aquifer as the ground-water table drops (usually after years of extensive depletion due to irrigation). For cottagers with wells, the best safety factor is distance; the problem can largely be prevented by locating wells as far as possible from salt sources. Keeping road salt out of surface water, such as your lake, means dealing with government bureaucracy, a subject beyond the scope of this book (and sometimes reality, for that matter).

CHEMICAL COMPOUNDS

At last count (not mine), humanity had concocted – intentionally or otherwise – more than two million known chemical compounds, with thousands more getting added to the list each year. VOCs (volatile organic chemi-

SWIMMING: COME ON IN, THE WATER'S FINE

For swimming, the quality of the water in North America is, with the exception of a few isolated pockets of pollution, very good. Both the Canadian and US federal governments have adopted a suggested faecal coliform count of 200 faecal coliforms (*E. coli* faecal coliforms, in the case of Canada) per 100 ml, although provincial and state governments may establish more stringent standards.

In most cases, chemical contamination of the water is not a problem for swimmers in North America. Normally, the amount of chemicals absorbed through the skin while swimming isn't considered significant enough to pose a potential hazard for the majority of people. The greatest risk of contamination occurs downstream from a chemical plant, pulp mill, or similar industry that uses and expels water into the lake or river. To avoid this risk, swim upstream from such industries.

Water quality in a lake or river will vary. The standards mean that the water is considered safe to swim in (not safe to drink) for the *majority* of people in the *majority* of water bodies. Because susceptibility to contamination varies widely in both humans and water, the final say as to whether a beach gets closed down or not falls on the shoulders of the local medical officer of health.

That a beach is closed at one location along the shoreline doesn't necessarily mean the water is considered unfit for swimming at some other area of the lake or river. And, obviously, the opposite also holds true. Generally, the farther you get from the shore, the less contaminated the water. On shallow lakes, for instance, you can reduce your risk of exposure just by entering the water from the end of your dock.

To find out more about the water quality for swimming at the cottage, contact the health department or health unit in your cottage jurisdiction.

---

cals), PCBs (polychlorinated biphenyls), THMs (trihalomethanes), PAHs (polycyclic aromatic hydrocarbons) – it's an alphabet soup of known and suspected carcinogens out there. Add to that dioxins and pesticides and, gee willikers, it's enough to make you sick just thinking about it, or at least a little confused.

Another cancer-causing agent that can also spice up the home brew is radon gas, a radioactive substance occurring naturally in the ground. Fortunately, this gas evaporates quickly, so it shouldn't pose a problem in surface water. However, it can turn up in dangerous quantities in ground water, evaporating from there into the air of your cottage.

Realistically, is there reason to be concerned about such persistent and potentially lethal substances in the water at your cottage? The fact is, in most cottage-country lakes, they may not be present at all, or be present in such small amounts you would probably drown long before you could drink enough to cause any harm. But note the words "most" and "probably".

So how do we know if this stuff might be waiting for us at the cottage? There are indicators – because, radon gas aside, such chemicals are the byproducts of certain types of human activities. A pulp and paper factory dumping its wastes upstream from the cottage intake line, for instance, is not a good sign; extensive agricultural activities bordering the lake's watershed are also a warning flag. If you're at all concerned, have a chemical analysis of the water done.

NUTRIENTS

Nutrients are essential to all forms of life. They are the mineral elements and compounds used by all living things to build cells. They exist in finite quantity. They can be transformed (broken down into their basic chemicals) or relocated, but never destroyed. The problem, therefore, is not with nutrients per se but rather the manner in which we carry out that transformation and relocation.

The nutrients of primary concern to cottagers are phosphorus, because of its effect on aquatic life in our waterways, and nitrogen, because of its potential health effect on humans. They also tend to travel together.

THE PHOSPHORUS PROBLEM

Most fresh-water ecosystems, like lakes, are phosphorus limited in their natural state, meaning that phosphorus is in relatively short supply in that system. So aquatic plant life is also limited. But as phosphorus is introduced into the water – the process being greatly accelerated by faulty septic and municipal sewage systems, continued use of phosphate-based soaps, detergents, and other products such as fertilizers, bad agricultural practices, the destruction of marshes, and the clear-cutting of shorelines – aquatic vegetation flourishes.

In severe cases, blue-green algae blooms will appear on the surface of the lake. While most algae are honourable members of the food chain, eating and being eaten, the blue-green gang is not. Blue-green algae (the only other organisms comparable in simplicity to bacteria) grow, die, and sink to the bottom to decompose, the bacteria responsible for their decomposition consuming water-dissolved oxygen in the process. This chain of events is called eutrophication, a lake being considered dead in extreme cases. And as the water loses dissolved oxygen, it enables additional phosphorus from bottom sediment to enter the water, exacerbating the problem.

By the way, the oxygen depletion of water doesn't lead to a basin of H_2s and no Os. The basic water molecule consists of two hydrogen atoms riding piggyback on one oxygen atom, hence H_2O. This molecule doesn't break down into its atomic parts very easily. The oxygen available for fish and other aquatic life, such as algae, is dissolved oxygen, O_2, a separate molecule from H_2O. Dissolved oxygen is also what's consumed when decomposition takes place in the water. The important thing to remember is excess nutrients lead to oxygen deficits which lead to a dead lake (as excess government spending leads to deficits which lead to a dead economy).

NITROGEN: SAME SOURCES, DIFFERENT EFFECTS

Other than affecting taste, phosphorus doesn't directly degrade the quality of water for drinking purposes. Nitrogen, however, is another matter. High levels of nitrates have been linked to methaemoglobinemia, a disease causing oxygen deficiencies in blood. In young infants, who have less blood than adults but similar capacities for nitrates, methaemoglo-binemia can lead to brain disorders. For the most part, the many variants of nitrogen get into our water systems in the same manner as phosphorus does – human and animal sewage and excess use of chemical fertilizers.

There is also an indirect link between nutrient enrichment and pathogens, the two often arriving at the lake via the same bus – sewage being the most obvious example. Microorganisms tend to flourish when nutrient levels are high because they feed on the nutrients. In fact, we take advantage of their dietary preferences, using microorganisms to eat sewage in the septic tank.

HOW NUTRIENT ENRICHMENT IS MEASURED

The degree of nutrient enrichment is determined by measuring the amount of chlorophyll in the water, chlorophyll being the green pigment in algae (and other plants), algae being the byproduct of the introduction of the nutrients phosphorus and nitrogen into the water. Essentially, it's a measurement of the lake's pulse.

Lakes registering the least amount of chlorophyll are clear, cold, and usually deep – good lakes for trout. In the spring when the water temperature still hovers around freezing, dissolved oxygen could theoretically reach its maximum possible concentration of 12 mg for every litre of water.

At the opposite end of the enrichment scale, high concentrations of algae make the water turbid, green, and odorous. It's no fun to swim in, water-skiing can be downright unpleasant, and it's certainly no match for Perrier as a beverage. As a lake degenerates to this level, the balance of aquatic life changes, with those species requiring the most dissolved oxygen dying off. The first fish species to go are lake trout (assuming the lake was deep and cold enough to support them in the first place), and then the perch and pickerel, to be replaced by catfish and sunfish.

Nutrient enrichment does more than lead to a premature death of the lake. Every time we either permit excess nutrients to flow into the watershed – through use of phosphate-based cleaners or by ignoring septic system problems, for example – or make it easier for nutrients to flow into the watershed (by clear-cutting shorelines, for instance), a portion of those nutrients are no longer accessible for use by land-based vegetation. This short-changes the plants, which in turn short-changes animal life (like us).

TURBIDITY

Turbidity is the cloudiness of the water caused by suspended solids such as sediment. It is often a byproduct of nutrient enrichment because as eutrophication increases, there tends to be more stuff in the water.

On the other hand, turbidity encourages nutrient enrichment; as sediment is washed into the lake, nutrients tend to tag along. This, of course, leads to the old chicken-or-the-egg debate, which in turn allows politicians to while away hours upon hours in heavy discourse without actually having to do anything about the problem.

Regardless, turbid water can have all the visual appeal of diarrhoea, and sometimes taste as bad as it looks. But beyond aesthetic concerns, turbid water can also signal the presence of other contaminants. Stowaways such as bacteria, pesticides, and phosphorus cling to the particles in droves.

Also, turbid water is more difficult to disinfect. The particles absorb disinfectants such as chlorine and iodine, and shield bacteria from the radiation of ultraviolet purifiers, diminishing the effectiveness of such destroyers of pathogens. Abrasive particles like sand can also destroy the seals on pumps and wreak havoc throughout the plumbing system. And not only does a high concentration of dissolved solids in the water reduce the effectiveness of soap, it also increases the odds that the cottage will be afflicted with the dreaded bathtub ring. (Heavens!)

Although some water problems, such as turbidity or high levels of minerals, can be detected by our senses, most of water's travelling companions cannot. The only accurate way to determine what's in the water is to have it tested.

A REPORT CARD FOR WATER

A bacteriological test, as outlined above, is usually available free of charge or for a nominal cost from local, provincial, or state health departments. It should be done quarterly if you're using the cottage year round, otherwise once in the spring and again once the water warms up will probably suffice. (Around the middle of August is good.) But such a test only reveals the water's potential for harbouring a pathogenic populace, nothing more.

To find out what other evils, if any, lurk in your drinking water, you need a thorough chemical analysis of your drinking water, which should test for and report on about 100 different variables. The price of such a test varies greatly from lab to lab. In my area, it costs $300 (1993 prices), including the accompanying report, which seems to be a bargain compared to what many labs across North America are charging.

Although pollutants can travel very long distances, if you have no reason to suspect agricultural or industrial contamination, a less-extensive examination looking for such things as hardness, acidity, lead, coliforms, nitrates, and solids may suffice. My local lab charges $85 for such a test, reporting on 18 variables. And if it's surface water you're testing, such as a lake, you may be able to share the expense with neighbouring cottagers.

DO-IT-YOURSELF TESTS

What about home test kits? In the trade, these are referred to as portable test kits and are available from many water-testing labs. For testing chloride levels (which will give an indication of salt contamination), pH, iron, and hardness, these kits work well. However, some contain hazardous materials and must be used with considerable caution. They are not for children. The problem with portable test kits for other types of contaminants is sensitivity – will they measure low enough levels to be of any use? For instance, the maximum allowable amount of lead in North America can vary from 10–50 parts per billion (check with your jurisdiction for local regulations). If the test kit won't accurately recognize and measure the presence of lead to at least the mandated level, it's useless as a drinking-water testing procedure. (Sensitivity levels should be listed on the kit's label.)

Many of the portable test kits that measure metals in the water look only for dissolved metals, whereas the criteria used for drinking-water standards usually asks for total metals, including both dissolved and suspended metals. This makes the kit of questionable worth if you want to know what's in the water. And there is no portable bacteriological test kit suitable for cottage or home use.

Aside from testing to determine chloride content, pH, iron content, and hardness, any analysis of your water should be done by a reputable independent laboratory. Tests offered for free or at a nominal cost by water-treatment retailers and distributors are highly suspect because of the unavoidable biases inherent in selling a product that purports to correct a problem that their testing equipment just might reveal. In fact, some of these tests are deliberately misleading.

Don't let a failed *legitimate* water report card get you down. There's bound to be some unpleasant stuff in there if somebody looks hard enough. What we want is water that is safe to drink, and that is an attainable goal. Because while water as the almost-universal solvent is keen to pal around with all sorts of earthly substances, it can usually be coaxed into parting with them too.

The glass of water I started this chapter with is now sitting on my desk, empty save for the few tiny grains of sand sitting on the bottom. I suppose I could have filtered them out before they even got to the pump but, the way I see it, why bother? We have had the water tested and for the moment are prepared to live with its aesthetic failings rather than mess with the taste. That's one of the beauties of a private water-supply system – the decisions of what gets added and taken away are solely ours. Think I'll pour myself another glass.

6 PURIFYING THE WATER

A guide to choosing a treatment device

Back to basics:
Boiling is the simplest treatment. All you need is a stove and a pot or kettle – and some time.

WATER IS LIKE A WORLD TRAVELLER WHO embarks on a trip having packed only the necessities, then picks up all sorts of stuff along the way. At each new border crossing, some overworked customs officer must check out this traveller's ever-expanding load of baggage. The officer must know what to look for, how to find hidden contraband, and what to do should any be found. The customs officer and the typical water-treatment device have much in common.

Water arriving at the cottage has already been a few places and picked up an incredible pile of souvenirs to show for its travels (see Chapter 5 for a rundown on what to expect), a testimony to humanity's unwillingness to control water quality in the public domain. Fortunately, as operators of private water systems, cottagers have the option of setting their own standards for what's acceptable in water pouring out of the cottage tap.

What is acceptable? As countries have standards for what it is permissible to import at their borders, most jurisdictions in North America have standards for water quality. A test of your water source will reveal how much, if any, your drinking water varies from those standards. Beyond that, it's largely up to the cottager. For contaminants that we choose to restrict, we need the equivalent of a customs officer. We need a water-treatment device or system – some form of purification method to remove the contraband from water's baggage.

In the majority of jurisdictions, the water-treatment industry is a loosely regulated one (Iowa and Wisconsin being two notable exceptions). And there is little consensus among legislators as to what works and what doesn't. For instance, some government agencies suggest that boiling is not an adequate means to kill bacteria and that only chlorination will work, while others, like the state of Utah, take the opposite point of view. And it's a marvel how this regulatory freedom and jurisdictional confusion feed the inventive spirit of copywriters for water-treatment brochures and advertisements. While it is human nature to believe – particularly when believing might save us a few bucks – if a water-purification device or system seems too good to be true, odds are it probably is. Should an EPA, CSA, or similar logo appear on a water-treatment device, these well-recognized stamps in no way reflect on the device's ability to treat water. They are for registration purposes or to show that the device has been approved for use in a plumbing system only – and *nothing* more.

Covering all the treatment gizmos and combinations thereof on the market would turn this chapter into a 24-volume water-purification encyclopedia, so only the most feasible alternatives for single cottage use (often referred to as point-of-use) will be dealt with here. The information is gathered from a great variety of sources, from microbiologists specializing in water purification to, at the other end of the scale, those aforementioned brochures. As suggested in Chapter 5, the science of water is not always exact, so definitive answers are not always available.

BOILING

Boiling is an acceptable method of water treatment when pathogens are the only known contaminant and only small quantities of drinking water are needed. It is the absolute minimum treatment for any surface water you intend to drink. Boiling requires planning so that a supply of boiled and subsequently cooled water is always on hand, the inconvenience increasing exponentially with the quantity of water required.

Boiling also consumes large amounts of energy while releasing heat and moisture into the air – potentially a real drag on a hot, humid day. But if you already own a stove and a pot, or an electric kettle (the electric kettle using about half the electricity to boil water as the stove-top alternative), start-up costs for this treatment method are nil.

HOW LONG DOES IT TAKE?

Boiling water kills the three groups of microorganisms that can be pathogenic: bacteria, protozoa, and viruses. One minute of boiling is usually sufficient to snuff out any micro-

organisms alive and kicking in your water (or whatever the micro-world equivalent of kicking is). What makes biologists nervous, though, is that some microorganisms go into a dormant state. Test the water after the one-minute boil and all appear dead, but the dormant crowd can later "reactivate". If you want to be certain you've done them all in, you should boil for 20 minutes, says an environmental-biologist friend. Yet this is up to four times longer than most government health departments suggest (at least, those willing to actually put a number on it). Being Canadian, and therefore genetically disposed towards compromise, I boil for 10 minutes.

Boiling has no residual effect. (See box, p. 76.)

Minimum requirements: *a pot and a heat source.*

DISTILLATION

A distiller is a close relative of the kettle, the main difference being that it is the evaporated liquid we make use of, not the heated liquid left in the pot. The process of distillation is used extensively in the industrial and scientific realm to isolate solvents from compound liquids. It's the means by which we refine crude oil into gasoline, how we get whisky, and also the *single* most effective way to purify that almost-universal solvent, water.

A water distiller heats the incoming water to its evaporation point, then allows the vapour to condense on a cooled surface where it is collected into a reservoir, ready for use. Anything that isn't killed by the boiling or doesn't vaporize is left behind – all the dissolved and suspended solids, minerals (both good and bad), radioactive substances, and the majority of toxic chemicals and disagreeable tastes and odours.

OPERATING COSTS AND DRAWBACKS

Distillers are reasonably expensive both to purchase and operate. The basic models that only my cheap neighbour Dave would buy start at about $400, the price quickly soaring into four digits as we add basic features such as built-in reservoirs with sight gauges, automatic cleaning systems, and a direct connection to the cottage pressure lines.

And while brochure talk of "pennies a day for pure water" sounds right up my impoverished alley, that statement is only true because pennies do indeed form part of dollars. Actual operating costs will depend on your local cost of electricity (which is only going to rise in the years between now and Armageddon) and on the quantity of purified water you need.

From an economic standpoint, distilling anything more than drinking and cooking water doesn't make sense because large-capacity distillers are very costly both to purchase and operate. Therefore, pollutants potentially damaging to the entire system, such as iron or iron bacteria, or just irritating, such as the rotten-egg stench of hydrogen-sulphide gas, would have to be removed by separate treatment methods. (Boiling also shares this shortcoming as a water-treatment method.)

Volatile contaminants such as VOCs can tag along with the water vapour during the distillation process and must be removed with the addition of an activated-carbon filter between the condensing surface (often a coiled tube) and the reservoir. Some distillers include such a filter as standard equipment. Still others (get it? – *still* others?) claim to vent a portion of the unwanted volatiles into the atmosphere before the vapour is condensed. As the atmosphere in this case would likely be the interior of your cottage, provide a means for these gases to vent outdoors – by opening a window, for instance.

You might want to open a window in any event because, in common with boiling, heat and humidity are by-products of the distillation process. And of course the purified water will need to be cooled before drinking.

Distilled water is essentially mineral free. Critics maintain it will consequently draw minerals out of your body as the water seeks to re-establish its balance of natural components. Advocates cite this same tendency as a benefit, the purified water supposedly "flushing" the body's system as it toddles on through to the toilet.

This latter receptacle seems the best place for either theory. Relative to the quantities your body needs (for instance, about 800 mg of calcium per day for adults), the amount of minerals in water just isn't enough to make a difference to your body (about 3 mg– 4 mg in a glass of lake water versus 275 mg in a glass of milk), especially when compared to the indisputable benefits of drinking unpolluted water. Drink and eat right and don't worry about it.

TYPES OF DISTILLERS

Water distillers fit into one of two broad categories: batch or continuous feed. A batch distiller purifies one batch of water at a time, requiring manual refilling of the boiling chamber as each batch is processed. Continuous-feed models (also known as automatic or direct connection) are tied into your plumbing system, so the reservoir is automatically topped up as you drain it. Continuous-feed models are more convenient – and more costly – while a batch distiller has the advantage of portability, making it relatively easy to transport between home and cottage.

An interesting variation on the batch distiller is the solar distiller. If you have ever had condensation on the cottage windows, then you are already familiar with the basic principle. Untreated water is placed under an angled piece of glass; the sun heats the water, vaporizing it, and the vapour rises, condensing on the underside of the glass. It then trickles down into a catchment trough, and from there into a bottle. Yield is minimal even on a clear day (about 7 L or 1.9 US gal.), and you could get a mite thirsty on a cloudy one; but for cottages without electricity, this is a dandy way to purify water: certainly the most environment-friendly purification system, bar none.

Distillation, like boiling, has no residual effect.

Minimum non-solar requirements: *electricity, and a pressurized plumbing system for continuous-feed models.*

Minimum solar requirements: *sunshine.*

ULTRAVIOLET RADIATION

Ultraviolet radiation, or UV, water purifiers are simple in concept: The water passes by the light; the light kills most microorganisms. Nothing is added to the water, meaning there is no residual effect, and nothing is taken away, meaning all the solids, minerals (good and bad), and any toxic chemicals or radioactive substances remain. If your water tests positive for anything other than the presence of coliforms, you will have to treat those other problems separately.

UV will not kill cysts, like *Giardia,* because the light cannot penetrate this pathogen's protective shell. Similarly, bacteria and viruses hiding behind suspended material such as sand or algae are shielded from the light's disinfecting ways, so at the very minimum, all water must pass through a sediment filter before reaching the UV light chamber. Following exposure to the UV light, if the water is then directed through an activated-carbon filter or a ceramic filter, all remaining microorganisms – including cysts – will be removed.

EXPOSURE TIME

For ultraviolet radiation to disinfect, the pathogens, and hence the water, must have sufficient exposure to the UV rays. The time required to kill the bacteria is variable, depending in part on their numbers and in part on the intensity of the lamp. While minimal exposure may appear to have killed all bacteria, it has been shown that as many as two-thirds of these "dead" bacteria can revive themselves as you pour the "purified" water into a container for storage in the refrigerator. This problem relates back to the "how long do we boil the water?" question – perhaps better rephrased as "What's it take to kill one of these little buggers anyway?" Most manufacturers recognize this problem and design the housing of the UV purifier to permit maximum exposure of the water to the killing ways of radiation. Because exposure time must increase as the microorganism count increases,

a UV device is not recommended when the faecal coliform count exceeds 100 per ml of water. Fluctuations in voltage, a potential problem in rural settings, can also reduce a UV's effectiveness.

Complicating the issue is the fact that the output of a UV lamp diminishes over time. A lamp is only good for about one or two years of cottage duty, perhaps less when operating under arduous conditions (such as when the water is turbid). Most UV devices have a tiny warning light that glows red when the lamp is kaput, but you need more lead time than that. Look for a unit with a monitoring device that allows you to keep track of the lamp's diminishing intensity, a must if you want to be sure the purifier is doing what it was designed to do.

UV rays can be blocked by dirt accumulating on the lamp, so a UV device must also provide a convenient way to access the lamp for cleaning (and replacement, for that matter).

Like distillation and boiling, UV treatment adds nothing to the water, and therefore nothing potentially nasty to your body or the environment. A UV lamp also consumes much less electricity than a kettle or distiller, and it can disinfect the water for the entire cottage plumbing system. This means drinking water will flow to every outlet, including the toilet, which will no doubt please the family dog. The price of a quality lamp and the required filters will set you back about $1,000; a replacement lamp is approximately $100.

Minimum requirements: *electricity and non-turbid water.*

FILTRATION

A filter removes an unwanted substance from water by preventing the flow of that substance through the filter medium. For filtration to be effective, we have to establish which substances we wish to stop, and then determine which filters can indeed stop these substances in an acceptable time frame. From the perspective of drinking water, the first criterion is easily satisfied by an extensive water examination as outlined in Chapter 5. However,

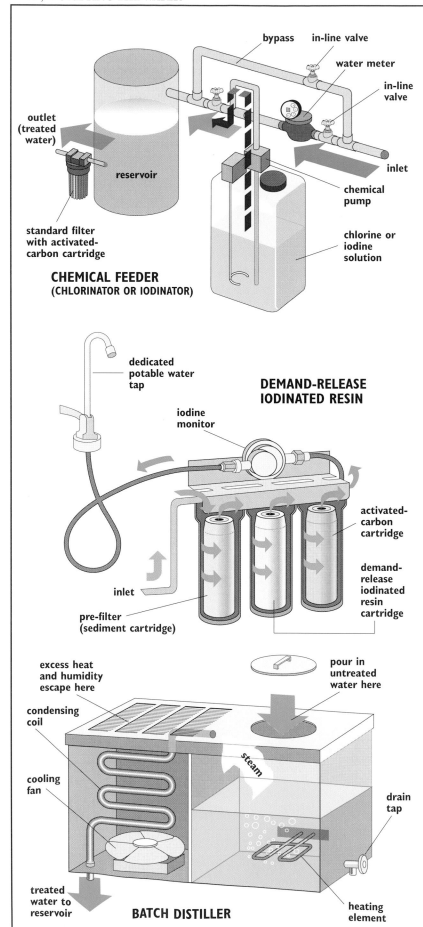

CHEMICAL FEEDER
(CHLORINATOR OR IODINATOR)

bypass in-line valve

water meter

in-line
valve

outlet
(treated
water)

inlet

reservoir

chemical
pump

standard filter
with activated-
carbon cartridge

chlorine or
iodine
solution

dedicated
potable water
tap

**DEMAND-RELEASE
IODINATED RESIN**

iodine
monitor

activated-
carbon
cartridge

demand-
release
iodinated
resin
cartridge

inlet

pre-filter
(sediment cartridge)

excess heat
and humidity
escape here

pour in
untreated
water here

condensing
coil

steam

cooling
fan

drain
tap

treated
water to
reservoir

BATCH DISTILLER

heating
element

choosing an appropriate filter can be more difficult than searching for truth in a platform of election promises. (Oh, those fantastical flights of brochure hyperbole.)

One measure of a filter's ability to stop contaminants is its porosity – the size of the holes in the filter medium that permit the water and whatever else to squeeze through and continue on their way. The size of material that a given filter can stop is measured in microns, one micron being equal to one-millionth of a metre (about three-millionths of a foot). A hair on your head is about 100 microns in diameter, while your average bacteria checks in at around 5 microns and a virus at about 0.03 micron.

Judged by Max's Arbitrary Rules of Simplification (MARS), there are three general categories of water filters applicable to cottage use: tank, standard, and dumb. Not included in this review are the combination water filter/water jugs that have proved very popular in the city. These filters are designed to remove the taste of chlorine and other additives from treated water, but aren't considered suitable for use with untreated water.

TANK FILTERS

Tank filters are large canisters averaging 20 cm (8 in.) in diameter by 125 cm (48 in.) high, but the dimensions can certainly vary. Each tank may contain more than one filter medium – which is usually a loose fill poured into the tank. Because the quantities of filter medium are large, the capacity of the filter to deal with contaminants is also large, which translates into longer filter life, the ability to handle increased flow, the ability to filter out more contaminants, or some combination of the three. Tank filters are generally used as part of a full-system approach to water purification, meaning you can drink the bath water (before you take a bath, of course).

Many tank filters have the potential to incorporate backwashing. This allows for periodic (and preferably automatic) flushing of the filter medium, again extending its life. Tank filters of any type should never be backwashed into a septic system, as the sudden

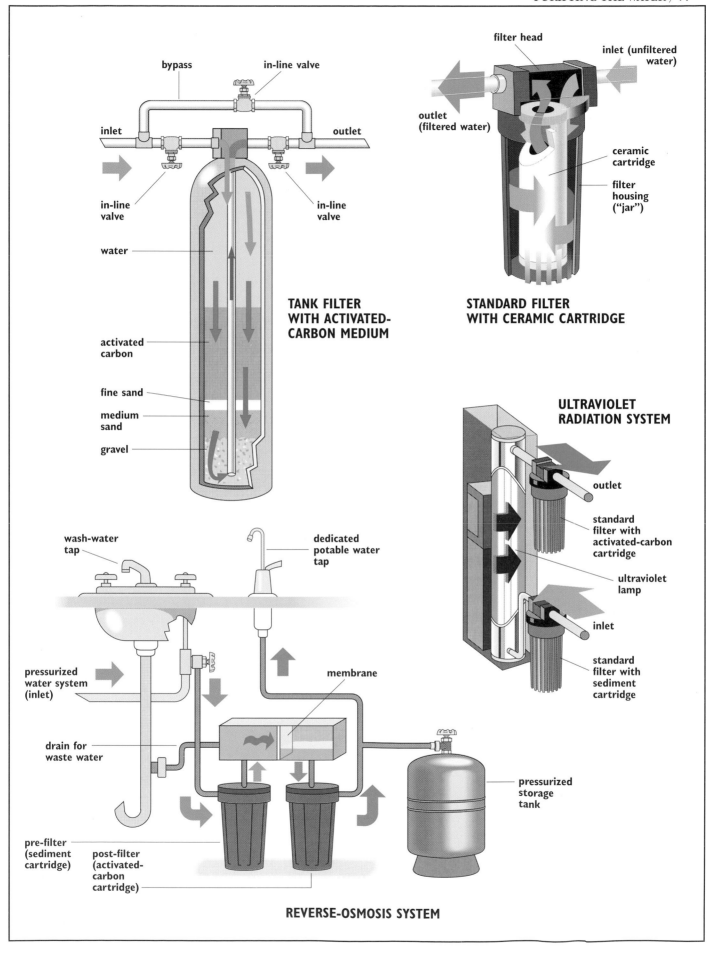

TANK FILTER WITH ACTIVATED-CARBON MEDIUM

bypass

in-line valve

inlet

outlet

in-line valve

in-line valve

water

activated carbon

fine sand

medium sand

gravel

STANDARD FILTER WITH CERAMIC CARTRIDGE

filter head

inlet (unfiltered water)

outlet (filtered water)

ceramic cartridge

filter housing ("jar")

ULTRAVIOLET RADIATION SYSTEM

outlet

standard filter with activated-carbon cartridge

ultraviolet lamp

inlet

standard filter with sediment cartridge

wash-water tap

dedicated potable water tap

pressurized water system (inlet)

membrane

drain for waste water

pre-filter (sediment cartridge)

post-filter (activated-carbon cartridge)

pressurized storage tank

REVERSE-OSMOSIS SYSTEM

and sizable influx of liquid may cause solids to wash out into the absorption area (see Chapter 7), nor should the backwash be discharged near any water source. Chemicals contained in the filter medium may also destroy the bacterial action in the septic tank.

The initial cost for tank filters (from about $500 to $5,000, depending on intended function and options) can quickly get scary, but that may be offset by longevity and convenience. The cost of filter replacement depends on type and quantity.

STANDARD FILTERS
Standard filters are much smaller, about 10 cm (4 in.) in diameter by about 36 cm (14 in.) high, and have replaceable cartridge-style filters. These often see duty hooked into a pressure line leading to a dedicated drinking tap next to the sink, although if water problems are minimal, they could conceivably tend an entire cottage system. Standard filters are also used extensively in tandem with each other, or with distillers, UV devices, or reverse-osmosis units. (More on these below.)

Some can get downright fancy, with all sorts of brightwork and uniquely sized filters – objects of industrial art. Of course you're going to pay dearly for fancy, both in purchase price (which can approach the lower end of large tank filters) and filter-replacement costs.

Fortunately, there are more plebeian filters that perform equally well. Look for a sturdy filter housing that accepts the standard interchangeable 9¾-in. cartridge, rewarding you with a far greater selection of filters to choose from. The standard filter housing is basically a glass or plastic jar that screws into the head, which is both the jar's lid and the water inlet and outlet. A nice feature to look for is a shut-off valve on the head, allowing you to change filters without turning off the water supply.

An entire filter will be in the $50 range, while replacement cartridges will usually run from $5 to $20.

DUMB FILTERS
Dumb filters simply clip or screw onto the end of your tap. With the water exposed to so little filter medium, the benefits of filtering are at best minimal – as is the filter's longevity in a typical cottage situation. Cheap to buy (usually less than $30), but not worth the price.

WHAT FILTERS YOU NEED FOR WHAT
The most basic filter type common to both tank and standard varieties is the sediment filter. This takes out big chunks – those in the 50–100 micron range. Obviously, a very fine filter would remove more contaminants, but it would also tend to clog quicker. Extremely turbid water may require a backwashing tank filter or two or more standard filters, each with a lesser micron rating than the preceding filter, to prevent premature clogging. While the sediment filter medium in a tank filter is usually a specialized loose-fill sand, standard filters have sediment cartridges made of foam, wound rope, or pleated plastic film. The pleated variety will usually last longer. The other two also have a greater tendency to support bacterial growth within their pores.

In addition to stopping sediment, a ceramic cartridge in a standard filter housing can also stop bacteria and protozoa, including cysts, when the faecal coliform count is less than 100 per ml of water. A ceramic filter will not stop viruses.

Because filters only block pathogens, not kill them, they must be scrubbed frequently to remove bacterial build-up. If the cottage is left vacant for the week, the warm environment within the filter housing is an ideal place for microorganisms to replicate, so the cartridge must be cleaned on your return. How do you clean it? Very carefully, folks, due to the fragility of the filters. Even near-invisible cracks are enough to let the micro-bugs slip by.

A ceramic filter used after UV treatment should stop all pathogens (assuming the water is clear, which can be achieved with an additional sediment filter before the UV unit). However, for water having a faecal coliform count greater than 100 per ml, test the treated water to ensure that the system is up to the task.

For water with a disagreeable taste or odour

(possibly from chlorine or iodine disinfection) or that has tested positive for organic chemicals or radon, an activated-carbon filter – also known as an activated-charcoal filter because it consists of highly refined charcoal – may be the answer. Through a process known as adsorption, activated-carbon filters attract and accumulate most of these waterborne contaminants. However, sediment will quickly clog the fine pores of a small carbon cartridge so a sediment pre-filter is required if the water is turbid. But a tank carbon filter will remove sediment without risk of clogging. Unfortunately, whether in a cartridge or a tank filter, charcoal attracts bacteria, allowing the microorganisms to proliferate in its pores. Therefore, water containing microorganisms must be disinfected (by distillation, UV radiation, ceramic filter, chemical treatment, etc.) prior to passing through a carbon filter.

The greater flexibility inherent in larger tank filters, because of size, backwashing, and the ability to include large quantities of more than one medium in one tank, leads to a greater variety of uses. These include water softening, iron removal, tannin removal, and neutralizing of acidic water.

WATER SOFTENERS AND SEPTICS DON'T MIX

Water softeners work by passing the water through a chemical that trades calcium for salt. Some governments, such as Alberta, express concern over the effects of this salt being introduced into a septic system absorption area, as excess sodium can reduce the permeability of the soil, increasing the possibility of leaching bed failure. Therefore, water softeners are *not recommended* for use in conjunction with septic systems. If they must be used, definitely do not allow the filter to backwash into the septic system and "under no circumstances should any water softener be used for iron removal," when the cottage is served by a septic system, states the Alberta government.

Avoid any filter medium that contains a phosphate compound – such as polyphosphate used for iron removal or potassium phosphate used as a water softener – due to their contribution to nutrient enrichment.

All filters deteriorate and require replacing, the exact timing all but impossible to call – except that it will likely occur *before* manufacturers' recommendations. A filter that is spent and not replaced could add contaminants to your drinking water.

Filtration has no residual effect.

Minimum requirements: *water pressure.*

REVERSE OSMOSIS

In a reverse-osmosis unit, water is forced through the pores of a fine membrane. Everything too big to squeeze through the pores gets left behind. In theory, anything bigger than a water molecule shouldn't make the grade, but in practice, because the size of the pores vary, some microorganisms make it through. Reverse osmosis will remove organic chemicals and toxic minerals, but not tastes, odours, or radon gas. To rid the system of pathogens, a UV device or ceramic filter would have to be installed in conjunction with the unit. Iron, manganese, sulphur, and turbidity can all dramatically decrease the life expectancy of a membrane, so the reverse-osmosis unit must be preceded by a sediment filter. If tastes and odours are a problem, a carbon filter will have to be installed after the unit. In most cases, the sediment and carbon filters are included in a reverse-osmosis system. Expect to pay about $1,500 (and up) for this system.

WILL IT WORK WITH YOUR WATER PUMP?

What rules out reverse osmosis for most cottages is the requirement of a minimum incoming water pressure of 35–40 psi. As the typical cottage water pump doesn't meet this standard, an auxiliary pump would have to be installed – which adds substantially to the price of an already expensive purification system.

Typically, a reverse-osmosis system takes about three or four hours to treat 4 L (1 US gal.) of water, and wastes 10 L–35 L (3 US gal.–9 US gal.) in the process. (The leftovers are known as the "brine".) At the cottage, this waste water invariably ends up in the septic system, an additional load it certainly doesn't need. (See Chapter 7.)

Reverse osmosis has no residual effect.
Minimum requirements: *consistent water pressure of at least 35–40 psi.*

OZONATION

Ozone is a gas, O_3, that can be formed by an electrical discharge passing through the air. Lightning will do the trick in the upper atmosphere where ozone protects us against excessive UV rays from the sun, or we can do the same down here by plugging in an ozonator. Ozone is a strong disinfectant that will kill bacteria, protozoa, and viruses given sufficient contact time. Excessive amounts of iron, manganese, and sulphur in the water will interfere with the disinfection process, so an ozonator must have add-on filters to remove turbidity. It won't remove cysts, so an additional filter is needed for that, too.

Ozonators are often used as purification devices in the bottled-water industry, but as of this writing, ozonators for cottage use have not yet proven themselves a practical alternative. Only small amounts of water can be disinfected at a time and the reservoir requires frequent cleaning. And while ozone high in the sky is good, ozone down here (known as ground-level ozone) is not, but some is released into the lower atmosphere nonetheless. Ozonators consume electricity and cost about $750 for a system with carbon filters.

Ozonation has a mild residual effect.
Minimum requirements: *electricity and water free of turbidity.*

CHEMICAL DISINFECTANTS

Thanks to the wonderful world of chemical compounds, cottagers have yet four more ways to conveniently slaughter microorganisms: chlorine injection; superchlorination; iodine injection; and demand-release iodinated resins (also known as pentaiodide).

CHLORINE

Chlorine gas is the disinfectant of choice for municipalities throughout North America.

This is an extremely dangerous substance, used during World War I to kill humans, but fortunately a much less toxic version of it is available for use at the cottage – sodium hypochlorite, better known as chlorine bleach. Usually, a chemical feeder (in this case called a chlorinator), automatically injects chlorine into the incoming water line, the percentage of the chlorine added to the water being constant regardless of how many microorganisms may be in the water at that time. (This system is not legal in all jurisdictions in North America.) For cottage use, *safe* doses of chlorine must be in contact with the water for about 20 minutes to be effective, so a large reservoir may be necessary if water use is high. At these levels, chlorine will not kill all cysts. A carbon filter installed after the chlorinator will remove any taste and odour of the chlorine, and the cysts. Turbidity will reduce chlorine's effectiveness (the particles adsorbing the disinfectant), as will high alkalinity (higher pH values). Chlorine can also increase the toxicity of some undesirable chemicals that may already exist in the water supply.

A complete chlorination system, which includes the chemical feeder, a reservoir, a sediment tank filter, and a carbon tank filter, will cost about $3,000–$4,000, while the chlorine itself costs about $20–$30 per gallon.
Minimum requirements: *electricity, water pressure, and water free of turbidity.*

In addition to disinfection, chlorination is used to precipitate iron, manganese, and hydrogen sulphide from water, the suspended material and chlorine taste then removed by filtration. This creates the problem of dispensing with high concentrations of chlorine compounds trapped in the filter medium.

Never backwash such a filter into a septic system: The chlorine will kill the bacteria necessary for the decomposition of sewage, and there's also a very high risk of forming THMs (trihalomethanes). So where's the safest place to get rid of it? Probably your local sewage hauler (honey wagon), if he or she will take it.

Costs for this system are the same as above.
Minimum requirements: *electricity and water pressure.*

CHARTING THE WATERS: TROUBLESHOOTING GUIDE

PROBLEM	PROBABLE CAUSE	POSSIBLE REMEDY *(see text for further explanation)*
COLIFORMS REVEALED BY BACTERIOLOGICAL ANALYSIS	composting vegetable matter or faeces from warm-blooded animals getting into water supply	–boiling –distillation –UV treatment –ceramic filtration –chlorination –iodine injection –demand-release iodinated resin
TURBIDITY *(suspended and dissolved solids other than those listed below)*	sand particles, algae, miscellaneous vegetable matter	–distillation –sediment filtration
RED STAINING ON FIXTURES, METALLIC TASTE	excess iron (often accompanied by manganese)	–distillation –chlorination –manganese sulphate/potassium permanganate filtration –manganese greensand filtration
BROWNISH STAIN OR SLIME ON FIXTURES, COFFEE AND TEA TURN BLACK AND BITTER TASTING	iron bacteria and/or manganese bacteria, or tannic acid	–annual superchlorination, followed by ongoing chlorination or demand-release iodinated resin –drill new well –tannin tank filtration
BAD TASTE AND ODOUR	methane gas, hydrogen-sulphide gas, chlorine, iodine, or composting organic matter	–aeration –boiling (if allowed to vent) –distillation –activated-carbon filtration
PLUMBING FIXTURES CORRODING, METALLIC TASTE	*a)* acidity (pH >5, <7) *b)* acidity (pH <5)	*a)* –neutralizing filtration (marble and/or limestone chip) *b)* –soda ash injection
NASTY TASTE, SCALING ON KETTLES AND PIPES, UNSIGHTLY BATHTUB RING	excessive hardness	–water softener (zeolite filtration) –distillation (clean boiling chamber often)
CHEMICAL ANALYSIS SHOWS PRESENCE OF: ORGANIC CHEMICALS *(VOCs, pesticides, petrochemicals, etc.)*	agricultural/industrial pollutants	–distillation (except VOCs) –activated-carbon filtration
RADON	Mother Nature	–distillation –activated-carbon filtration
TOXIC MINERALS	industry/Mother Nature	–distillation –activated-carbon filtration
NITRATES	agriculture/faulty septic systems/Mother Nature	–distillation

SUPERCHLORINATION

Superchlorination is a technique used to disinfect wells. As the name implies, it involves large dosages of chlorine being dumped into the well and run through the cottage water system. Regrettably, there is no other acceptable means of purging an entire plumbing system of bacteria, a crucial and (you hope) once-in-a-lifetime step after the well is capped. Superchlorination is also the only means anyone seems to have devised to deal with iron bacteria or manganese bacteria. A cottage well infected with either of these has to be treated once each spring, with continual chlorination or demand-release iodinated resins required between the annual doses. There is no doubt that superchlorination kills pathogens, but it also dramatically increases the risk of subsequent side effects, such as the formation of THMs. For single-dose superchlorination, a bottle of bleach is the only cost.

Minimum requirements: *a well or water system in need of disinfection.*

One of the things we like about chlorine is that it hangs around. This means that as a disinfectant, it has a respectable residual effect, and as a chemical in glues and building materials, it provides durability. But its propensity to persist also means it hangs around in the environment, something we're not nearly as keen on. Chlorine is very reactive: It's a chemical streetwalker – always looking for a mate, and you know it's going to cost. For instance, chlorine mates with organic compounds to form dioxins and THMs. Because the water we treat inevitably ends up in our septic system, which is essentially an ocean of organic compounds, the likelihood of forming these potentially carcinogenic compounds is high, as is the likelihood of some of these newly created toxins leaching out into the environment.

IODINE

Like chlorine, iodine can also be injected into the water supply to disinfect water. Unlike chlorine, no evidence is available on the long-term effects of usage, although it is suspected of causing thyroid problems and affecting people prone to allergies. Iodine does not re-act with organic compounds to form potential carcinogens, nor are its disinfection properties diminished as pH levels increase. It does, however, require 50% more contact time with the water than chlorine, and costs about 20 times more, but it kills all pathogens, including cysts. And should a nuclear holocaust occur while you're at the cottage, iodine will slow some of the effects of radioactive fallout. Handy. Just like chlorine, it has a residual effect on microorganisms, and its potency can be diminished with turbidity. The taste and odour it imparts to water can be removed with a charcoal filter, which also reduces potential side effects. Iodine injection systems are comparable in price to chlorination systems.

Minimum requirements: *electricity, water pressure, and water free of turbidity.*

DEMAND-RELEASE IODINATED RESINS

Demand-release iodinated resins are relatively new on the water-treatment market and hold some promise as being an efficient means of dealing with pathogens with minimal side effects. The iodinated resin is held in a car-

RESIDUAL EFFECT AND STORAGE

A method of water purification is said to have a residual effect when it continues to function as a purifier after the initial contact with the contaminated water. For example, chlorine hangs around, bumping off bacterial invaders, while boiling only kills what's there at the time.

These post-purification bacterial invasions can be curtailed by proper storage. The best place for disinfected water is in a cool, dark place, like the refrigerator, and it should be consumed within a couple of days following initial purification. Water left in the cottage water system between visits (and usually at temperatures considered ideal for bacterial growth) should not be considered safe to drink.

The container material of choice is glass. Water will pick up the taste, and sometimes the chemical constituents, of plastic containers, with the possible exception of clear polycarbonate. Do not use an aluminum pot to either store or boil water in, as aluminum can leach into the water. The accumulation of aluminum in nerve cells has been associated with Alzheimer's disease.

tridge, similar in concept to a cartridge filter, the water coming into contact with the disinfectant, rather than the disinfectant being added to the water (hence the term demand-release). The advantage to this system is that the required contact time to kill the incoming microorganisms is reduced to about two or three seconds, which means much less disinfectant is needed to do the job, so less of it ends up in our bodies and the environment. As with iodine injectors, turbidity will diminish its effectiveness and shorten the life of the resin, so sediment pre-filters will likely be required. The resins also eliminate the handling and mixing required with chlorine and iodine injection methods. For cottages without electricity or running water, gravity-feed models are available. A typical cottage unit with pre-filter will cost about $230–$600, and replacement resin cartridges cost about $130–$375, although the price can approach that of a full chlorination system depending on the quantity of purified water required.

Minimum requirements: *electricity, water pressure, and water free of turbidity, unless using a gravity-feed model, in which case only water free of turbidity is required.*

Just before leaving the world of chemical compounds: Highly acidic water (having a pH level less than 5) can be neutralized with a solution of soda ash fed into the incoming water using a chemical feeder similar to those used for chlorine and iodine solutions.

Minimum requirements: *electricity and water pressure.*

BOTTLED WATER

Another option that makes sense if your drinking-water needs are small or the cost of purifying your well or lake water proves exorbitant is to purchase bottled water and schlep it into the cottage. Sporadic exposés conducted by consumer groups and government agencies have brought to the public's attention, usually via front-page headlines, the news that not all bottled water is created equal, and some of it is created rather poorly indeed. While such announcements are usually followed by hot

and heavy debate over the testing methods used and the legitimacy of the findings, a very important point is regrettably overshadowed by all the brouhaha – some bottled water, the stuff that passed these notorious tests, for instance, is unquestionably of very high quality.

Bottled water undergoes treatment using variations of the systems discussed above, only on a grander scale. My own preference is for distilled bottled water – perhaps because I have a lot of difficulty rationalizing spending money for something called "pure spring water" or the like when I draw my own water from an artesian spring that, while safe to drink, is anything but pure. Personal prejudices aside, buy from a reputable dealer.

A FREE IDEA

While the family snoozes through the night, all sorts of stuff can be happening in the cottage plumbing system – such as toxic metals leaching from the pipes into the water and microorganisms partaking in an all-night orgy of replication. All this and more could be waiting to greet the dawn at a tap's first opening. So first thing in the morning – and when you first arrive at the cottage – run the water for about a minute to clear the pipes.

FINAL THOUGHTS ON WATER TREATMENT

All purification equipment is going to require maintenance, usually more often than indicated in brochure insinuations. If your water source is seriously contaminated, it may be more economical in the long run (and certainly more convenient) to drill a new deep well. Of course, there's no guarantee water from that source will be trouble free, but at least the odds are with you.

7 DEALING WITH SEPTIC SYSTEMS

A guide to what happens when you flush at the cottage

Cafeteria for bacteria:
In the septic tank, anaerobic bacteria assist in decomposing the sewage; in the leaching bed, aerobic bacteria finish the job.

ON AVERAGE, EACH PERSON LIVING IN NORTH America produces between 275 and 350 litres (75–95 US gal.) of sewage per day from all sources. I don't know who measured it or how, but those are the figures – our combined individual contribution to the dilemma of dispersal. Where does it all go? One flush (or maybe two) of the toilet and it's gone, thank goodness. And it's the same with the stuff we chuck down the kitchen drain. Does it really matter where it ends up?

At the cottage, chances are good it's headed for that neglected and misunderstood friend, the septic system – and from there, into and often onto the property where the cottage sits, and then perhaps into the waterways we swim in, and sometimes even into our drinking water. So a flush at the cottage only removes sewage from our immediate sight; it doesn't make it disappear. Call it sleight of can, an illusion only if we choose to ignore the potential degradation of the cottage environment.

While it's easy to distance ourselves from the workings and failings of a public sewage system, a septic system, our private sewage-treatment plant, sits just a few feet from the cottage door. It is an integral part of the cottage landscape. And since we are the owner/operators of this system, it is perhaps the most significant area where individually, and without undue inconvenience, each of us can make a noticeable difference in maintaining (or improving) the quality of cottage country.

In order to assume your obligations as owner/operator, it is necessary to understand how your sewage system is supposed to work. Exact construction details and approvals will still have to come from the government authority presiding over such matters in your cottage locale – hereafter referred to as the sewage police – but the following overview should assist you in understanding what is required, and how to minimize the system's impact on good old Mother Earth.

Most private systems are a variant of the septic tank system, consisting of two major components: the septic tank and the absorption (or leaching) area, the size of both being determined by local standards that are usually related to the number of bedrooms in the cottage, the number of cottagers, soil conditions, or some combination of these variables.

WHAT GOES ON IN THE SEPTIC TANK

In a properly designed system (a necessary qualifying phrase), first stop for the effluent once it leaves the cottage is an approved septic tank (the tank usually stamped with a CSA, NSF, or appropriate governing body symbol and approval number). The tank has two primary functions in life: to serve as a temporary storage bin for some of the things you send down the drain and, at the same time, to operate as a cafeteria for anaerobic bacteria. These microscopic epicures eschew oxygen but chew sewage – assisting in its decomposition – and then they die. (Not surprising with a diet like that.) These bacteria and their corpses become part of the fluids in the tank.

TYPES OF SEPTIC TANKS

The majority of modern septic tanks are prefabricated, made from concrete, fibreglass, or plastic. Steel is permitted in some areas but, generally, concrete or plastic is preferred. Some jurisdictions will permit poured-in-place concrete or concrete-filled, steel-reinforced concrete block. Although a skilled tradesperson can, in theory, build a higher-quality tank than most off-the-rack vendors can provide, the prefab route is much easier (and usually less expensive) if you are doing it on your own. Plastic has the advantage of being very light, making it easier to handle in tight areas and easier to transport to sites referred to by tradespeople as "inaccessible" when they're already busy with easier jobs. Plastic tanks can even be floated to the site. Fibreglass tanks can be floated too, but are a little heavier and more fragile, requiring that considerable care be taken during installation. Concrete tanks are usually less expensive than either plastic or fibreglass ones and much less likely to be punctured during installation. (Puncture a fibreglass or plastic tank and it's junk.) However, a concrete tank must be delivered and lowered into place by a crane-equipped truck, making it unsuitable for many cottage locales.

As with any popular cafeteria, interior design plays an important role in the tank's success. Inside, small diversionary baffles are located at the entrance and exit pipes of the tank, while the main dining area is usually divided by one or more larger baffles. (Picture the ubiquitous office divider with holes punched through the midsection.) The purpose of the baffles is to slow the flow, allowing sewage solids to sink to the bottom, where

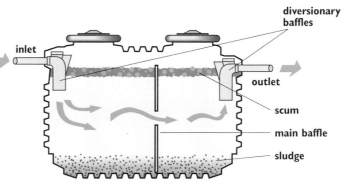

they are christened "sludge", and greases and fats to float to the top, to acquire the title "scum", leaving a turbid liquid in the middle. The larger the tank, the more time the solids have to separate into sludge and scum. While all this may sound a bit analogous to certain congressional or parliamentary systems, there are important differences. For example, with a properly maintained system, the sludge and scum are held in the tank before getting pumped out every couple of years, leaving the space open for new sewage. No excrement gets re-elected. Take a pass on this pumpout, however, or skimp on the tank size and sure as shootin' the sludge and scum will cause the ruination of any system, no matter how good it may have been at the beginning.

In a properly designed and maintained septic tank, the sludge settles to the bottom and the baffles keep the scum floating above. Meanwhile, the odorous liquid sandwiched in between runs out the tank's exit pipe and into the absorption area. There are two principal methods employed in dispersing this effluent – the leaching (or seepage) bed and the seepage pit (not always permitted) – although research for this book turned up

Tank theory:
Concrete and plastic are generally the preferred materials for septic tanks. Inside, baffles slow the flow so solids and grease settle out before the liquid sewage moves on to the absorption area.

countless variations approved for use in specific jurisdictions or special circumstances. Check with the local sewage police should your cottage site not lend itself to the more popular methods outlined below.

Absorption areas only work as planned when the permeability of the soil meets acceptable levels. Permeability is determined by a percolation test. Approved methods for this vary (although they all tend to yield the same results) so, again, check with the sewage police for details. (For percolation-test basics, see Chapter 10.)

THE LEACHING BED

By far the most common type of effluent-dispersal mechanism in cottage country is the leaching bed. The bed is a dedicated area of the cottage lot that facilitates the seepage of effluent from the tank into the soil in a controlled fashion. It is here that aerobic bacteria dispense with nasty pathogens and the like.

To visualize what a typical system is supposed to look like under the soil, picture a giant pitchfork buried flat in the bed: The handle represents the pipe connecting the tank to the bed; the horizontal rod to which the tines are attached is the bed's 3 in.–4 in. diameter header pipe; and the tines are the 3 in.–4 in. diameter distribution pipes through which the liquid sewage passes. Sometimes, where the "handle" meets the header, a distribution box is installed to encourage equal volumes of effluent to flow through each of the distribution pipes (usually not necessary when the header feeds an even number of distribution pipes). This picnic-basket-sized box (usually made of concrete) has holes punched in the sides for individual leads to each distribution pipe, the holes being at slightly different levels. With either method, the ends of the distribution pipes may be capped, or joined together by an unperforated cross-pipe.

Each distribution pipe (or run) consists of either several 1-ft.-long clay tiles carefully placed to allow narrow gaps to remain between them (an older practice rarely used now) or lengths of perforated plastic pipe glued together (the current preference). Through the gaps in the tiles or the holes in the pipes, the sewage oozes out into an envelope of ¾-in.

SUGGESTED MINIMUM SETBACKS AND CLEARANCES

ABSORPTION AREA SETBACKS *(check with local authorities for approval)*

Bottom of absorption area to high ground-water table*	1.2 m (4 ft.)
Open water or spring (including cistern or reservoir)	30 m (100 ft.)
Wetland	15 m (50 ft.)
Drilled well with watertight casing 6 m (20 ft.) deep	15 m (50 ft.)
Dug or driven well	45 m (150 ft.)
Pump intake (suction) line	30 m (100 ft.)
Dwelling, pool, or hot tub	6 m (20 ft.)
Property line	3 m (10 ft.)
Driveway	3 m (10 ft.)
Distance from slopes greater than 25%, cliffs, or rock	8 m (25 ft.)

TANK SETBACKS *(check with local authorities for approval)*

Open water, spring, wetland, or well (including cistern or reservoir)	15 m (50 ft.)
Pump intake (suction) line	15 m (50 ft.)
Dwelling, pool, or hot tub	3 m (10 ft.)
Property line	3 m (10 ft.)
Distance from slopes greater than 25%, cliffs, or rock	5 m (15 ft.)

A consulting engineer or the relevant local government authority can determine your high ground-water table.

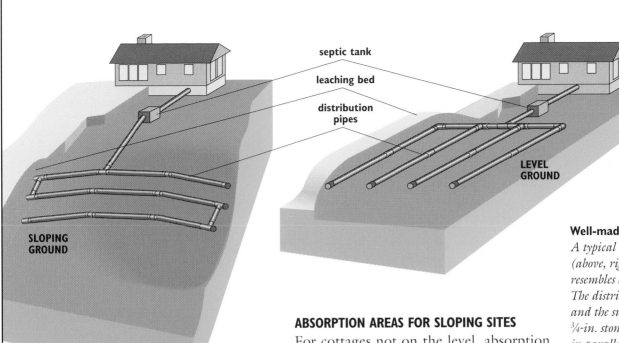

septic tank

leaching bed

distribution pipes

LEVEL GROUND

SLOPING GROUND

Well-made beds:
A typical leaching bed (above, right) resembles a pitchfork. The distribution pipes and the surrounding ¾-in. stones are laid in parallel trenches. If a cottage isn't on level ground, the leaching bed is set up more like a slalom ski run (above, left), with each successive trench set lower on the slope than the one above.

stones. From there, the sewage seeps into the soil where bacteria and bacterial leftovers from the anaerobic cafeteria are gobbled up by aerobic bacteria. (These bacteria like oxygen.)

The traditional leaching bed is referred to as a "tile bed" or "trench-type bed". Parallel trenches approximately 0.6 m (2 ft.) wide are dug in the existing soil about 1.5 m–1.8 m (5 ft.–6 ft.) apart. To take advantage of the aerobic bacteria naturally occurring in the upper layers of the soil, the depth of the trenches should not exceed 0.6 m–1 m (2 ft.–3 ft.). The pipe (levelled and supported at frequent intervals by wood or concrete blocks) is placed in the trenches, surrounded by its envelope of gravel, covered with a blanket of building paper or straw, and then topped off with soil. Because the effluent is supposed to seep into the soil, not pour out onto it, the pipes are set level, or at a maximum slope of 5 cm in 10 m (2 in. in 30 ft.). (Check local requirements.) The blanket keeps the upper layer of soil from washing into the gravel and plugging the gaps or holes in the tiles or pipes. (Besides, every bed needs a blanket.) It's a simple and relatively inexpensive filtration system to install, suitable for level sites with soil that meets acceptable percolation standards.

ABSORPTION AREAS FOR SLOPING SITES

For cottages not on the level, absorption trenches can be installed that follow the contour of the land, each successive trench or run set lower on the slope than the preceding one. This style of leaching bed is a bit like a slalom ski run for bacteria and other microbes, or maybe one of those giant water slides seen at finer amusement parks everywhere ("Step right up, bacteens, and ride the famous Sewage Slide!")

To picture what lies underground, you have to scrap the pitchfork imagery for this bed, since the pipe from the tank connects directly to the first distribution pipe at its centre point, and is perpendicular to it. One end of this perforated distribution pipe is capped, the opposite end being connected to a non-perforated cross-over pipe that feeds the next distribution pipe down. The effluent travels the full length of that pipe before meeting another cross-over to the next run and so on, the final run being capped at the end.

SEEPAGE PITS

In principle, the seepage pit (also known as a leaching pit in some jurisdictions) serves the same purpose as the leaching bed. However, instead of a leaching bed's group of pipes set in gravel-lined trenches, the seepage pit has one or more containers constructed in gravel-lined pits. The containers are usually built on site from uncemented stone, brick, or con-

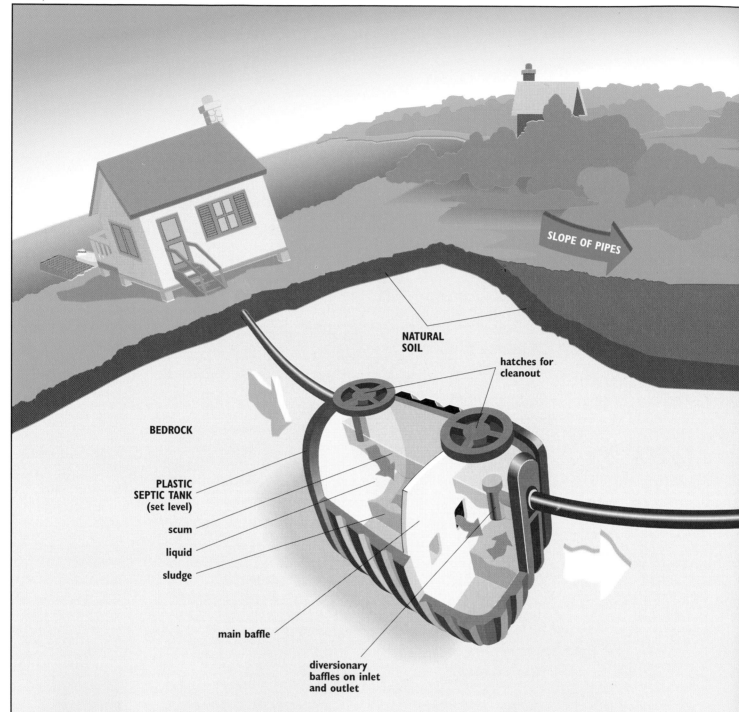

SLOPE OF PIPES

NATURAL
SOIL

hatches for
cleanout

BEDROCK

PLASTIC
SEPTIC TANK
(set level)

scum

liquid

sludge

main baffle

diversionary
baffles on inlet
and outlet

TYPICAL RAISED-BED SEPTIC SYSTEM

*First stop for the sewage is the septic tank, where solids and grease settle out.
From there it moves to the leaching bed, where it is dispersed through a
series of perforated distribution pipes, slowly oozing out into an envelope of
stones and from there into a layer of imported soil.*

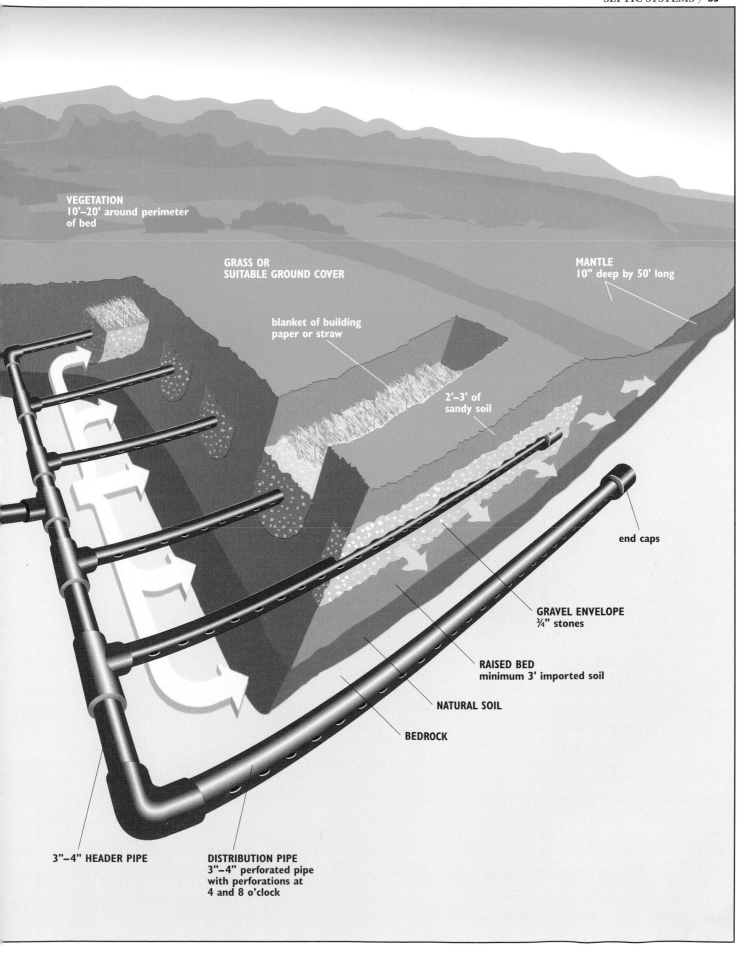

VEGETATION
10'–20' around perimeter
of bed

**GRASS OR
SUITABLE GROUND COVER**

MANTLE
10" deep by 50' long

blanket of building
paper or straw

2'–3' of
sandy soil

end caps

GRAVEL ENVELOPE
¾" stones

RAISED BED
minimum 3' imported soil

NATURAL SOIL

BEDROCK

3"–4" HEADER PIPE

DISTRIBUTION PIPE
3"–4" perforated pipe
with perforations at
4 and 8 o'clock

crete block. (The standard 8 in.–12 in. concrete blocks are sometimes laid on their sides to take advantage of the large holes running through them.) The gaps and holes in the pit wall serve the same function as the gaps in clay tiles or the holes in plastic pipe in a leaching bed. If more than one pit is required to handle the quantities of sewage, the flow of effluent to each pit must be equal (just as the flow must be equal through distribution pipes in a leaching bed). Therefore, the pipe exiting the septic tank has to branch out to each pit individually, just as it does to the distribution pipes in the leaching bed. The sewage cannot flow first to one pit and then to the next.

In design, the seepage pit is very much like a grey water leaching pit and the type of cesspool some jurisdictions allow to handle composting-toilet overflow. Although seepage pits were once quite prevalent in some parts of the continent, now they are usually approved only when a cottage lot does not have sufficient room to install a leaching bed. But there are better septic alternatives for restricted lots. (Read on.)

THE RAISED BED

Because cottages tend to be located in scenic areas, it's normal to encounter soils with high clay content, bedrock just below the surface, and high water tables. So it is not unusual for such sites to flunk the percolation test. One solution to this dilemma is to "import soil", a euphemism for having sand trucked in and piled up on your property to create what is known as a "raised bed". Depending on the ability of the existing soil to absorb liquid, 1 m (3 ft.) or more of this imported soil may be required before the distribution pipes, each one surrounded by its gravel envelope, can be laid out over the sand and then covered with an additional 0.6 m–1 m (2 ft.–3 ft.) of sand and topsoil.

Because the bottom of a raised bed usually rests on an impermeable surface like rock or clay, an additional mantle of imported sand is sometimes required at the end of the bed. Without a mantle, when the sewage reaches the rock or clay, it simply runs along the surface and out onto open ground. The mantle, a layer of approved soil approximately 15 m (50 ft.) long by 25 cm (10 in.) deep, helps to keep the effluent below the surface for a longer period, affording it further opportunity to slowly seep into less-permeable soils and for its nutrients to be used up by whatever vegetation is growing on top.

A variation on the raised bed is the treatment mound, in which the distribution pipes are set in a single, large bed of gravel (picture several hotdogs in one big bun), then covered with soil like a standard bed.

NEED A LIFT?

Should the septic tank or the distribution pipes in the raised bed end up being higher

An imported bed:
If your soil flunks the percolation test, you'll need to have suitable soil brought in to create a raised bed. An extra mantle of this soil is sometimes required at the end of the bed to keep the sewage from running out along the surface.

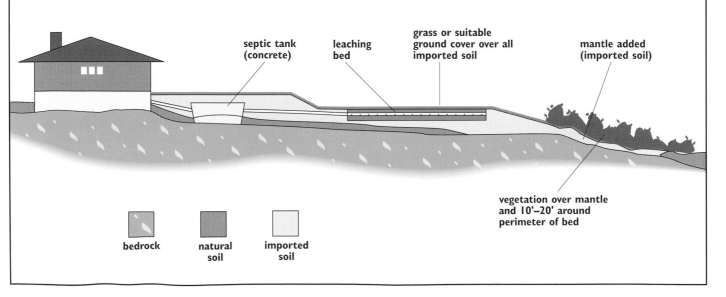

septic tank (concrete)

leaching bed

grass or suitable ground cover over all imported soil

mantle added (imported soil)

vegetation over mantle and 10'–20' around perimeter of bed

bedrock

natural soil

imported soil

than the toilet, kitchen sink, or other source of sewage, the sewage will need to be pumped up to the bed. (The effluent is always pumped up to a treatment mound.) Any levels of the cottage that are above the bed can still use gravity-fed plumbing, while an individual sewage lift pump can serve the fixtures or appliances below bed height. Some toilets, such as the Saniplus, have built-in lift pumps that can handle an entire bathroom's worth of waste water; or a separate sink pump for water-only fixtures, like sinks and showers, can be installed, usually in a sewage well. This well is a small, sealed holding tank, about 20 L–40 L (5 US gal.–10 US gal.) in capacity, the pump inside being activated by a float. It works much the same way as does a sump pump in a suburban basement.

If the entire cottage plumbing system needs a lift, a sewage pump would then be required to push the sewage uphill to the septic tank, the absorption area, or the holding tank, depending on site requirements. This type of pump is similar in concept to a centrifugal water pump but designed more for volume than pressure, our main goal here being to get the quantities of effluent out of the cottage rather than enjoy a good shower in the stuff. A sewage pump is designed to handle liquid and sewage-style solids, and is usually submerged in the septic tank or a sewage well. (And you thought servicing the cottage water pump was a distasteful job.)

WHERE TO PUT THE SEPTIC SYSTEM

Septic tanks and absorption areas both have minimum legal requirements for setbacks from buildings, lot lines, open water, and wells. The accompanying chart (p. 80) gives most of the preferred minimum setbacks, but check with the sewage police who patrol the area in which your cottage is located for any anomalies that may apply to your particular jurisdiction. These folks will also be able to supply you with all the technical poop and pertinent regulations governing the length of pipes, the distance between them, the minimum depths of gravel above and below the pipes, as well as the permissible slope of the pipes.

If a raised bed is used, applicable setbacks should be increased by at least 0.6 m (2 ft.) for every 0.3 m (1 ft.) of added height.

The topography that attracts us to cottage country – rock outcrops and steep slopes – can work against us when it comes time to squeeze a septic system onto the property, or update an existing one. Sometimes, the legal minimum clearances for a raised bed or trench-type bed cannot be realized. Fortunately, there are alternative septic systems for tight quarters: the aerobic system, the filter bed, and the holding tank.

OTHER OPTIONS
AEROBIC SYSTEMS

An aerobic system is a modified septic tank in which air is pumped into the sewage. If you've ever indulged in the fine art of blowing through a straw to make a chocolate milk shake bubble, you already understand the basic principle. The air bubbles encourage aerobic bacteria to take up residence in one's sewage. (Hint: Use an approved aerobic system, rather than a straw, for introducing bubbles to your septic tank.) Aerobic sewage eaters work more efficiently than their anaerobic pals, consuming more sludge, so the sewage gets broken down more before making its run out to the leaching bed.

Because this less-viscous liquid requires less filtering, some jurisdictions allow the total length of distribution pipe to be reduced to as much as two-thirds of that required for a bed fed by a regular (anaerobic) septic tank. Aerobic systems are expensive, complex, and require electricity. In recent years, they have lost favour as private sewage-treatment facilities because of their high cost (both to purchase and maintain) and, more significantly, because of the advent of the filter bed.

A SMALLER TYPE OF LEACHING BED

What differentiates a filter bed from the traditional leaching bed is that it uses specially selected sand that meets specific granular size requirements. As in the treatment mound, the pipes are laid in a continuous layer of gravel, rather than in individual trenches. Material costs are greater, but the size of the bed can be reduced by a third to a half that of a conventional bed, and maintenance costs are no greater than those of a conventional system. (Clearances for both aerobic tanks and filter beds remain the same as those for conventional septic systems, as does the frequency of tank pumpouts.)

HOLDING TANKS

The holding tank is a temporary parking zone for sewage; there is no provision for filtering. When the tank is full, the sewage must be pumped out. Some municipalities are reluctant to approve holding tanks since the sewage is usually trucked to a local treatment facility which may already be operating at or near capacity. Others will only approve a holding tank if the owner can provide proof of an approved method of disposal, which usually means a signed contract with a certified hauler of sewage. However, some jurisdictions, like Saskatchewan, require that any cottage located within 450 m (1,500 ft.) of the high-water mark of any surface water shared with an urban municipality or recreational area *must use* a holding tank. Holding tanks are also used extensively in areas that experience extreme winter temperatures, like the northern Canadian Prairies or the Northwest Territories, as absorption areas in such climates may not be able to retain enough heat for decomposition to take place. And a holding tank is sometimes the only sewage-system alternative where no space exists for an absorption area or the slope of the land exceeds what is permitted locally for contour-style absorption trenches.

Every holding tank must be equipped with an alarm to alert owners to impending pumpouts (What's brown and sounds like a bell? DUNNNNNG!), which, depending on use, can be a frequent expense.

WHY SYSTEMS FAIL

So which is the best system? It's not the *type* of system so much as its *condition*. Odds are, the best system is the one that is both new and properly maintained. Two major faults exist with any septic system that relies on Mother Earth to soak up its sins: natural obsolescence and an inability to deal with nutrients. Yet the biggest problem with septic systems is our attitude towards them – out of sight, out of mind. If the system occasionally gets a bit smelly or messy on the surface, Mother Earth will take care of it as soon as the weekend crowd leaves the cottage, right? Wrong.

The sad reality is that any absorption area will eventually fail. The lifespan of a system used year round is estimated to be 10–15 years; a system subjected only to seasonal use would in theory last longer. All absorption areas are destined to failure because the effluent flowing out from even a properly maintained septic tank carries some sludge through the exit pipe with it. The turbidity in this effluent tends to separate out at its earliest convenience, which in a new leaching bed corresponds to the first metre (3 ft.) or so of perforated pipe. The sludge coagulates in the gravel and plugs the pipe's holes. Over the years, the flow of sludge particles slowly moves down the pipe's length, gradually plugging up the gravel and holes along more and more of the pipe. When the effluent can no longer find speedy access to the surrounding soil, it will pond.

Ponding is a pleasant way of saying that liquid sewage is coming to the surface. Ponding pushes the oxygen out of the bed, and hence the aerobic bacteria die. When this happens – even if just once – the system is no longer doing what it was designed to do. This process of self-destruction is greatly hastened by a failure to pump out the tank regularly. That's because as solids build up in the tank, there is less space for incoming sewage, and therefore less time for sludge and scum to settle out before the sewage seeps into the absorption area. Robbed of this opportunity, the sewage will quickly plug the bed and destroy it. And clogged distribution pipes are more likely to freeze, which means more ponding. Also, gases given off by sewage left in the tank for long periods of time will deteriorate tank baffles, which in turn allows the sewage to run straight through to the absorption area and your yard. Regardless of cause, when the absorption area or tank is kaput your only recourse is to bite the bullet and have either or both replaced.

REGULAR PUMPOUTS ARE THE KEY

Due to their owner's ignorance, stubbornness, false economy, or whatever other rationalization or excuse, septic tanks are rarely pumped out when they need to be. It may be helpful to think of the septic tank as a large flow-through chamber pot: you still have to empty it, but because of its size and design, not quite as often. On average, a tank should be pumped out about once every three years – more often if the system is old or undersized for the load. The best time for a pumpout is early summer after the high ground-water levels of spring have subsided. This gives the entire summer and autumn for the bacterial action to re-establish itself. (Bacteria, like most cottagers, prefer warmer weather.) Emptying any sewage tank (septic or holding) in the fall may not allow enough time for decomposition to begin in earnest before winter's coldest temperatures take hold, putting the contents of the tank at risk of freezing, which not only stops the treatment process but could also seriously damage the tank.

Even if a pumped-out septic tank sneaks through the winter without turning into an indoor rink, it may still encounter problems. Because our contributions to a tank's contents are usually minimal in the off-season, an empty tank in the fall is still an empty or near-empty tank in the spring. Buoyed by water-soaked soil, the tank may float and could actually pop out of the ground (the lighter plastic tanks being more susceptible to this "welcome back to the cottage" surprise), which explains why early spring is also not a good time for a pumpout.

Some jurisdictions have, or are considering, legislation to enforce regular cleanouts and inspections, laws which will inevitably become universal. An inspection is the only way to determine if the need for a pumpout is imminent, and a licensed contractor is the best person to carry out this task. Most jurisdictions advise against owner/operator trips to the inside of a tank because every year, some unsuspecting home handyperson succumbs to the gases of his or her own effluent. Only anaerobic bacteria find honour in death by the septic tank.

A pumpout is not an expensive luxury, usually less than what you would pay for sewage taxes back in the city. But too many folks call the "honey wagon" only after things start to smell or the ground gets soggy over the septic field. By then, it's too late; your system is plugged. And contrary to the hyperbole of some advertising, no amount of additives can save it.

THE ISSUE OF SEPTIC ADDITIVES

The common element of these "miracle" septic savers is the assertion that the product will keep your system trouble-free and odour-free, or words to that effect. Some even leave no question in the consumer's mind that the product in question will stop the pumper truck. Maybe, if you pour the stuff into the truck's fuel tank rather than your septic tank.

Every jurisdiction in North America contacted regarding these additives advises against their use; but faced with the reality of a failed system, some cottagers continue to pour this stuff, and their money, down the drain. Most of the products *do* activate bacterial growth in the tank, as claimed. But according to all the biologists I contacted, simply adding more sewage does the same thing. Any product that claims to do more – like unclog pipes, for instance – could be in the hazardous-chemical category, in which case, it should *definitely not* go into any septic system because you can bet your long-term disability fund that it too will eventually end up in the water supply.

Another "additive" I was made aware of just a few years ago, one which seems to have some history behind it judging from the age of the person espousing its virtues, is to "Shoot two squirrels and dump 'em into the tank before you use it. Gets the bugs working." I

PRIVATE SEWAGE SYSTEM TROUBLESHOOTING GUIDE

(Note: While maintenance is not only allowed but encouraged, in most jurisdictions a permit is required for any repairs or modifications to the system.)

PROBLEM	CAUSE AND SOLUTION
SLOW FLUSH OF TOILET, OR SEWAGE BACKING UP INTO COTTAGE	**Pipes leading to septic or holding tank clogged:** Call a plumber or rent an auger and clear out the pipe yourself. **Tank full:** Get it pumped out, and be tankful it wasn't the absorption area. **Absorption area failure:** Call the sewage police and arrange for a new one. If the area cannot be relocated to another suitable location on the lot, then digging up the old area and importing new, approved fill might be required.
ODOURS IN COTTAGE	**Vent stack clogged:** The most likely cause of this is birds or squirrels nesting in the top. Climb up on the roof and evict the freeloading beasts, installing a screen over the end of the vent stack, which sometimes discourages them from returning. If problems with these squatters persist, it may be necessary to fabricate a cap for the stack (similar in concept to a chimney cap). **Vent stack not high enough:** The top of the stack should be at least 0.3 m (1 ft.) above the roof. If you are in an area susceptible to downdrafts, this clearance may have to be increased. **Fumes entering cottage directly from tank:** Tank may be full and require a pumpout, or drainpipe traps in cottage plumbing are incorrectly installed or leaking. Check that the septic-tank lid is making a tight seal to the tank. It should be sitting flush (no pun intended) with the top of the tank. Dirt between the lid and tank can also result in a bad seal. **Wind blowing the fumes in off a ponding absorption area:** Call the sewage police and arrange for a new absorption area.
SOIL WET ANY-WHERE ALONG LINE FROM COTTAGE TO TANK TO ABSORPTION AREA	**Broken pipes leading to the tank or absorption area:** Locate the leak, determine the cause of the failure (for example, the marine railway runs over the pipe as it leaves the cottage) and rectify (move the railway), then replace the damaged pipes and connections. **The tank is overflowing:** Get it pumped out. **Absorption area failure:** Call the sewage police and arrange for a new one. **It's raining:** Wait for a dry spell and check again.
SEWAGE COMING TO THE SURFACE AT A POINT AWAY FROM SEPTIC SYSTEM	**System failure or improper placement of system** *(for example, too close to a grade or bedrock)*: Time for a new septic system.
SEWAGE PUMP MALFUNCTIONING	The sewage pump being a variation of the centrifugal water pump, see the pump troubleshooting guide in Chapter 4.
HOLDING TANK ALARM AND/OR LIGHT ON	**The holding tank is full:** Get it pumped out. **There is a fault in the alarm system:** Have it checked by a plumber or an electrician.

asked whether substituting a single porcupine would work as well, seeing how these pesky varmints had recently mistaken my cottage for a meal plan, but the elderly sage replied that no, "Squirrels are better 'cause you can flush them down the loo." Now I haven't been able to find any scientific evidence to substantiate this claim, nor do I endorse the shooting of squirrels (porcupines I'll reserve judgment on for the moment); I only mention this within the context of septic additives. However, based on after-the-fact roadside observation, this method does appear to have one thing in common with the additives above: I wouldn't count on a squirrel to stop a pumper truck.

Overloading the system has the same effect as not pumping it out. Many cottages draw water directly from the lake and therefore enjoy an unlimited supply. Yet what we don't realize is that the septic system has to cope with all the incoming liquid (out of sight, out of mind), and the more liquid we feed it, the greater the likelihood that solids and anaerobic bacteria will be carried into the bed to plug distribution pipes or seepage pits. Besides shortening the life of the absorption area, this constant flushing of the septic tank also means reduced decomposition in the tank, which lowers the inside temperature, which in turn decreases efficiency and increases the risk of freezing in cold weather. So regardless of supply, minimize your water consumption.

HELPING THE SYSTEM COPE

REDUCE THE FLOW OF WATER INTO THE TANK

At 22 L (5.8 US gal.) per flush, the toilet is by far the number-one user of water at the typical cottage. Up to 50% of toilet water consumption can be saved by using a low-output toilet. Products that reduce consumption in existing toilets, either by using a two-stage flush mechanism to regulate flow (allowing the flusher to use about half the normal allotment of water when sending liquid-only wastes on their way) or via a baffle (which re-

duces water for every flush) provide an economical route to water reduction. Many water-saving techniques are free, like the old adage, "If it's yellow, let it mellow; if it's brown, flush it down." Some can even be fun, like showering with a friend. And remember, every time you don't use water, you don't use electricity to operate the pump.

Keep the run-off from roof drains or drainage tiles away from your septic system, and don't drain hot tubs or pools into it either. Filling a dishwasher before turning it on and doing laundry throughout the week rather than all on the same day (or taking it back home to city plumbing) also lessen the load.

Don't build additions or add washrooms or even appliances without checking with the sewage police to ensure that your system will handle the load. It probably won't, yet many cottagers continue to demand more and more from a system that through natural degradation can only give less and less. In some jurisdictions, it is against the law to enlarge or alter a cottage if it will negatively affect the operation of the sewage system.

WHAT YOU SHOULDN'T PUT INTO THE SYSTEM

Don't put paints, thinners, degreasers, or toxic cleaners down the drain. Aside from the very real danger of these products (some of which are known or suspected carcinogens) leaching out into the water table, they can also diminish the effectiveness of sewage decomposition by killing bacteria or breaking down the scum, allowing greases and solids to leach out into, and plug, the absorption area. Even chlorine bleach will destroy some of the bacteria in the tank. Acids used to rid toilets of lime deposits can corrode plumbing and septic tanks and, worse, can leach into wells and waterways. Remove the toilet (two bolts and it's free, plus maybe a new gasket) to clean it, neutralizing the acid afterwards with baking soda.

Ignore all tales of how coffee grounds are good for the system; coffee grounds simply create more sludge. They belong in the compost heap, not down your drains.

Do not put anything into the septic system that will not easily decompose. This includes cigarette butts, cooking fats, greases, disposable diapers, paper towels, and facial tissues. Put them in the garbage. To determine if your preferred brand of TP will decompose readily, place a few sheets in a jar half full of water. Cap the jar and shake it vigorously. If the TP breaks up into little pieces, it's suitable for use with a private septic system.

Absorption areas are great level playing fields for croquet or badminton matches, but the only vehicle that should ever cross the area is a lawn mower – and that means no lawn tractors. Keep everything from boat trailers to delivery vans away (including winter toys like snowmobiles). The weight of vehicles can crush absorption-area pipes or knock them out of level, and will compress the soil and snow above the pipes or pits. This reduces the natural insulation, which puts the system at risk of freezing. (See Chapter 12.) Fence the absorption area off if necessary, perhaps with a nutrient-hungry hedge, to keep innocent or deliberate trespassers away.

THE NUTRIENT NEWS

As users of septic systems, our contribution to pollution is a double-edged sword: pathogens and nutrients – each coming from the same source, each doing its own damage. (See Chapter 5.) Septic systems were never designed to remove nutrients, nutrient overload not being widely recognized as a problem much before the '70s. Anything we do that has a deleterious effect on our septic system only exacerbates the problem, increasing the nutrient load in our waterways and ground water. Fortunately, there are some simple things we can do to reduce nutrient loading from septic systems.

Number one on the list is get that darn tank pumped out! Frequent pumpouts are the single most effective way to prevent an absorption area from clogging, extending the life of the area, which in turn allows the nutrients more opportunity to be taken up into vegetation before reaching the waterways. It may be the most important thing you can do as a cottager to protect your environment, investment, and family. Use phosphate-free cleaners. Soaps and detergents with phosphates are one source of phosphorus, the nutrient most waterways are in short supply of, and the one needed for aquatic plant life to begin flourishing – which starts the eutrophication process that can lead to a dead lake. (See Chapter 5.) Keep the clearing of your lot to an *absolute* minimum. The more trees and vegetation you have between your septic system and the lake, the better the chance that the nutrients are going to be taken up in land-based biosystems rather than exported into the lake.

A healthy lawn or ground cover is important over the absorption area, but don't fertilize it – let the septic system do it. For those who pride themselves on a well-manicured yard, a vegetation buffer zone between the septic and the lake doesn't have to resemble untamed bush. Plant shrubs and trim them into an impressive shape – like your favourite aunt. The important thing is that vegetation is in place to take up the nutrients before they reach the waters. (Trees should be kept about 3 m–6 m or 10 ft.–20 ft. away from the perimeter of the absorption area so that root structures will not interfere with the distribution pipes, tiles, or seepage pits.)

THE OWNER/OPERATOR INSPECTION

A quick walk onto your septic system's absorption area can sometimes reveal potential problems. During August when lawns turn a bit brown, the nutrients leaching out of distribution pipes cause the grass above them to grow green. If this occurs within the first few feet of a leaching bed, chances are that the bed is functioning correctly, the sewage percolating into the soil through unrestricted holes or gaps in the pipes.

But if the green stretches to the end of the bed, it's possible that the flow has become restricted, and instead of the sewage seeping out as soon as it reaches the leaching bed, the full length of the pipes is required to distribute it. If this is the case, get the system inspected by a licensed contractor or the sewage police. If the leaching bed is wet, you don't need an inspection, you need a new system.

Your nose can also help evaluate the system's state of health. Sometimes, sewage odours from vent pipes can waft over the absorption area during a downdraft. If the foul odour persists, try taking a bath. If that doesn't solve the problem, head out to the absorption area and look for ponding. If effluent is seeping to the surface, chances are it's going to raise a stink.

BIGGER IS BETTER

When a new system is deemed necessary, one of the best things you can do is put in the biggest tank that will fit into the available space, while still getting it pumped out on a regular basis. This gives the solids more space to separate out from the sewage, resulting in less crud getting into the absorption area. And while you are at it, go for a bigger absorption area too. Without question, a bigger septic system is going to last longer and have less impact on the environment. The costs of going bigger when you're putting in a new system are substantially less than the costs of replacing a spent system. For approximately $100 extra, I was able to install a tank double the required size at our cottage, and for a few dollars more, the absorption area was increased by one third, all the while maintaining at least double the minimum setbacks. It makes both economic and environmental sense to overbuild, and it also lessens the odds of future cottage additions overtaxing the system.

If someone began taking swacks at your cottage or boat with a sledgehammer, naturally you would be a mite upset. Yet research in some jurisdictions has shown that up to 70% of us who own septic systems are participating, by operating faulty systems (sometimes knowingly), in the destruction of the cottage-country waterways that mean so much to us all. Obviously, where our sewage ends up is more important than any building, boat, or other symbol of the cottage experience – for without the lakes and rivers, the other elements of the picture are worthless.

8 THE INS & OUTS OF OUTHOUSES

Everything you wanted to know about privies – and a few things you didn't

Backhouse, biffy, *privy – whatever you choose to call it, an outhouse is inexpensive to build and operate, open for business all year round, and environment-friendly to boot.*

ONCE UPON A TIME LONG, LONG AGO, Grandma left the farm to visit her daughter (Mom, to me and my brothers). It was an arduous and lengthy train ride from northern Manitoba to the city in southern Ontario, but that didn't bother her. Nor did the hectic pace of an urban existence. In fact, there wasn't much she missed about the farm that had consumed most of her life – where she and Granddad had built their log home and barn, raised 16 kids, and survived the Depression. Surprisingly, Grandma didn't even seem to miss Granddad, who had opted to stay in Manitoba to round up the cows with his brand-new '51 Studebaker. No, Grandma loved the city, and might have stayed there except for one thing: our wretched indoor plumbing.

Truth was, Grandma sorely missed the joys of kicking open the backhouse door to watch the stars stitch a night sky together, to see the swirling rainbow negligees of the northern lights or the acres of wheat set aglow by a red-ball sun kissing the horizon good morning or good night. To hear Grandma tell it,

even the barnyard drenched in all-day rain had it all over staring at our avocado tub with matching shower curtain. So Grandma packed up her yearnings and took the train back to the farm and her outdoor loo.

There are those who might pooh-pooh such romance as the foolish nostalgia of an

---

OUTHOUSE SETBACKS

SUGGESTED MINIMUM SETBACKS AND CLEARANCES FOR OUTHOUSES
(check with local authorities for approval)

Bottom of pit to high ground-water table	1.2 m (4 ft.)
Open water or spring	30 m (100 ft.)
Wetland	15 m (50 ft.)
Drilled well (watertight casing 6 m deep)	15 m (50 ft.)
Dug or driven well	30 m (100 ft.)
Pump intake (suction) line	30 m (100 ft.)
Dwelling	6 m (20 ft.)
Property line	3 m (10 ft.)

old woman, but they miss the point of the outhouse, its *raison d'être* in these modern, and decidedly indoor, times. The porcelain john is a 24-hour convenience, built for the Ex Lax pace of city dwellers. An outhouse, on the other hand, is the original restroom: a place to sit, think, and sometimes stink. Just yesterday morning I frittered away a moment in silent repose, outhouse door jammed open as it usually is, contemplating absolutely nothing as seven ruffed grouse balanced awkwardly on the top twigs of the closest birch tree, doing the same as me. Beyond lay the meadow and wetland draped in morning mist, enveloped in the mysterious sounds of the woods. From this hilltop vantage point a hop, skip, and jump from the cottage, I could almost see our leaching bed. It's tough to beat the view.

ADVANTAGES OF THE PRIVY

Yet the pleasures of the outhouse are not restricted to grand views. A neighbour brings his reading material to ours, claiming squatter's rights for at least as long as it takes him to get through a chapter or magazine article. Other users declare it to be the best spot to enjoy that second cup of morning coffee. And, lest we forget, it also serves as an admirable receptacle for bodily wastes.

Which brings up the point: Although I'm sure Grandma didn't know and probably wouldn't have cared, there are sound, logical reasons for owning an outhouse.

Contrary perhaps to public perception, an outhouse – backhouse, biffy, privy, or whatever one chooses to call it – is an environment-friendly way to dispose of human body waste. Because backhouse sewage is not nearly as fluid as the household mix we send to a septic system, the leaching of nutrients into surrounding soils and from there into our waterways is greatly reduced. We know that many septic systems aren't up to snuff. Also, research conducted by enlightened government agencies has revealed that the flow of sewage from a cottage (equipped with all the amenities of home) to the septic tank can be reduced by as much as 40% if an outhouse is used.

It therefore stands to reason that, spared the task of handling human body wastes, an existing septic system of questionable efficacy may be able to cope quite nicely. And without the human solid-waste factor to deal with, the life of a brand-new leaching bed is extended, as it is less likely to become plugged. Plant a biffy outside an unplumbed guest cottage, and again you reduce load on (and line-ups at) the main system. And – here comes the clincher – outhouses are inexpensive to build and operate.

Still not sold? Indoor plumbing systems rely on hydrodynamics to operate, so all pipes must constantly be kept above freezing if the system is to remain operational. The cost and impracticalities of heating the cottage (and often the incoming water lines as well; see Chapter 12) when no one is there usually leads to the annual draining of the pipes and, therefore, no pot to pee in during winter visits. But an outhouse is open for business all year, encouraging trips to the snowbound (and refreshingly quiet) cottage.

CHECK FOR RESTRICTIONS

You would think that any device that allows you to spend more time at the cottage while reducing the environmental impact of your stays would be greeted with considerable enthusiasm by those government agencies in charge of public dung.

Regrettably, this is not generally the case. Many jurisdictions have an outright ban on outhouses, while others limit use to seasonal cottages in remote areas, specifying type and size. You may also be required to have an approved septic system or at least a grey water system to handle liquid household wastes. And local authorities often place additional restrictions on use. So check for all building and backhouse bylaws that pertain to your cottage locale before beginning construction.

These governmental concerns over outhouses are not all hot air. Health problems have been associated with outhouses that were located too close to drinking water supplies, or built so as to allow rodents and insects into the works to pick up pathogens and thereby spread disease. And outhouses are not the ticket in highly populated areas. Yet could not the same criticisms be levelled against the septic system? In both cases, the key to minimizing impact is good planning and careful siting.

THREE VARIATIONS ON AN OUTHOUSE THEME

There are three types of cottage outhouses – the pit privy, the vault privy, and the pail privy – all looking essentially the same from the floor up. The pit privy is the original enclosed frontier john, basically the traditional outhouse structure built over a pit or hole in the ground. Although this allows some sewage to leach out into the surrounding soil, most of it remains trapped in the pit. The bottom of the pit should be at least 1.2 m (4 ft.) above the high ground-water table, the hole surrounded on all sides and the bottom by no less than 60 cm (2 ft.) of earth. The sides also need to be reinforced to prevent cave-ins (very embarrassing if you happen to be engaged in outhouse activities at the time). Recycled concrete blocks, laid in place dry with no mortar between the joints, work well, as does building a crib out of 4 in. x 4 in. (or similar) fir. By the time the fir rots, the hole will likely be full, necessitating a move to a new site. The earth around the base of the house must be built up 15 cm (6 in.) or more above the surrounding ground level, the ground in turn being graded away from the pit to keep rain and melting snow from draining into the dungeon of dung.

The vault privy is like a pit privy except that all excreta are held in a vault, or tank, below the outhouse. It's much like an outdoor version of the holding tank in that no leaching of sewage occurs; the sewage is merely stored temporarily and must be pumped out when the guck rises to about 30 cm–45 cm (12 in.–18 in.) below the outhouse floor (keeping in mind that an empty vault may float during spring melts or rainy seasons). Where a vault privy is not the government-mandated style of backhouse, it should still be considered when soil conditions do not permit adequate clearance from the high ground-water table. In some areas, the mandatory setbacks for privies are reduced if a vault privy is installed. The vault itself is usually built of concrete (or a similar watertight material) and has an external rear hatch about 0.6 m square (24 in. square) to facilitate cleanout.

The pail privy is like a vault privy with drastically reduced capacity. A pail sits below the seat (or the two are combined) directly on the floor. When the pail is full (which could be quite often), it must be emptied – and who wants to lug around a pail full of dung? And where do you dump the stuff? If you have an approved spot on site, why not do the job there in the first place? All very revolting (not to mention dumb), and running counter to the romance espoused by Grandma.

THE HOLE MATTER

What should go down the outdoor loo hole other than human body waste? Soiled pages of catalogues, toilet paper (TP), and that's about it for pit privies. In other words, no vegetable matter, diapers, sanitary nappies, or grey water. This will no doubt be a bit of a bummer for those who favour the traditional corncob

Privy counsel:
A pit privy (near right) consists of the traditional outhouse structure built over an open hole in the ground. With a vault privy (far right), the sewage is held in a tank (or vault) which must be pumped out when it gets full.

PIT PRIVY

for completing the toilet ritual. Generally, the same rules apply for vault privies, although some jurisdictions do allow the grey water from kitchen sinks and hand basins to drain into the vault.

The US Department of Agriculture (USDA) Farmer's Bulletin #1227 (circa 1928) claims that, on average, each American (and probably those with landed-immigrant status too) is responsible for expelling just under half a ton of personal body sewage each year. Today, in the true spirit of cross-border co-operation, it seems reasonable to presume that this figure would apply to Canadians as well, minus a small percentage to account for the difference in monetary exchange rates. (Granted, this estimate of excreta does seem a bit high – in all senses of the word – but when you consider that politicians are included in this faeces census, it's not out of line.) No matter how you look at it, it's still a lot of dung. So how big a hole does a backhouse need to accommodate this mountain of digested decadence?

Fortunately for cottagers, the annual per-capita contribution to the cottage outhouse is decidedly less than the USDA estimate because the outhouse is usually not subject to constant year-round use. Still, the longer it

takes to fill, the less often an outhouse will have to be moved or, in the case of a vault privy, pumped out.

Some jurisdictions solve the size dilemma by stipulating a minimum capacity rather than dimensions. When such minimums are not set, for pit privies a hole 1 m (3 ft.) square by 1 m (3 ft.) deep should see most cottagers through a lifetime of holiday contributions; but if you have any doubts, make the hole deeper, keeping in mind that a high water table or the presence of bedrock may restrict pit depth. At the very minimum, the hole should be 60 cm (2 ft.) deep. This yields a mere 30 cm (1 ft.) for movements before the building needs moving, the remaining 30 cm (1 ft.) being required for capping off the abandoned hole.

If the terrain won't permit at least that depth, find a new spot or switch to a vault privy. Vault size is usually set by legislation, but in jurisdictions where capacities are not stipulated, figure on a minimum of 2 cu. m (25 cu. ft.) per person per year.

Both aerobic and anaerobic bacteria are working diligently on your behalf to reduce the volume of family wastes but, even when aided by evaporation and seepage, the mountain beneath you still grows. We inherited our cottage privy from previous owners who left no record as to how deep the hole was and, to be honest, we didn't check current depths with the real estate agent before we bought. ("Er, excuse me, can I borrow a tape measure?") Two years later it was darn near standing room only in the backhouse, a situation compounded by the fact that the structure was sinking slowly into its own pit. So we dug a new one – a wonderful hole just shy of 2 m (6 ft.) deep by 1 m (3 ft.) square shored up with old concrete blocks and discarded railway ties – and moved the old building to its new home. By my calculations, we'll be too old to make the trek out there by the time it needs to be moved again.

(By the way, a backhoe is an indispensable tool when it comes to moving the ca-ca castle. Waldo – that's the name of our hoe – dug the new hole, hoisted the house off its old

VAULT PRIVY

footings, and placed it onto the new foundation. Actually, it wasn't quite that simple; we almost lost friend and neighbour Dave when the ground gave way around the old pit as he deftly guided a swaying airborne backhouse eastward. But we got him out. I'm sure of it. Didn't we? Yo, Dave. Hello?)

Cover abandoned holes with at least 60 cm (2 ft.) of fill to keep pests out and dung in. (Some jurisdictions demand that the pit be pumped out first.) We stuck a small tree on top of everything at our old site, and it's doing fine, thank you.

HIND SITE: WHERE TO PUT THE PRIVY

Choosing a site for the outhouse is sometimes more difficult than digging the hole. First, it must be on the same property as the cottage it serves, so that narrows it down some. Then, most jurisdictions have minimum setback requirements similar to those listed in the chart on p. 92, so that eliminates a few choices. It should also be down grade from any well and not placed in an area prone to flooding. Although regulations in some areas permit the building of an outhouse smack dab against a cottage wall, consider that although this certainly would cut down on the walk, winds do carry odours. So give yourself at least 6 m (20 ft.) between living quarters and spending a penny, but keep the path under 60 m (200 ft.) unless you plan to have the chauffeur drive you there during bouts of inclement weather. ("Shut the motor off, James. I may be a while.")

Once having delineated all possible locations, you should choose the one with the best view. A valley, the sky, a peek at the lake, a small clump of favourite trees – virtually any scene that breathes relaxation will do. A panorama of plugged highways won't do, whereas a single sumach might be just dandy. And whenever possible, the outhouse door should face due east, letting solar heat warm the seat first thing in the morning when the day's coldest temperatures are out to greet bared flesh.

View being a reciprocal thing, privacy is another good reason not to face a highway, whether that thoroughfare be on land or on water. The path leading up to the backhouse should be sheltered from onlookers too, with trees, shrubs, or latticework carpeted in climbing plants lining the approach, all vegetation preferably of the type providing year-round coverage. Visiting an outhouse is a very intimate act, unless it's someone else's act – in which case, at the drop of a beer-bottle cap, a gathering of the inane can be counted on to break out in a chorus of "We know what you're doing, we know what you're doing...." But things could be worse: That gathering could be black flies or mosquitoes.

Another hot tip regarding the path is to "have her go past the woodpile". This sage bit of advice comes from Lem Putt, the fictional outhouse builder extraordinaire whose collected wisdom on the subject appears in *The Specialist*, a booklet first published in 1929 (actually written by American humorist Charles Sale). This practical approach to routing accomplishes two things: the gathering of wood for the stove or fireplace, and the concealment of the real reasons for one's venture down the garden path.

DESIGNING THE OUTHOUSE

In the past, biffy architecture often reflected the design themes of adjacent structures. Brick walls (as in "built like a brick..."), peaked roofs, barn roofs, gingerbread trim – even the influence of famous architects like Ludwig Mies van der Rohe and Frank Lloyd Wright can be traced to outhouse design. If you like company or prefer a selection of sizes (one size doesn't fit all), try a multiple-holer. Two's company; six is a party.

But for the ultimate in one-upmanship, insist on a two-storey job. These gems evolved in areas that received sufficient snow to block the lower entrance. Although the upper deck did have its own chute leading to the pit one and a half storeys below, turn-of-the-century plumbing wasn't as watertight as today's, giving new meaning to the phrase "Look out below!" Guaranteed, a double-decker will keep the neighbours talking for years.

A shed-roofed outhouse is the simplest and least-expensive style to build. It also works well from an ergonomic standpoint, being higher at the front where you enter, and lower at the back where you sit.

NO PLYWOOD, PLEASE

As for building materials, the bottom sill or anywhere the outhouse comes in contact with the ground is one of the few places I wholeheartedly endorse the use of pressure-treated wood, specifically the type designated PWF (preserved wood foundation). However, some jurisdictions – Indiana, for instance – insist on nothing less than a concrete floor. (In fairness, it should be noted that the outhouse regulations of the Hoosier state also call for "comfortable seats", without question a praiseworthy goal.) Above ground, use a wood (and colour scheme) that will complement the exterior finish of your cottage. If you're a traditionalist who doesn't fancy the modern hinged toilet seat, use a hardwood such as oak for the combination bench and seat top; elsewhere, any construction-grade wood will do – except plywood. Stay away from plywood and similar glue-and-wood combinations for anything but the roof since porcupines and other gnawing rodents love to munch on the stuff. Deprived of their preferred diet, though, these pesky varmints may feed on any wood, including the sacred bench. We spread a coating of cayenne pepper (in paste form) over

A BRIEF ON BETTER BACKHOUSE BUILDING

The following is a short guide to construction techniques for a traditional shed-roofed, one-hole pit privy with wood floor, 4 ft. wide x 4 ft. deep x 7 ft. tall (at the front). All dimensions – and the hole count – can be expanded to suit cottage requirements and the stylistic inclinations of the builder.

Use 2 x 6s on edge for floor framing, and a 4 x 4 for the Lem Putt corner post; standard construction-grade 2 x 4s serve well for the remainder of the framing.

A distance of 7 ft. between the floor frame and the roof frame at the front and 6 ft. at the rear (making for a gentle slope of 3-in. rise in 12-in. run) provides adequate headroom for most cottagers, the lowest part of the roof being directly above the sitting area. However, professional basketball players may want to increase these dimensions.

Seat height (from the floor to the top of the lowered seat) should be between 12 in. and 16 in. (depending on family ergonomic preferences), the frame of the bench consisting of 2 x 4s on 16-in. centres front, top, and back. (Keep the space directly above the hole wide open and clear of obstructions.) Install the galvanized metal liner before nailing the top framing members in place; if you try to install it after the seat frame is built, you'll have to tip the outhouse on its side. Set the hole about 2½ in.–3 in. back from the front seat riser.

The 2 x 4 wall studs can be placed on 24-in. centres, tying in with the seat front. Headers are required at the top and the bottom of the walls (such headers are called top and bottom plates) and above and below a window. A door needs only a header above it. Wall sheathing can be applied horizontally directly over the framing, but if vertical siding is to be used, the framing will need to be strapped (24 in. on centre) to provide sufficient nailing spots.

The roof should be approximately 68 in. square, leaving a 10-in. overhang at the sides, 9 in. at the rear, and 9½ in. at the front. The roof frame is made from 2 x 4 rafters running front to back on edge, with single 1 x 6s at the front and back of the roof to act as headers. Sheathing can be plywood or 1 x whatever boards. If you want a skylight, use a sheet of Plexiglas 16 in. wide by whatever length seems reasonable (like 16 in. for a square skylight). This allows the skylight to sit over a 14½-in. opening cut between the centre rafters with no additional framing needed. Install the Plexiglas (or similar plastic) as you would a shingle – that is, the bottom overlapping the shingles below, the upper edge being overlapped by the shingles above, and screw it in place (predrilling the holes). Use silicone caulking to seal it to the shingles and to seal out the weather. Use rubber vent gaskets where the vent stacks penetrate the roof, incorporating them into the shingle pattern as well.

The easiest door to make is 1 x 4 or 1 x 6 shiplap or tongue-and-groove boards butted together, with a Z-shaped support glued and screwed to the back, using 1 x 6 wood. A space of ⅛-¼ in. between the door and its frame, and also between the two halves of the Dutch door (if used), allows the door to function without binding. Overlapping the frame of the lower section of a Dutch door with the lower bracing of the upper section by an inch or more will help keep the weather out.

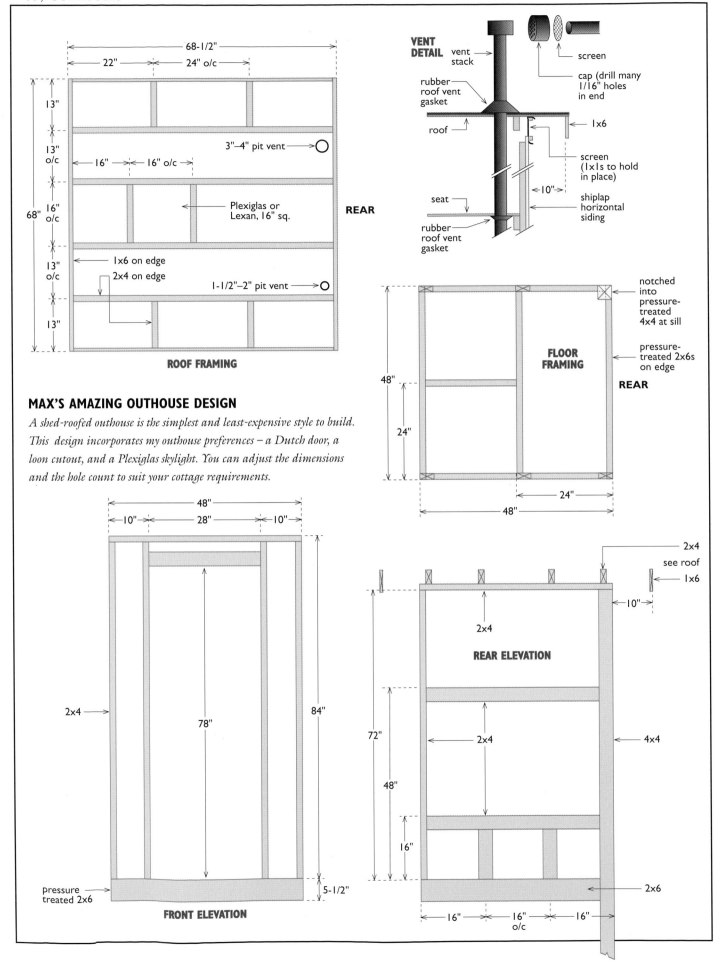

ROOF FRAMING

68-1/2"
22" 24" o/c
13"
13" o/c
3"–4" pit vent
16" 16" o/c
68"
16" o/c
Plexiglas or Lexan, 16" sq.
REAR
13" o/c
1x6 on edge
2x4 on edge
1-1/2"–2" pit vent
13"

VENT DETAIL
vent stack
screen
cap (drill many 1/16" holes in end)
rubber roof vent gasket
roof
1x6
screen (1x1s to hold in place)
seat
10"
shiplap horizontal siding
rubber roof vent gasket

FLOOR FRAMING
notched into pressure-treated 4x4 at sill
pressure-treated 2x6s on edge
REAR
48"
24"
24"
48"

MAX'S AMAZING OUTHOUSE DESIGN

A shed-roofed outhouse is the simplest and least-expensive style to build. This design incorporates my outhouse preferences – a Dutch door, a loon cutout, and a Plexiglas skylight. You can adjust the dimensions and the hole count to suit your cottage requirements.

FRONT ELEVATION
48"
10" 28" 10"
2x4
84"
78"
pressure treated 2x6
5-1/2"

REAR ELEVATION
2x4 see roof
1x6
2x4
10"
2x4
72"
4x4
48"
16"
16" 16" 16" o/c
2x6

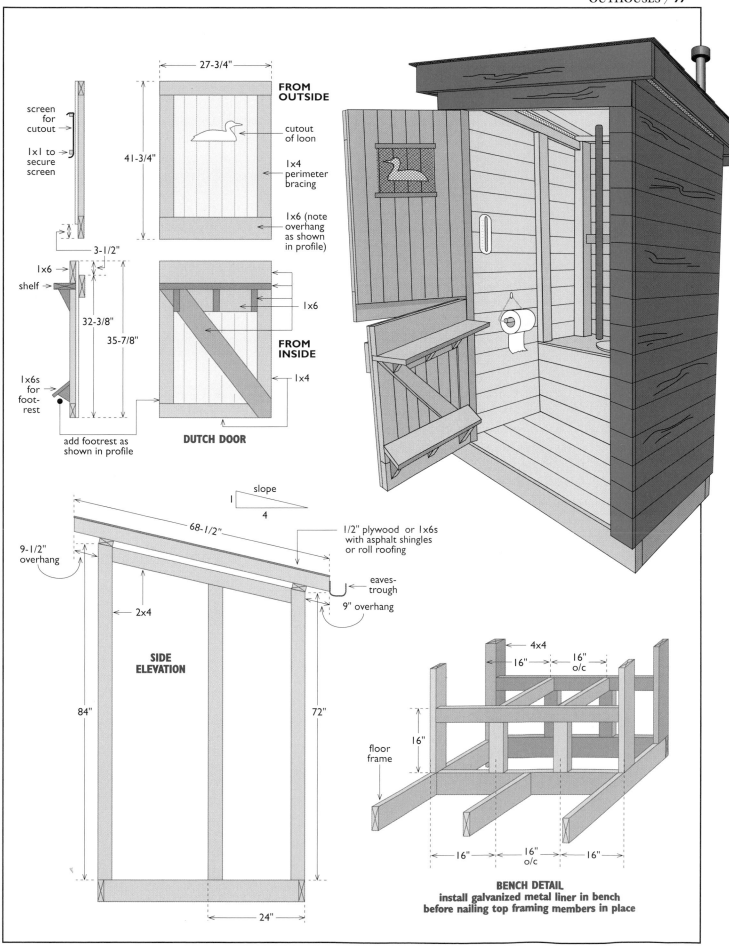

screen for cutout

1x1 to secure screen

3-1/2"

1x6

shelf

32-3/8"

35-7/8"

1x6s for footrest

add footrest as shown in profile

27-3/4"

FROM OUTSIDE

cutout of loon

41-3/4"

1x4 perimeter bracing

1x6 (note overhang as shown in profile)

1x6

FROM INSIDE

1x4

DUTCH DOOR

slope 1 / 4

68-1/2"

1/2" plywood or 1x6s with asphalt shingles or roll roofing

9-1/2" overhang

eaves-trough

9" overhang

2x4

SIDE ELEVATION

84"

72"

24"

4x4

16"

16" o/c

16"

floor frame

16"

16" o/c

16"

BENCH DETAIL
install galvanized metal liner in bench
before nailing top framing members in place

the lower quarter of our outhouse, which discouraged the porcos enough that they transferred their culinary interests to the cottage. Other deterrents include a few rows of asphalt shingles around the bottom (shingles also being the best waterproof cover for the roof) or a bottom edging of galvanized sheet metal, for those into glitter.

Galvanized sheet metal is also the material of choice to line the interior sides of the bench to protect the wood above ground from rot. The metal should extend just beyond the lower edge of the bench, down into the hole.

Lem Putt suggests that every outhouse of any standing have a 4 x 4 corner post running from the roof down 5 ft. into the soil, making it very difficult to push the building over. Better safe than sideways, I guess.

A measurement that often falls short in outhouses is the space between the bench and the door. Regardless of gender, you need room to stand up and tuck in without bumping into bits of building. A foyer approximately 24 in. from door to bench and 48 in. from side to side does the trick for a one-holer.

DOOR DO'S AND DON'TS

Many jurisdictions require that the door be self-closing. This runs counter to Grandma's (and my) requirement for a view. Not that I generally subscribe to civil disobedience, but one way around the problem is to hitch the door open with a string tied to a nearby tree. The door stays open when you're aboard, then slams shut when unhitched. A solution perhaps more palatable with the privy police is to install a self-closing screen door in addition to the normal one. This offers the advantage of a full view, and it holds the bugs at bay. Obviously, one of the doors would have to open inward (not allowed in some areas), which tends to intrude on the working area; so if you opt for this route, leave extra room inside.

My personal favourite outhouse door is the so-called Dutch door, which is divided horizontally in two, allowing the top to be opened independently from the bottom. This is the door you see on stables in paint-by-number kits, usually with a horse sticking its head out of the top half. Self-closing hinges are installed on the lower section, the upper section being hinged in a normal fashion to the structure. The two sections are connected by a latch bolt so that when bolted together they operate as one, and the door is self-closing. But unlatch the top, and that portion swings open. You get privacy and you get the view. The height of the lower door is about 36 in., but verify it before cutting by sitting down on the bench, checking the view, and taking measurements.

FROZEN ASSETS

If you've got your sights set on four-season service, beware the rising mound of frozen excrement that continues to build skyward all winter like a faecal variation on the Tower of Babel. (Should the tower rise to intrude on sacred ground, outhouse visitors have been known to call out in a language foreign to most folks of proper upbringing.) The remedy is to wait for spring thaw or use a long stick to topple the tower. (This latter act explains the historical significance behind that well-known expression about getting the unsavoury end of the stick.)

Without question, the most important cold-weather survival gear an outhouse user can own is the expanded polystyrene foam ring, sometimes referred to at our cottage as the "polystyring", but probably known to you as that white foam doughnut the kids use for floating about in the water. Serious outhouse users know it as a seat. It never ceases to amaze me – and other outhouse visitors – how well this plebeian device works for a job it never applied for. Thirty below zero and the ring remains warm to the touch of bare buttocks, even when left out all night. Colder than that, it tends to frost up if left out, so we bring ours in as the Fahrenheit and Celsius scales start to converge, carrying it back out each trek until the thermometer rises again. A double caution: The extra height of the ring compounds any problems related to poor hole design, and the inner surface of the ring can acquire a coat of wake-me-up-quick frost if left sitting over the hole during severe cold snaps, so hang it up between duties.

By the way, the outhouse is a swell place to hang a thermometer. Not only does it bring you up to date on a regular basis, it supplies plenty of fodder for those competitive hard-times tales exchanged between friends.

The upper edge of the lower door is also a great place to put a shelf just big enough to hold a coffee cup. An angled footrest attached to the bottom of the door, within easy reach of weary feet, will be appreciated by those with shorter legs.

In colder climates, the door latch should allow for fluctuating alignment due to frost heave. As the building moves, the hole that the latch is supposed to mate with moves, and the door won't shut. The solution is to elongate the hole, making it easier for the rambling latch to find its way home. Or you could opt for the simple and time-proven hook and eye for an interior latch.

CONTROLLING ODOURS

Not so long ago, miners carried a caged canary down the mine shaft with them, the bird being more sensitive to methane gas than people are. If the canary croaked, the miners ran for the nearest exit. There's no reason to suspect that this fowl play would not work in the outhouse, but a much better way to handle fumes, especially from the canary's point of view, is via ventilation. A 3-in.–4-in. plastic pipe running from just under the bench to about 0.6 m (2 ft.) above the roof, installed either inside or outside the house, will let pit or vault gases bypass the outhouse interior on their way to the atmosphere. A 1½-in.–2 in. pipe, similarly installed, will let fresh air in to replace the exiting fumes. Both pipes need to be screened at the top to keep bugs out.

The outhouse proper should be vented too, preferably at the sides just below the roof line (the roof overhang helping to keep the rain and snow out), and the vent openings should be screened, of course. In some jurisdictions, you may also be required to install louvred vents just above the floor to increase air flow (not a big advantage during cold spells).

What about a window, which provides not only ventilation, but also light and a view? The problem is where to put it. The back wall is out because you can't see out but I can peek in – and what's the point of peeking if nobody knows you're doing it? If you have a side with plenty of privacy, by all means stick

a window there. My own preference is the flat, Plexiglas, non-opening skylight for light; a Dutch door for keeping in touch with nature; and upper vents for closed-door interior ventilation. The cutout on the door lets some air in too, but its original purpose was to serve as a system of outhouse classification, the quarter moon signifying ladies, the star (or sunburst pattern) signifying men. A loon or deer shape (screened again) might serve to welcome all cottagers.

Small quantities of a type of lime known as calcium hydroxide can be occasionally added to the outhouse mix to control odours. It's used in stables for that purpose, is inexpensive, and is sold through feed stores. An even less-expensive alternative is ash from the wood stove. It's not as effective as lime, and may be harder to come by when odours reach their height – in the heat of summer.

A GENDER-BIASED OPTION

Through the ages, outhouses acquired a reputation as places of filth and disease because many of them were – and still are – filthy. We scour our bathrooms, down on hands and knees scrubbing the floor, wiping the very bowl, yet rarely does even the swish of a broom grace the outhouse floor. There is no requirement, government or otherwise, that an outhouse assume the sewage-lagoon ambience of a service-station john. This sanitary neglect is the pity of the privy, because a spiffy biffy makes a body feel welcome.

Speaking of which, let us address the delicate subject of urine as it pertains to good outhouse design. (Parental guidance may be necessary for the next few paragraphs.) The outhouse's Creator never intended for men to urinate in his (or her) handiwork. Men were expected to find open-air relief. So a bench conducive to stand-up peeing was not a requirement. Vertically inclined readers know, however, that to hit a hole consistently and accurately without assuming the posture of a humpback, males need to splay their feet around the front of the bowl, a position seen in better indoor toilets everywhere. This is obviously impossible with a bench.

One solution, often employed in those plastic portable pooh-booths, is to have a separate urinal attached to the wall. Basically, this consists of a trough connected to the bench via a small-diameter drainpipe. It works, but it's not much fun to sit next to. I opted for a smaller, more discreet device – a recycled plastic litre-sized Mobil 1 oil container, actually, the spout accepting the standard 1-in. fittings of your garden-variety hose. The front of the container is cut open, leaving one side and the back for splash guards. One galvanized roofing nail holds it on the wall opposite the toilet paper, splash-guard side towards the bench. A garden hose runs from Mobil 1 to the pit via a hole drilled through the riser (front side) of the bench. The smaller size of this urinal requires more attention to the job at hand, the success of the device being somewhat dependent on the user's dexterity. But it's a real trick item and a guaranteed conversation piece.

POSITIONING THE TOILET SEAT

Cottagers with deep-seated preferences may question the need for such a dedicated apparatus when man is perfectly capable of sitting too. Which actually is a tactless lead to the problem of urine on the bench.

Traditionally, the hole in the bench had a lid, much like the one on a Hallowe'en pumpkin. The user removed the lid and then sat down right on the bench itself, the perimeter of the hole being bevelled for greater comfort. Nothing touched the seat but skin. Now, an indoor-style toilet seat (preferably a tight-sealing version to keep bugs out and fumes in when closed) usually tops the hole, which most consider to be a great advance in comfort, although it's unlikely my Grandma would have approved. Anyway, the problem of this modern addition is that many handyman specials do not allow for the variety of angles expelled urine can embark on from a seated position. Now to be honest, I know of no research to back me up on this point; I am only assuming this to be the case based on years of after-the-fact observation in poorly designed outhouses.

It all has to do with the modern toilet seat/old-style bench interface. If the bench hole is not of the right size, shape, or position in relation to the toilet seat and lid above it, urine originating from any gender can miss its mark. This is especially true for younger cottagers, but certainly not restricted to them. Proper delivery to the pit will only result if the hole is pear-shaped, not circular. If the hole is going to be topped by a toilet seat, make the hole as large as possible, leaving enough material around the perimeter to adequately support the seat plus the weight of any occupant. (You wouldn't want any falling-outs with your friends.) This should work out to about 11 in. long x 9 in. wide (at the fat part of the pear) but, if you're in doubt, let the indoor porcelain bowl be your guide.

Should you decide to do without the seat, choosing to go with the traditional hole in bench with lid, reduce the hole dimensions by about an inch in all directions.

While we're on the topic of open holes over sewage-filled pits, young children should never be allowed to use an outhouse without adult supervision.

OPEN-AND-SHUT CASE

Having already advised readers on how to circumvent the law regarding self-closing doors, I will now boldly expand my criminal activities into the realm of self-closing seat lids. In some locales, a self-closing seat lid is mandatory. This is a law fabricated by some ass whose cheeks have never touched an outhouse bench. For a lid to be self-closing, it cannot of its own free will remain up and out of the way. This much is obvious, yet it seems a point lost on those legislative assemblies in North America that have deemed such matters worthy of their attention. A visit to any law-abiding outhouse would require an occupant to manually hold the lid up until seated. Then, with back to the wall, the occupant is attacked by the lid as it clamps down on its victim like some giant man or woman-eating clam, pinching any exposed nether regions as it snaps shut when the occupant rises in panic. And for cottagers equipped with the optional stand feature, the contortions required to keep the lid and seat up just to have a leak are enough to get you arrested.

When statutes start accumulating more dung than your average outhouse, it's time to empty them and install a self-closing feature on the law books.

THE WHITE PAPERS

If mice are a problem in your neighbourhood, TP will need to be stored in a lidded container. The mice around our place don't seem to take much notice of our TP, perhaps because we use the cheap, recycled stuff. Regardless of brand loyalties, keep an extra roll handy in a weatherproof container. We use a plastic shopping bag from our local grocer, and I'm sure he's grateful for the free advertising. When the extra roll gets used, the bag comes in and is hung by the door with care, with a new roll ready inside for the next trek to the privy. Failure to notify the world of TP consumption in accordance with these rules is punishable by death.

An old dish drainer, cut in half, makes a dandy magazine rack. The open concept discourages mice from taking up residence in the reading material. And every outhouse needs one or two coat hooks, particularly if you want to hang up your hat and enjoy the view for a spell.

9 ALTERNATIVE TOILETS

John by any other name

Be forewarned:

When it comes to alternative toilets, government regulations vary widely. Check what's allowed in your locale before you buy.

FIRST, IT'S IMPORTANT TO DEFINE WHAT IS meant by an "alternative toilet". Technically, it could be anything that differs from the norm, the norm in North American cottage country being the indoor plumbed loo with companion septic system or an outhouse. But in order to squeeze the topic into a chapter, such time-honoured alternatives as diapers, crouching over a nearby log, or trekking down the lake to a restroom marked "For Marina Customers Only" must be passed over in order to deal solely with the three principal alternatives to the indoor plumbed loo: the composting toilet, the incinerating toilet, and the chemical toilet.

Each is a variation on the traditional bowl theme. Like the outhouse, each can handle humanity's excreta but none is capable of dealing with grey water. In concept, each is an attempt to provide the cottager with the convenience of the indoor crapper without the expense (or convenience) of a full-blown septic system. Each is a marriage (of sorts) of porcelain and privy.

No question, such mixed marriages can be wonderful things, but only if all parties concerned are willing to resolve the difficulties that inevitably arise. Let's look at these three marriages one at a time before lumping them together for an overview of their pros and cons.

COMPOSTING TOILETS: HOME FOR BACTERIAL BREAKDOWN

The composting toilet has three basic elements: a place to sit, the composting (or storage) chamber, and a drying tray. Some models also offer a separate evaporation chamber as part of the unit. Seating and storage can be amalgamated into a single component (in which case the toilet can be rather bulbous in appearance, showing strong artistic influences from the Mutant Ninja Toilet school of design). Or seating and storage can be separated, with the part you sit on inside and a much larger remote storage chamber located outside, usually underneath the cottage (in which case the part of the toilet you see when paying your respects resembles a svelte city john devoid of its rear water tank). With either type, the drying tray is located directly below the composting chamber, and can be removed for emptying.

A composting toilet relies on aerobic bacteria for decomposition, so some way of aerating the sewage must be provided. This aeration is accomplished by stirring or turning the sewage inside the composting chamber, usually via a hand-operated crank mounted on the outside of the unit, although some electric models will do the churning for you automatically.

THE ODOUR EXIT

Every composting toilet has a vertical section of pipe pointing skyward to vent fumes, odours, carbon dioxide, methane gas, and excess moisture outdoors. On nonelectric models, the heat produced by the composting material is supposed to provide sufficient updraft to exhaust the fumes up the vent, much as a smouldering fire in a fireplace or woodstove is supposed to send smoke and fumes up a chimney. But any passive vent transporting minimal heat, like a chimney over a dying fire or a toilet vent without a fan, is subject to downdrafts that can drag what normally goes up back down into the cottage. Fortunately, again as with chimneys, adding more length to the vent stack will often improve the draft enough to encourage fumes into upwardly mobile action. But this is not always enough to overcome atmospheric inversions.

Some companies offer optional battery-operated fans on nonelectric models, while electric composting toilets incorporate fans as standard equipment. The fans serve a dual function: to force the fumes up the vent and to circulate air around the sewage.

WINTER USE

The bacteria responsible for decomposition work best in a warm climate, about 15°C (60°F) being the preferred minimum. In fact,

if the temperature dips below 5°C (40°F), the bacteria go on strike and all decomposition stops, so the composting chamber must be well insulated and kept in a heated space if regular winter use is contemplated. To hasten decomposition and evaporation of excess moisture, many composting toilets have small built-in heaters, the heat being circulated by the fan. Some heaters are thermostatically controlled, allowing the operator to vary the amount of heat (and electricity) used.

In common with an outhouse, a composting toilet can be used during the winter, even

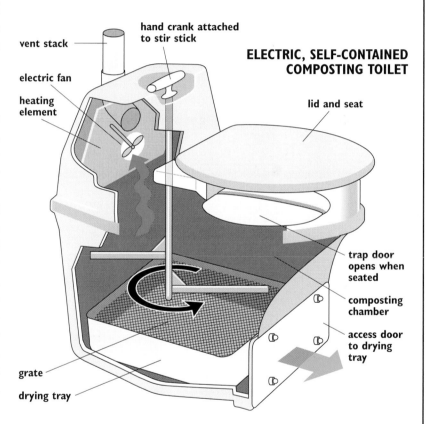

ELECTRIC, SELF-CONTAINED COMPOSTING TOILET

vent stack

hand crank attached to stir stick

electric fan

heating element

lid and seat

trap door opens when seated

composting chamber

access door to drying tray

grate

drying tray

if it's left unheated. The sewage will freeze, but this should not present a problem *if* visits to the cottage, and the related contributions to the compo-loo, are kept to an absolute minimum, and *if* the cottager follows the manufacturer's recommendations for the annual rites-of-spring start-up (for example: emptying any composted material already in the tray, adding topsoil, and reading your manual). Should too much dung be added over the winter ("too much" being determined by the model of the toilet, the climate, and perhaps

Taking a turn:
The sewage in a composting toilet must be aerated for decomposition to occur. This is usually done by turning the sewage with a hand-operated crank, although some electric models do the turning automatically.

the phase of the moon), the composting chamber may have to be emptied out and cleaned in the spring – a hell of a job. Because you are dealing with raw sewage at this point, not some environmentally benign humus, such a cleanout should *only* be done by a licensed contractor experienced in handling sewage, known up our way as a honey-wagon operator. Although, considering what the job entails, a lawyer might be appropriate for the task too. Check local regulations.

COMPOSTERS THAT FLUSH

Some jurisdictions will permit a low-flush variant of the composting toilet, perhaps more appropriately described as the variable-flush toilet. The flushing action is usually initiated by pressing down on a foot-activated lever. The lever lets the water flow into the bowl while also opening a small spring-loaded gate (a trap door) or a ball valve (see Chapter 4 for an explanation of ball valves) to let the mix of water and miscellanea drain out to a remote chamber similar to the one on some standard composters.

While manufacturers tend to label these toilets as "one-pint flush" units, the amount of water scooting through the bowl depends *totally* on how long you keep your foot on the lever. If restraint is not your forte, a composter's ability to convert your sewage to humus could quickly be overwhelmed, leaving you with a bin full of icky poo-goo – and that means contacting the honey-wagon operator on his cell phone again.

When shut, the gate or ball valve theoretically keeps a small quantity of water in the bowl after each flush, this puddle of water creating an airtight seal, which in turn keeps odours from sneaking back up into the bathroom. In practice, the gate or valve, and the gasket between either and the bowl, are both subject to wear. Once they're worn, the seal is kaput, allowing the water to drain out between flushes and the odours to seep in. Bits of TP hung up in the gate or valve can have the same effect. On these toilets, ball valves generally last longer and seal much better than gates.

THE MATTER OF MAINTENANCE

A composting toilet requires a minimum of maintenance, but it must be done for the toilet to function as intended. To aid the decomposition process, peat moss, rich topsoil, and vegetable matter must be added. One manufacturer suggests that you pretend there is a rabbit living in your toilet and that you feed him daily. (This leads to all kinds of questions, such as how will the pretend animal-rights activists feel about this? Should we give the rabbit a name? And how do we know it is a he? What if it's a she and it mates?) Feeding of the rabbit must also be accompanied by regular aeration of the dung heap.

How often these tasks must be performed is governed by factors such as toilet use, the pretend rabbit's appetite, the climate, and the effectiveness of the nonsewage additives in promoting bacterial growth. It's the operator's responsibility to monitor the state of the dung heap, using the toilet's manual as a guide to maintaining good composting action. Usually, for weekend cottagers, a twist of the crank on arrival and another on departure are all that is required in the way of aeration. The drying tray needs to be emptied maybe once or twice a year.

Do not dump anything into the toilet that the manufacturer does not specifically recommend, especially chemicals or toxic cleaning solvents. Bleaches and similar agents to curb smells or clean the bowl will kill the bac-

CESSPOOL SETBACKS

SUGGESTED MINIMUM SETBACKS AND CLEARANCES FOR A CESSPOOL
(check with local authorities for approval)

Bottom of pit to high ground-water table	1.2 m (4 ft.)
Open water or spring	30 m (100 ft.)
Wetland	15 m (50 ft.)
Drilled well (watertight casing 6 m deep)	30 m (100 ft.)
Dug or driven well	60 m (200 ft.)
Pump intake (suction) line	30m (100 ft.)
Property line	3 m (10 ft.)

teria, leaving you with a chamber full of sludge and a bill for the necessary cleanout.

HOW TO HANDLE THE COMPOST

Composted material must be removed from time to time to make room for new arrivals into the storage bin above. Usually, this material is collected in the drying tray over the duration of the summer. Depending on the model, additions to the tray are made either automatically or at the owner's discretion (the latter based on the dung level in the composting chamber). If the composter is working correctly, the "humus" in the tray appears to be a moist (but not wet), dark topsoil, what some manufacturers refer to as fertilizer. While this nutrient-rich material would no doubt help your vegetables grow, composting *does not* rid sewage of disease; encysted pathogens are able to survive for years, waiting patiently for the appropriate host in which to revive themselves. And the material has not always been fully composted by the time it reaches the drying tray. In either case, any disease-carrying microorganisms are quickly taken up by plants, especially root veggies such as carrots and potatoes. Under no circumstances should anything that has spent time in a composting toilet be added to a vegetable garden; in fact, it's illegal to do so in many jurisdictions. *Fully* composted, the stuff is great for trees, shrubs, and flowers – but again, check with local authorities to verify such use is permitted.

A composting toilet's ability to handle our faeces and urine is rated by suggested number of users. Exceed the maximum and the unit could overflow. On models with adjustable thermostats, the liquid content can be monitored and baking time set to suit input and required evaporation. Other manufacturers install overflow pipes on their units. How a cottager disposes of the leachate resulting from this overflow depends on local laws, most jurisdictions insisting that it be disposed of in an approved septic system or public sewage system.

In some areas, it is permissible to let the overflow drain into an approved cesspool similar in design to the grey water leaching pit in Chapter 10, but this is a poor second choice since the walls of the pit tend to plug very quickly, preventing dispersal of the liquid. If a cesspool is your only reasonable option, build it to the higher standards of a seepage pit (see Chapter 7), which is better equipped to handle sewage. Overflow should never be dumped onto the ground or collected in a five-gallon pail, as one composting-toilet manufacturer suggests. The pail presents the same problem as the pail privy – what do you do with it after it's full? This is, after all, a pail full of liquid sewage. (Okay, who wants to carry this insidious slop around? Volunteers? Anyone?) Only a licensed hauler of sewage should handle raw sewage.

Prices for composting toilets run about $1,000–$1,600.

INCINERATING TOILETS: THE WASTE GOES UP IN SMOKE

Using either electricity, natural gas, or propane as its energy source, an incinerating toilet heats the sewage to about 650°C (1200°F) or so, boiling away the liquid and then converting the residue to a powdery ash. (According to rebellious members of my family, this process bears more than a casual resemblance to my bouts at the cottage barbecue.)

All incinerating toilets must have an approved chimney to vent the smoke and combustion gases to a safe point above the cottage roof line.

ELECTRIC-POWERED UNITS

With electric models, incineration takes place after each dump. Close the lid, flick a switch, and a radiant heater starts cooking the excreta, TP included. The ash collects in an ash pan below, which should be emptied at least once a week, or more frequently depending on the amount of use the toilet gets. A fan blows the smoke and fumes up the chimney and helps cool the unit following incineration. This in turn reduces the temperature of the gases flowing up the chimney, so depending on local building codes, electric models may require only a PVC plastic pipe for venting.

Should the need arise ("Clear the decks, I've got the green-apple quicks!"), incineration can usually be interrupted by a switch or similar device, but the fan must remain on until the unit has cooled. At least one electric model has a catalytic device (similar in concept to the catalytic converter on an automobile's exhaust) to help reduce smoke and odours. Being heat-activated, the catalyst depletes with each use, and therefore the quantity of catalyst remaining must be monitored and topped up as required.

PROPANE-FIRED TOILETS

Gas or propane-powered units rely strictly on high combustion temperatures to vent the smoke and fumes up the chimney, so local building codes may demand a 6-in. metal chimney, with insulated sections where it passes through a wall or ceiling (a good idea even if not required by law). Since no fan is required, a propane-fired loo may make sense for the nonelectric cottage. However, as with nonelectric composting toilets, its chimney is a passive vent, so odours could be a problem between firings.

Rather than store the ash as electric models do, gas or propane-powered incinerators usually have some limited capacity for storing the excreta (about 16 L or 4 US gal.), allowing cottagers to bank a few deposits before initiating the faeces flambé. The cook tosses in a packet of anti-foam (to keep the poo-brew from boiling over), secures the lid in the locked position, ignites the burner, and about 4½ hours later the lock releases.

Remove the ash (there will be about a cup of it) after each incineration to avoid corroding the container, and the toilet is ready for action again. One of those small, hand-held vacuums works well for this task. If the burner is turned on after everyone has gone to bed, down time shouldn't be a problem. Besides, it teaches good self-discipline.

Those who have to schlep supplies into a remote site should know that a 50-lb. bottle of propane is good for about 300 deposits.

DISPOSING OF THE ASH

Because the by-product of any incinerating toilet in good working order is sterile ash, assuming local regulations don't state otherwise, can ash can go into the ash can, or anywhere else you might get rid of the ashes from a woodstove. However, the concentration of nutrients per ounce of ash is high, so the ash must always be disposed of as far away from the water as possible.

Incinerating toilets are waterless and not dependent on ambient temperature, and are therefore open for business all year round. Which brings up the point that, with some units, you may even be able to heat a super-insulated cottage simply by incinerating your dung. (Picture the family standing in a circle with their backs to the toilet, singing campfire songs as Aunt Mabel fuels the stove. And should the weather take a turn for the worse, you can always hand out Ex Lax.) Of course,

All fired up:
Incinerating toilets can be powered by electricity, propane, or natural gas. After incineration, you're left with sterile ash; local regulations permitting, you can dispose of it as you would ashes from the woodstove.

lid and seat   flushing bowl   cover moves when "flush" activated

ash pan   heating element   vent stack   electric fan

ELECTRIC INCINERATING TOILET

this sure isn't much of a plus in the summer.

Toasty toilets cost about $2,000 and up, including chimney.

A TOILET WITH REAL CHEMISTRY

Chemical toilets come in many shapes and sizes and are alike only in ideology: each is a chemical bathtub for excreta. The chemicals vary some, but usually can be classified as caustics, dyes, perfumes, preservatives, or some combination thereof.

Sodium hydroxide (caustic soda) and lye, both caustics, work by burning and corroding organic tissue, liquefying the solids and killing bacteria in the process. Dyes change the colour of sewage (chemical toilet aficionados apparently preferring blue or green to natural brown) while perfumes merely mask the smells. Dyes and perfumes do nothing to reduce the pathogens in sewage, and are usually added in conjunction with a caustic or preservative. Preservatives such as formaldehyde kill bacteria, but they also prevent decomposition, leaving us with the dilemma of what to do with a bowl full of dung.

The problem of disposing of the effluent from chemical toilets – or from composting or incinerating toilets, for that matter – has not been realistically addressed by many jurisdictions. The contents of a chemical toilet, unlike those of other alternative toilets, will destroy the bacteria a septic tank, absorption area, or cesspool depend on to function. So even cottagers with a septic system on the property (who have a chemical toilet, say, in an unplumbed guest cabin) cannot use it for disposing of the contents of the chemical toilet. The only realistic solution is to call the honeywagon.

As the quantity of sewage from a chemical toilet does not diminish through decomposition or leaching, frequent pumpouts can be required – which can get expensive when the toilet has minimal storage capacity. (Some are not much more than a pail privy on drugs.) Fortunately, some models of chemical toilets have remote storage chambers (similar to the remote chambers of some composting toilets), or are designed to work with holding tanks; both these arrangements increase the time between pumpouts.

For many cottagers, the main objection to most chemical toilets is the smell. Perfumes or no, these toilets are often a real drag to share sleeping quarters with. Their odoriferous reputation is due in part to their portability, which makes it difficult to install an effective venting system. Low-flush variants of the chemical toilet with remote storage chambers are available. Such models are supposed to have less of an odour problem and offer a modicum of self-cleaning action; however, on any of the models I have observed in action, these benefits seemed to be more brochure braggadocio than fact. And of course, adding more liquid to the brew will increase the frequency with which pumpouts are required.

Splashback can also be a problem on some models lacking remote storage tanks. Considering that the exposed portions of a seated cottager rank among humanity's most prized possessions, at least in the seated cottager's opinion, who would knowingly put such highly regarded organic tissue at risk of corrosion? (Maybe a little preservative wouldn't hurt on occasion, but is this the best way to apply it? And how do you explain those weird stains from the dye to an inquisitive mate?) Fortunately, toilets with built-in splash pans are not as likely to besprinkle those on the throne.

As chemical toilet shapes and sizes vary, so do prices. They start at about $100 for the port-a-bucket variety, while models with remote sewage chambers are competitive in price with composting toilets.

OTHER POINTS TO CONSIDER

OPERATING COSTS

Beyond the purchase price of any alternative toilet are the costs of operating the unit. For instance, there are the aforementioned costs of frequent pumpouts for chemical toilets, as well as the costs of adding – and the hassles of handling – dangerous chemicals. And, with the exception of chemical toilets and nonelectric composting toilets, alternative toilets consume significant amounts of energy. Incinerators, especially, can be quite costly to operate – about 40 cents per dump in my neck of cottage country. Composting units used much in the winter will need to be heated constantly, which costs again. A GFI (ground fault interrupter) may be required for any bathroom appliance (like a toilet) using electricity, a point overlooked in most instruction manuals. (The basic rule is that any bathroom outlet within easy reach should have a GFI.)

Also, the cottage electrical system may not be up to the added draw of a heated composter, let alone an incinerating model. If you have any doubts about the system or the necessity of a GFI, have the cottage checked out by an electrician or the electrical power company serving your cottage area.

VENTING WARNING

Operating a standard bathroom vent (sometimes required by building codes) or even opening the bathroom window may result in backdrafts. For air to exhaust out of a building, there must be air coming into the building to replace it, called make-up air. Air tends to exhaust through the hole offering the least resistance, make-up air being drawn in through the next-biggest hole. For instance, it may be easiest for bathroom air to leave through an open window, the make-up air then being drawn in down through the vent stack, and then wafting over the sewage and into the cottage. So keep the window shut, auxiliary fans off, and the bathroom door shut, leaving enough room under the door for fresh air to be drawn in.

Alternative toilets equipped with fans are better at venting but can be irritatingly noisy, especially in a typical cottage where bathrooms sit smack dab against bedrooms, with few sound-deadening materials between them. Speed controls can reduce the noise, but slowing the fan also reduces its efficiency, increasing the risk of odours.

Like outhouses, many of these units can be difficult or even dangerous for small children to use unattended, which can sure put a lot of extra mileage on an adult's sneakers.

KEEPING THE BOWL CLEAN

Another trait many share with outhouses is an unobstructed view of past contributions, not a pretty sight for anyone who lacks an interest in such matters. Toilets with remote storage chambers are not as likely to suffer from this affliction, and incinerators that are fired after each sitting get rid of the problem entirely.

And while I'm on the topic (why do I always get myself into this sort of mess?), what about skid marks? A modern toilet hooked up to a pressurized water system uses substantial amounts of water to flush things down, yet even then our droppings will occasionally mar the bowl. Granted, this is only a temporary blemish, but how does an alternative toilet cope? Composters with an 8-in. duct leading directly to a remote chamber below escape most of these unsightly marks, but with most of the others, it's a burden you have to learn to live with. Or you can clean the pieces of faeces off with a small amount of water and a *dab* of mild nontoxic detergent, like dish soap. In recognition of this unsightly problem, one model of electric incinerator has paper liners that are inserted into the bowl before each go, a bit of a bother actually. And at 10 cents apiece, isn't this putting unnecessary inflationary pressures on the concept of "spending a penny"? Some models of composters have a removable "funnel" to facilitate cleaning. Gas and propane incinerators usually torch skid marks into oblivion, but only after the chamber has garnered sufficient contributions to warrant firing ol' Betsy up.

Steve (friend, long-time cottager, and art director for this book) plans to use a Super Soaker (a water gun with a hand pump for pressurizing the ammunition) to blast the marks into another world, or at least into the remote chamber of his composting toilet. Although untested as of this writing, it seems a dandy idea – low volume, high pressure, and good fun. Just be sure to wear eye protection. And, who knows, it might even work as an alternative bidet.

CHECK WHAT THE LAW HAS TO SAY

Contrary to some manufacturers' statements, these devices are not universally approved for use. Nongovernment approvals such as CSA, UL, or NSF are certainly good things to have, but do not in themselves guarantee that the unit is approved for use in every jurisdiction. In some cases, an approval means only that a portion of the product – the electrics, for instance – have passed inspection for use, *not* the entire product.

As with outhouses, governmental approval and conditions for use vary for each jurisdiction. For example, in some jurisdictions alternative toilets are approved for abatement purposes only (meaning as a stop-gap measure to reduce the load on a failed septic system or outhouse), but not for new construction. In other jurisdictions, they're approved for use in cottages without pressurized plumbing, in seasonal dwellings only, or in cottages situated on lots large enough to accommodate an approved septic system should the need arise.

Many jurisdictions state that a cottager must apply for and receive a waiver from existing regulations before installing any of these toilets. And all jurisdictions permitting the use of alternative toilets demand that the cottage have some form of approved grey water treatment system, ranging from a full-sized septic system to a leaching pit.

Some government agencies even express open reservations about alternative toilets. For instance, according to Nova Scotia's Division of Public Health Engineering, "Problems such as odours, maintenance, and flies have been reported with all these disposal systems," while Massachusetts' Division of Water Pollution Control states that it has been the division's "experience that not all of the equipment which falls into this category performs as advertised," causing the division to "proceed very cautiously" with approvals.

But perhaps the biggest area of confusion, for governments and users, is in the disposal of the treated and untreated sewage from these toilets. There's no consensus among legislators as to what to do with the stuff. Massachusetts says bury it all under two feet of clean earth; in Wyoming you must have a licensed contractor come tote it away to an approved treatment facility; Ontario allows disposal of it into an approved cesspool; some jurisdictions will let you put it in a bucket or dump it anywhere you want, except maybe down a well or into the lake. It's all legal depending on your cottage locale. And to add to the confusion, in at least one instance policies within the same government agency contradict one another.

NO FLIES ON ME: INSECTS AND ALTERNATIVE TOILETS

There's no question that excreta attract flies. This in itself might not be a problem if it weren't for the tendency of the same flies to visit our food stocks without washing between flights. So for health reasons, not to mention avoiding the unpleasant experience of having them buzz our undercarriages while we are seated and engrossed in deep thought, the pesky insects need to be kept away from the contents of the toilet.

Incinerating toilets are not as disposed to fly colonies as composting toilets because the dung and everything else aboard get scorched regularly. Composting toilets (especially the nonelectric variety) and chemical toilets are more likely targets for insect stopovers. The best way to keep out flies is to prevent access. The tops of vent stacks (on non-incinerating toilets only) can be covered with a fine mesh screen, although this may restrict air flow, ne-cessitating a larger-diameter, or taller, stack. (Your nose will tell you if it's not venting properly.) Obviously, for reasons too disgusting to even mention, screening is not the ticket for the toilet opening, so keep the lid down when the toilet is not in use.

Flies can be discouraged from entering the bathroom by making sure the cottage is well screened and the bathroom door remains closed (which also aids stack ventilation). Check all joints in the pipes leading from a toilet to a remote chamber, and ensure that the lid of the chamber seals tightly when closed. Flies are also less likely to be attracted to composting toilets that are functioning correctly, so follow the manufacturer's recommendations regarding startup and regular maintenance.

And finally, equip the cottage with fly swatters and encourage their use. Use chemical sprays only as a last resort, and never on the dung heap itself.

READING BETWEEN THE LINES

Of course there's scarcely a hint of this problem in the manufacturers' brochures. Alternative toilets seem to suffer from the same brochure hyperbole as water-treatment devices do, the cottager having to be wary at both ends of the cottage water system. I can handle the endless brochure pictures of folks beaming with ecstasy at their toilets – after all, people are supposed to have fun at the cottage. Fuzzy photos of cute fawns are also harmless, although the connection between fawn and toilet does seem somewhat tenuous. However, I have difficulty with ridiculous claims, such as "no pollution", that leave cottagers with the impression that their excreta are suddenly having no effect on the environment. The only way to stop a human rectum from polluting is to put a cork in it. None of these devices can rid dung of nitrates, phosphates, or toxic metals, and some cannot even guarantee the killing of pathogens. Most will, however, *reduce* pollution. Insinuation often sidesteps fact in brochure land, steering an uninformed reader to erroneous conclusions. For example, a photocopied insert stuck in one brochure says that the finished product of the company's toilet should not be used to fertilize a vegetable garden. However, the accompanying glossy, full-colour brochure has snapshots of happy customers proudly displaying their crops fertilized with that very same toilet extract. There's also much to-do made over the fact that the unit has been classified as a "Class One" system by a government environmental agency. Although this sounds like quite an accomplishment, all it means in reality is that the government in question has seen fit to rank the toilet on a par with the outhouse. Stuff and fluff, what's a poor cottager to do?

BEFORE YOU BUY

Before buying any alternative toilet, get approval *in writing* from all the government bodies that preside over your cottage locale for installation and use of the exact model you intend to purchase, and for any other related systems required in conjunction with the unit (like grey water systems, cesspools, etc.). This may include getting permission from local health units, building inspection departments, municipalities, states or provinces, maybe even Elvis. (If there's no answer at Graceland, try the local all-night doughnut shop.)

Because of the expense and bulk of these units, few retail outlets are willing to stock and display them, so chances are most cottagers will only be able to inspect them at a consumer show such as a boat or cottage show. Most of the manufacturers offer "show specials" at these affairs, which can translate to savings of a few hundred dollars. But unless you have received all the necessary government approvals prior to visiting the show, do not yield to temptation. Instead, talk to the people displaying the product, and ask for and *read* copies of the warranty, installation manual, and troubleshooting guide *before* buying and taking delivery of the unit. This reduces the potential for surprise.

No matter how you look at it, our dung is our mess. It stinks, it's full of pathogens, and it attracts flies. A well-designed alternative toilet allows us the opportunity to personally do something about the mess before it creeps into the watershed and returns to the cottage via our drinking water. No city sewage system, septic system, or outhouse offers us that advantage. For this reason alone, alternative toilets are worth considering.

But be forewarned that the effectiveness of any alternative toilet depends as much on our willingness to do what is required to keep it working as it does on good design. Those who are not interested in such a commitment should steer clear.

10 DEALING WITH GREY WATER

A grey area in the plumbing regulations

Leaching pits
are usually approved only when the cottage is a seasonal residence and only when it's equipped with a nonflush loo.

WHILE THE PRECEDING THREE CHAPTERS illustrate humanity's ongoing search for the ultimate dedicated dung-disposal device, regrettably not nearly so much effort has been applied to the problem of what to do with the grungy water that's left after washing up. Not that this should come as a surprise; after all, it has long been recognized that humans are more disposed to profound thought when seated, the act of "thinking on one's feet" being considered a rare and enviable talent. So it seems natural that solutions to treating human excreta would be more abundant than what to do with dishwater, other than avoid creating it. Yet any cottage with a privy or waterless-type toilet must also have a means of dealing with grey water.

Grey water (also known as sullage) is the mix of water, soap, and miscellanea we create whenever we rinse or wash something – all the cottage's liquid waste, excluding the faecal and urinary stuff handled by the toilet. While the main contaminant in grey water is phosphorus, principally from modified soaps and detergents, the list of ingredients is only limited by what is available to scrub off; it often includes bacteria (like faecal coliforms), protozoa, viruses, animal greases, and petroleum-based whatevers (which can include everything from man-made edible goodies to paints and solvents). In fact, all of this and more can blossom from a single wash-up after dinner. So how do you get rid of it?

In many jurisdictions, you don't have a choice: Even if you own and operate the latest

LEACHING PIT SETBACKS

SUGGESTED MINIMUM SETBACKS AND CLEARANCES FOR LEACHING PITS
(check with local authorities for approval)

Bottom of pit to high ground-water table	1 m (3 ft.)
Open water or spring	30 m (100 ft.)
Wetland	15 m (50 ft.)
Drilled well	15 m (50 ft.)
Dug or driven well	30 m (100 ft.)

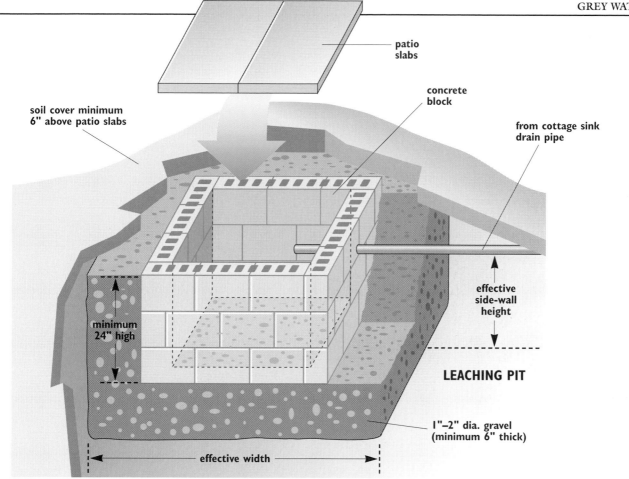

patio slabs

concrete block

from cottage sink drain pipe

soil cover minimum 6" above patio slabs

effective side-wall height

minimum 24" high

LEACHING PIT

effective width

1"–2" dia. gravel (minimum 6" thick)

in nonflush toilet technology, you still must have an approved septic system to handle your grey water. Some jurisdictions will allow alternative-toilet users to reduce the size of the required septic system, a few limiting that modest concession to the absorption bed only. (In such cases, the tank must remain full-size.) Some states specify performance criteria rather than quantitative regulations for alternative grey water systems. For instance, New York asks that such systems be "designed upon a flow of 75 gal. per day per bedroom and meet all the criteria previously discussed for treatment of household wastewater", leaving the manufacturer or installer responsible for proving that the device being proposed meets those "previously discussed" conditions.

As a means of dealing with a few buckets of dirty dishwater, any of these restrictions constitutes severe overkill. But for cottages equipped with pressurized water systems that encompass hot-water tanks, tubs, showers, and maybe even a dishwasher, anything less would be woefully inadequate. So fans of the minimalist cottage get stiffed. Unless, of course, your cottage is located in an area, such as Ontario, that permits the use of a minimal-flow system dedicated to grey water use.

THE LEACHING PIT

Although giving grey water a toss into the bush was once considered appropriate technology (we called it wash water back then), it became apparent that such freestyle waste-disposal methods weren't in the best interests of humanity or the environment. So we devised the leaching pit. Simplicity is the pit's biggest advantage – essentially we're dealing with a sink (normally in the kitchen) draining through a pipe via gravity into a hole in the ground.

Inside this hole, four walls are constructed of stone, concrete block, or brick, dry laid without mortar to allow for outward seepage of the sullage. In some jurisdictions, a perforated container, such as a barrel riddled with small holes, can be substituted for the ma-

Pit parameters:

A basic leaching pit consists simply of four concrete block or brick walls dry laid without mortar and surrounded by a 15-cm (6-in.) envelope of gravel. Top it with a couple of cement patio slabs and then cover with soil.

sonry walls. Leaching pits are usually approved only for cottages that are not year-round residences, and only for those that are equipped with nonflush loos.

The walls of the pit should be a minimum of 60 cm (24 in.) high, built on a floor of 1 in.–2 in.-diameter gravel a minimum of 15 cm (6 in.) thick. The same type and thickness of gravel should also surround the outsides of the four walls. The easiest way to top off the pit is to lay square cement patio slabs over the opening (your choice of 14 decorator colours), and mound dirt (such as the pile you accumulated digging the hole) up over the top at least 15 cm (6 in.) high, so that rainwater gets the hint to drain away from the pit. Also for drainage reasons, the pit should never be located in a depression where rain and grey water are likely to collect, nor should it be placed under the cottage where it is difficult to service.

CALCULATING PIT SIZE

The total size of the pit, also known as its effective size, is determined by the permeability of the surrounding soil and the estimated volume of grey water you plan on pouring in. Effective pit size is the area available for leaching, which includes the surrounding gravel. Similarly, the effective side-wall height is the distance between the bottom of the pit, including gravel, and the bottom of the inlet pipe. The permeability of the soil is determined by a percolation test. (See box at left.) We then throw simplicity into the bush instead of the grey water, and test math skills that have lain dormant for years.

Assessing your soil:
In order to determine how big your leaching pit needs to be, you have to do a percolation test. It's easy – just dig a hole, pour in a bucket of water, and time how long it takes for the water level to drop.

HOW TO DO A SOIL PERCOLATION TEST

A percolation test establishes the permeability of your soil, which governs the required size of your pit. Dig a small-diameter hole (15 cm–20 cm or 6 in.–8 in.) about 1 m (3 ft.) deep (a post-hole auger works well for this); pour a bucket of water into the hole, and time how long it takes, in minutes, for the water level to drop by 1 cm or 1 in. (depending on your metric or imperial inclinations). In the formula for establishing leaching-pit size, the percolation time is referred to as T.

MATH IS THE PITS: HOW TO DETERMINE THE PROPER SIZE

If you are working in metric, use this formula for determining the side-wall area of the leaching pit in square metres:

$$\frac{\text{per-capita flow in litres} \times \text{number of cottagers} \times \text{number of bedrooms}}{(400 \div T)}$$

For example, the estimated flow at Joe Canuck's cottage is 20 L per person per day, and there are three people fighting over two bedrooms. T is equal to 10 minutes per cm (T must always be equal to or greater than 4). Therefore, 20 x 3 x 2 = 120, and 400 divided by 10 = 40, so 120 divided by 40 = 3 sq. m in side-wall area. If the pit has an effective side-wall height of 0.6 m – 0.45 m from the bottom of the block wall to the bottom of the inlet pipe, plus 0.15 m of gravel – the perimeter would be 5 m (the side-wall area divided by the height, or 3 divided by 0.6).

This translates into a rectangle 1 m wide by about 1.5 m long, if we want to keep it the right width for easy installation of the patio-slab top. If you want the perimeter of the pit to be smaller, the side walls will have to be higher, which means getting out the shovel to dig a deeper hole.

If you are using the US system of measurement, the following formula applies for determining the area of the side walls in square feet: per-capita flow in US quarts x number of cottagers x number of bedrooms, divided by 100 over T (T being equal to or greater than 10 for this formula). For example, the estimated flow at Frank's cottage (Frank being Joe's American cousin) is 20 qts. per person per day, and there are three people fighting over two bedrooms. (People do that regardless of how you measure things.) T is equal to 25 mins. per in. Therefore, 20 x 3 x 2 = 120, and 100 over 25 = 4, so 120 divided by 4 = 30 sq. ft. in side-wall area. A pit with an effective side-wall height of 2 ft. would have a perimeter of 15 ft., so a 3 ft. x 6 ft. rectangle would more than fill the bill. (Bimeasural folks will note that Joe's and Frank's requirements are about the same; therefore, so are the leaching pits.)

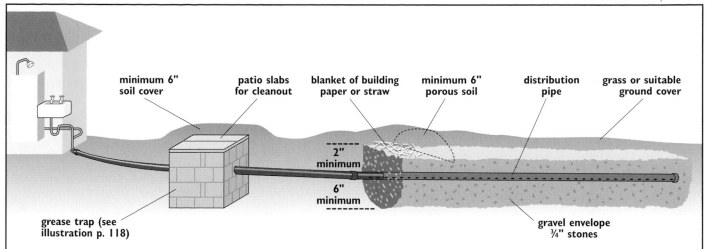

minimum 6" soil cover | patio slabs for cleanout | blanket of building paper or straw | minimum 6" porous soil | distribution pipe | grass or suitable ground cover

2" minimum

6" minimum

grease trap (see illustration p. 118)

gravel envelope ¾" stones

First, estimate how much water is likely to be used in a day; then divide that quantity by the number of people usually in attendance at the cottage to get the per-capita flow per day. Keeping in mind that a leaching pit is for *minimal* water use only (not much more than what drains from the kitchen sink) where the cottage is fed by an unpressurized water system, figuring out water consumption is pretty easy. For instance, how many buckets do you bring up from the lake or well per day? How big is the bucket? At our family cottage, two people used approximately 30 L (8 US gal.) per day, giving us a per-capita flow per day of only 15 L (4 US gal.). Granted, this is substantially less than average, the normal leaching pit per-capita use being 20 L–140 L (5 US gal.–37 US gal.) per day, but it does illustrate both the method of calculation and how little water one can get by on. The final bit of information you need is the number of bedrooms in the cottage – best counted by having a nap in each one.

With the above figures calculated and on paper ("I thought *you* were writing them down!"), we just plug the numbers into the formula given in "Math Is the Pits" (previous page) and *voilà*, we get the required side-wall area of the pit. From the area, we can calculate the dimensions of the pit walls suitable for our grey water outpourings.

Although it is inexpensive and easy to build, a leaching pit has limited capacity. Also, because greases and solids are sent directly to the leaching mechanism (that is, the pit) without first being separated out, the side walls of the pit are easily plugged. Therefore, there

are better options for a grey water treatment system (and this is especially true in jurisdictions that permit the use of leaching-pit-style cesspools to catch the overflow from composting toilets).

THE SEPARATE-TANK SYSTEM

When it comes to grey water, the province of Nova Scotia does it better. Realizing the need for a system that can handle greater quantities of grey water, the province allows what is in concept a miniature septic system, complete with downsized tank and absorption area. It is not meant to handle the effluent from automatic clothes washers or dishwashers, but it will handle grey water from all sinks and even a shower – making it perfect for most cottage needs.

First stop for the grey water is a grease trap (or grease interceptor), a single-chamber tank about 225 L (60 US gal.) in size. Like the larger septic tank, it can be concrete, concrete block, plastic, or fibreglass. (Check with local authorities for the requirements in your area.) Grease is held in the trap, and the trap is pumped out when full (just like the septic tank), while the rest of the grey water travels on to a leaching area. Depending on local regulations, this leaching area could be a pit filled with gravel, similar in design to the leaching pit described above, or an absorption area with distribution pipes, similar in design to that of a septic system, but reduced in size.

The advantage of this two-tiered grey water system is that by separating the grease

Going one better:
A two-tiered grey water system is kind of like a miniature septic system. The grey water first goes through a grease trap, then travels on to a leaching area. This setup is easier on the environment and lasts longer than a basic leaching pit.

from the rest of the grey water, thereby keeping it out of the leaching area, you greatly extend the life of the system – assuming, of course, that the trap is maintained by periodic pumpouts. The system is more expensive than a leaching pit, and more work to install. But if your grey water use is relatively high – greater than 75 L or 80 US qts. per capita

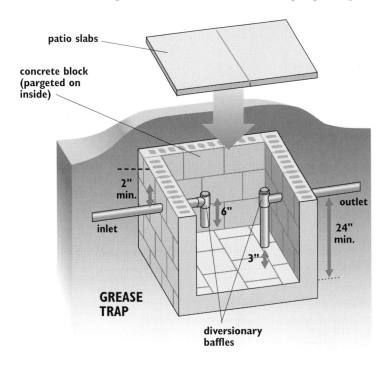

patio slabs

concrete block (pargeted on inside)

2" min.

inlet

6"

outlet

24" min.

3"

GREASE TRAP

diversionary baffles

Grease buster:
You can build your own grease trap out of standard concrete blocks. The downward-pointing intake and outflow pipes serve as diversionary baffles, allowing the grease to form a scum above the liquid rather than flow directly out to the absorption area.

per day – a grease trap and leaching area is much easier on the environment than a limited-flow leaching pit. And with the blessings of the local sewage police (and to the relief of your friends), you get to have a shower too.

BUILDING A GREASE TRAP
Should your cottage reside in an area that suffers an absence of commercially available grease traps (try the local plumbing-supply outlets), here are some construction tips for building your own. The trap walls and floor can be built from standard 6-in. or 8-in. concrete block, or even brick, pargeted on the inside. This is not a difficult task, but if you are unfamiliar with block-laying techniques, or are fond of your hammock, a mason should be able to assemble a trap at little cost. As with the leaching pit, cement patio slabs make for

a sound, inexpensive cover. Inside the trap, the intake must be above the outflow, while the lower edge of the outflow pipe (at the point at which it exits the trap) should be at least 0.6 m (2 ft.) above the bottom of the tank. To control flow and prevent grease from escaping, both intake and outflow pipes should point downward like an elephant's trunk. The lower edge of the intake downspout should be 15 cm (6 in.) below the intake pipe's centre line, while the outflow's snout should end about 8 cm (3 in.) above the bottom of the trap. Allow at least 5 cm (2 in.) above the intake pipe for grease build-up. Again, as with the leaching pit, mound earth at least 15 cm (6 in.) high over top of the trap to keep out rain.

PUTTING IN THE ABSORPTION AREA
The absorption area for this type of grey water system is constructed in the same manner as absorption areas for septic systems. (See Chapter 7.) For the average cottage, approximately 15 m (50 ft.) of distribution pipe in an absorption trench will usually do the trick. Use the clearances and setbacks for septic systems as the standard for grease traps and the grey water absorption area, although local authorities may allow some reductions.

Because a waterless john (like an outhouse or an alternative toilet) in conjunction with an effective grey water system uses dramatically less water than any conventionally plumbed system, it dumps much less effluent into the environment. This combination of dry toilet and minimal water use is the most environment-friendly way to deal with personal wastes in cottage country. It is a shame that such an approach to reducing pollution should be so restricted or totally forbidden by governments, rather than encouraged. When forced to install fully plumbed septic systems, people inevitably use more water, and nature picks up the tab. The less we dump on nature's shoulders, the easy it is for her (or him) to cope.

Maybe if engineers, by law, had to do the dishes, they might give more thought to what to do with the grey water. I must suggest that to my father-in-law next time I'm at the in-laws' cottage.

II CLOSING AND OPENING UP

Or how to decrease the odds of nasty spring surprises

The basic rule
for closing the cottage is to protect the system from freezing. Which means: Drain absolutely everything.

ALTHOUGH MANY COTTAGES ARE BECOMing more like second homes and making the traditional role of the cottage as a seasonal vacation residence a little fuzzy, most cottagers still pack it in for the winter months. So the twin rituals known as closing up and opening up have evolved, providing emotional and labour-intensive bookends to the cottage season. These are perhaps the only two times cottagers with running water envy those without.

GENERAL PRINCIPLES FOR A SUCCESSFUL CLOSING

It's the terminology that troubles me most about closing up the cottage. "Closing up" makes it seem so final – like maybe we're not coming back, so who cares if the chores aren't done right? To my mind (a warped one, admittedly), the idea of putting the cottage into storage seems infinitely more appropriate. The word "storage" carries with it the implicit notion that the period of disuse is only temporary. The cottage, the boat, the memories – nothing is really closed; it's simply preserved for future service.

Yet it has been my observation that often cottages are neither stored nor closed up but instead abandoned. When the delinquent owner returns, miracle solutions are sought to erase the inevitable degradation caused by weather and time. Unfortunately, there aren't any miracle solutions. If we want to be up and running with a minimum of fuss in the spring, the cottage needs to be stored properly before leaving it down and stopped for the winter. And this is especially true of the cottage plumbing system.

DRAIN EVERYTHING

The basic rule is: Protect the system from freezing. Most liquids, when they become solids, contract and become more dense. Water, however, is one of nature's weirdos. When it solidifies (becoming ice), it expands and becomes *less* dense. That's why ice floats. The other rebellious aspect of water is that as it freezes, it expands and therefore needs more room, about 11% more actually. This expansionary policy can put tremendous pressure on the walls of any container, pushing those walls outward. If the walls lack elasticity, they break. From reinforced-concrete cisterns to cast-iron water boxes on pumps, to plastic or steel pipes, to ceramic toilet bowls, nothing at the cottage is immune to the power of ice.

The best way to ensure that water will not freeze, expand, and force its way out of or through some cottage treasure (like the indoor toilet) is to rid the cottage entirely of water. In other words, drain *everything*.

ANTIFREEZE GUIDELINES

Some folks top up the system with antifreeze. While there are some spots where this may prove to be the best option (specifically, places that are a pain to drain, the toilet being the principal villain), understand that antifreeze does not prevent water from freezing; it merely lowers the freezing point, usually by interfering with the formation of ice crystals. If the temperature dips below this altered freezing point, the water will freeze and expand. Some types of antifreeze deteriorate with age, thereby increasing the risk of frozen pipes and fixtures over the course of a winter. An empty pipe or fixture doesn't run these risks.

But of greater concern than antifreeze's ability to stave off the formation of ice is its toxicity levels. A mere taste of methyl alcohol, for instance, can cause blindness; a 30-ml (2-tbsp) slurp can kill. So if antifreeze is to be used in any part of the plumbing system, from water lines to waste lines, make sure it is propylene glycol, also known as RV antifreeze. Propylene glycol is nontoxic, an approved food additive, a constituent of many cosmetic creams, and a pretty good antifreeze. Used in the quantities recommended on the label, it will not harm cottagers or even the bacteria in the septic system. Any other type of antifreeze can. And do not confuse propylene glycol with ethylene glycol, which is the stuff we add to a car's radiator, nor with windshield-washer antifreeze, nor with any other antifreeze. If you can't remember the chemical name, look for the RV and nontoxic indications on the container.

DRAINING YOUR SYSTEM, STEP BY STEP

INTAKE LINES: TAKE THEM OUT AND STORE THEM AWAY

Plastic and metal, the stuff pipes are made of, become brittle in the cold. This is particularly true of the cheaper grades of pipe. (I have a theory that the only reason manufacturers make cheap pipe is so they can say "I told you so" to all the cheap cottagers who buy the wretched stuff.) Regardless of type or grade, a pipe's susceptibility to damage is increased by cold weather, particularly if it's exposed. Perhaps it's no surprise then that the pipe voted most likely to fail over winter is any intake line taking an overland route to the cottage. Even if drained, a pipe and any connections left out under the snow are at the mercy of snowmobilers, cross-country skiers, hikers, and animals out for a stroll. (A deer's hoof can easily put a hole in poly pipe that's cold and brittle.)

Then there's pack ice. Technically speaking, pack ice is the variously sized pieces of frozen salt water that drift about freely in ocean currents and winds, so you wouldn't think it would be much of a problem at those cottages situated between polar circles. However, come spring the ice on many lakes mimics the reprehensible conduct of pack ice, piling up on shorelines, driven there by the force of winds and currents. So up our way we call it pack ice. Nobody seems to notice the lack of salt, penguins, or walruses.

A few springs ago, my in-laws arrived at their cottage to discover the remnants of a pack-ice welcome mat. The ice had crept over the shoreline rocks, pushing aside everything in its path like a Caterpillar D9 bulldozer. Had the intake line not been properly coiled and stored under the deck, the ice would have twisted and broken it up as easily as a child's hand plays havoc with a drinking straw. But because the line was stored properly, it escaped damage from winter's unexpected onslaught. The in-laws' aluminum boat, however, wasn't as fortunate. (Surprisingly, it still floats, although it now planes with a bit of a limp – the kind of boat where no one on board needs to be coaxed into wearing a life jacket.)

With or without the threat of pack ice, should your cottage's intake line run above ground to the lake or river, taking the line up and storing it some place out of harm's way is your best buy in "easy opening up" insurance. If done correctly, the job involves no annual cash expenditures and, more importantly, it greatly reduces the risk of having to locate and repair weak joints and hairline cracks in the line, a task that often melds frustration and tedium into a ruined weekend.

STORAGE STRATEGIES

Storing the pipe entails disconnecting it from the pump, then dragging the pipe out of the lake or river. Finding a safe place for long, straight lengths of pipe is difficult, unless the cottage is equipped with its own bowling alley, so usually poly pipe is rolled up in a coil for storage. There's no way to make this job easy, other than to con somebody else into doing it, but PolyGrip fittings, because of their ease of use and leak-proof design (see Chapter 4), will at least make the task less arduous. If the incoming line is metal, switch to poly if local codes permit. Metal corrodes and, besides, it's a heck of a thing to roll up for storage, although nobody told pack ice it's not easy to bend.

The moment you disconnect pieces of incoming line from each other or from a device like a pump or pressure tank, plug the open ends. The amount of dirt, sand, and small stones that can sneak into an open pipe end when you aren't looking has got to rank as one of the great aggregate wonders of all time. Naturally, this trespass won't become apparent until next spring when the pump won't prime and you spend a weekend or two looking for leaks in the line before finally getting the nerve to take apart the pump, at which point you find the injector, or impeller, or whatever is plugged with grit. A plastic grocery bag wrapped several times around the open end of a pipe, then taped in place with black electrical tape, is usually sufficient to keep debris out.

LEAVING THE LINE WHERE IT LIES

If pack ice has not historically been a problem at your cottage, and you don't mind gambling that history will continue to repeat itself, it may be possible to disconnect the line at the dock (perhaps at the T-junction mentioned in Max's Amazing Easy Prime, below), leaving the end with the foot valve to winter underwater. If the line to the lake or river is buried, or even placed inside a protective outer shell (see Chapters 4 and 12), you may be able to leave the entire line in place, drained to the surface of the water source. If you do so, it would be wise to increase the amount of anchorage to discourage the ice from tampering with the line. Try running the line through more concrete blocks, maybe one every foot or so, keeping in mind that anchors mean little to ice. Use only the best in poly pipe, and don't call me if it breaks, for the antics of ice are unpredictable.

Of course, the beauty of leaving the incoming line where it lies is that you don't have to struggle with sedentary sections of pipe. But if the line is subject to freezing, it must be made free of water. Ideally, it should be installed to allow gravity to do the draining. For this to happen, the incoming line must have sufficient slope down to the water source (about a 2-cm drop per 1 m of horizontal run, or ¼ in. per 1 ft., minimum). Then, to drain the line, all you have to do is turn off the pump, open a tap located just before the foot valve (see below), open the taps in the cottage, and let the water drain out of the lines back down into the lake, river, well, or whatever your water source may be. Nothing to it.

A friend of a friend of my uncle's neighbour's daughter's boyfriend (it's important to keep track of such things in cottage country) doesn't even bother with a foot valve, instead opting for a check valve located on the intake line just before the pump. The water is drained out of the cottage pressure lines through the drain tap located at the lowest point (at the pump); then the check valve on the intake side is disconnected, letting air into the line as the water flows back to the lake. (However, taking a pass on the foot valve means you're going to need a pump with some tolerance for air; see Chapter 3.)

The crucial point with either method is that *all* the water be removed, which is possible only when a water line has no peaks or valleys in the entire length of its run. If you have any doubts, a hand-operated diaphragm pump (see Chapter 3 again) can be used to force the water out (filling the pipe with air). Another way to flush out the water is to use a small tank of pressurized air. Unless you have easy access to an air pump to replenish the tank as its pressure depletes, the diaphragm pump is the preferable choice. It never runs out of air and it's also a more versatile cottage tool.

DEALING WITH INTAKE LINES WHEN YOU'RE WORKING WITH A WELL

Cottagers with wells and a buried intake line don't have to worry about pack ice pounding the plumbing. However, if the line is not buried below the frost line, which in the northern states and Canada ranges from 1 m–1.5 m (3 ft.–5 ft.), the line from the cottage to the well will still have to be drained. In a dug well, the easiest way to do this is with a T-junction and tap located just before the foot valve, although if the leg of the T is higher than the water line, the line will not completely self-drain and the remaining water will have to be removed, either by forcing it out from the pump end or by drawing it out at the T-junction. Again, it's tough to beat the hand-operated diaphragm pump for this kind of work.

After years of struggling with low-grade poly pipe each spring and autumn, my in-laws finally broke down and had a well drilled. Although the line to the cottage does not sit below the frost line, it does follow a gradual slope up from the well. At the end of the sea-

son, the well seal (or well cap) is removed and the pitless adapter is lifted up just enough to break the seal between the adapter and the well casing, letting the water drain back into the well. Then the adapter and well seal are replaced. Come spring, the submersible pump is started and the line fills with water. While this technique certainly has simplicity on its side, any time the well is opened there is a risk of contaminating the water. For this reason, some jurisdictions forbid such tampering with wells, while others may insist that the well be disinfected after each opening of the well seal. Also, in theory this could put additional wear on the seal of the pitless adapter, as it really wasn't designed to be a tap.

An alternative solution would be to install a T-junction and tap in the intake line just before it enters the head of the well, using the hand-operated diaphragm pump again to assist with emptying the line. However, whether you're using the pitless adapter or T-junction and tap, the water will remain in the pipe from the designated point of draining down to the foot valve (or the check valve on a submersible pump). If this section of pipe is long, and exposed to winter's temperatures, it's at risk of freezing and cracking. If you aren't prepared to take those risks, the intake line must be withdrawn from the well, drained, and stored.

EMPTYING THE HOT-WATER TANK

Shut off the power to the hot-water tank *before* doing the same to the pump. This allows you to use up whatever hot water remains in the tank (which you've already paid to heat), maybe for a final dish wash. And because the pump will then refill the tank with cold water, the tank's contents won't be dangerously hot when it's finally drained. Draining the tank not only prevents freezing, but it also removes sediment once a year, prolonging tank life. The tank should be drained *after* you have drained the pressure lines. (See below.)

To rid the tank of water, turn off the pump, attach a hose to the tank's drain tap, and lead the other end to a cottage storm drain or somewhere outside. (Overloading the septic system with water is not good practice at any time, but can be especially deleterious to the septic tank just before it's abandoned for the winter.)

If the water seems merely to dribble out of the tank, sediment may be restricting the drain tap. You can sometimes solve this problem by poking a thin wire up into the drain tap. If the blockage won't clear, you may have to remove the tap and clean it out.

DRAINING THE REST OF THE SYSTEM

With the pressure lines installed as suggested in Chapter 4, turn off the pump, open all the taps and in-line valves, flush the toilet a couple of times to empty most of the tank (the residual water in the tank will need to be mopped

---

DRAINING MATTERS: A STORAGE QUICK LIST

☐ Shut off the power to the hot-water tank and use up the existing hot water.

☐ Shut off the power to the pump.

☐ Drain the intake line, storing exposed line.

☐ Open taps and in-line valves and then drain the pressure lines, flushing the toilet to empty its tank.

☐ Drain the hot-water tank, any water-treatment devices, and the pressure tank if it's not a bladder or diaphragm type.

☐ Drain and, if necessary, store the pump.

☐ Drain any appliances (washing machines, etc.), and add RV antifreeze.

☐ Drain waste-line drain traps; put RV antifreeze only in those traps that can't be drained.

---

up with a rag), and let gravity drain the water out of 99% of the system. (There are no 100% guarantees in life.) If your cottage is fed by a centrifugal pump (like a jet or submersible) and there are no check valves in the lines (or bypasses with in-line valves installed to permit the water to drain around the check valves), this auto-drain method can be used to empty the entire water system, including pressure lines and the incoming line all the way back to the water source. Folks with other types of pumps (like piston pumps or cen-

trifugals with check valves) will have to drain the incoming line (from pump to foot valve) and the inside pressure lines (from taps to pump) separately. Where water and gravity fail to cooperate, as when an intake line follows a path reminiscent of my stock portfolio (mostly down, but with the occasional upward trend), you'll have to blow the water out with air, using either a hand-operated diaphragm pump or compressed air.

Bladder and diaphragm pressure tanks will self-drain with the rest of the system. Older-style tanks in which air and water share the same space should be drained through the drain plug provided to remove any last vestiges of water after the rest of the system has been drained. For those who don't know which type of tank they own, the plain pressure tank has a drain plug at its lowest point and is always galvanized. Bladder and diaphragm tanks don't have, or need, drain plugs.

All water-treatment devices also need to be drained. Because they differ so much in design, a manual is a real help here. If you left the manuals back home in the city, look for drain plugs. None of the water contained in any purifier – and especially a large-capacity tank filter such as a water softener – should be drained directly into the septic system. (See Chapter 6.)

Appliances like automatic washers and dishwashers can be a problem. Most aren't designed with cottaging in mind (maybe there's a message there), little if any attention having been paid to the need for periodic draining. If the appliance has drain plugs (check your manual or disconnect the power and peek underneath with a flashlight), by all means use them. Regardless, my advice is to disconnect the water lines and pour RV antifreeze (propylene glycol) into the incoming line. Then turn on the machine for just enough time to circulate the antifreeze through the nooks and crannies that invariably exist inside, and that should suffice.

PUTTING THE PUMP TO BED

While all the lines should now be empty, enough water can remain in the pump's innards to freeze and crack the casings, so this must be tended to as well. Although some folks leave the drain plugs out all winter, I always replace bolts and plugs and such so I know where they are next spring, and where they're supposed to go. Whether you replace or store them, putting a dab of vegetable oil on the threads of a plug will discourage rust from attacking the threads. (Avoid toxic greases anywhere in the drinking-water supply system.)

Hand pump: To rid a traditional hand pump (displacement variety) of water, push the handle down, slowly, and then hold it in the down position to keep the bottom flapper open while the water drains out. You may have to wiggle the handle a bit, but you'll hear the water running out the bottom when you get it right.

Piston pump: A piston pump requires the most work to store. To drain the water box, undo the drain plug. (It's usually at the bottom of the box or on the bottom edge of a side, but check your manual if you can't find it.) However, if a piston pump is merely drained and then left until spring, the leather dries and becomes hard. This dramatically increases wear the next time the pump is stirred into action, making it more difficult to prime. And should iron be present in the water, scale will accumulate under the valves, making it necessary to take the pump apart and clean it before any water will reach the cottage taps. To avoid such shenanigans, the owner's manual usually recommends pulling the piston out and storing the piston leather in liquid (such as linseed or vegetable oil) at the end of the season. A reasonable (and easier) alternative is to fill the empty water box with RV antifreeze (propylene glycol), which will protect it from freezing and keep the piston leather and valves soft.

Centrifugal pump: A centrifugal-type pump, such as a jet pump, requires draining only, usually via a plug in the bottom of the water box. Some pumps have a number of plugs, all of which must be removed to enable the water to drain out.

Submersible pump: A submersible pump can stay submerged all winter, with no drain-ing necessary, as long as ice conditions aren't severe enough to reach down to the pump.

WASTE LINES: ONLY THE TRAPS REQUIRE ATTENTION

Waste lines, the big ones that transport the used and abused water and miscellaneous bodily fluids out of the cottage, are naturally self-draining. Of course, there is always an exception, and in this case the drain traps are it. These are 180° elbows placed in the line just below open drains – such as sink, tub, and floor drains. The trap holds water continuously, forming an airtight seal within the pipe, thereby preventing fumes from venting back up the waste lines and into the cottage. Newer ABS plastic traps often have a drain plug at the lowest point of the elbow, making draining and cleaning out goop a simple task. Older metal traps may not have such plugs. Traps in toilets are built into the plastic or ceramic mould, accessible on a once-in-a-lifetime basis with a sledgehammer.

Drain traps under sinks are usually accessible from underneath, normally through the cupboard below the sink. Traps under tubs are often hidden behind ceilings, although open floor joists in basements and cottage crawl spaces may provide access.

If a trap can be drained, do it. An empty pipe won't burst from freezing no matter how cold it gets. (Again, I like to replace any plugs after draining so I always know where they are.) For traps without drain plugs, like those in toilets, antifreeze makes sense. Remember to use RV antifreeze (propylene glycol), pouring in only enough to replace the water with antifreeze. (The water has usually been pushed out when the liquid in the trap is the same colour as the liquid in the antifreeze container.)

OPENING UP: JUST REVERSE THE STEPS

Having completed all the necessary tasks of cottage storage – thereby greatly reducing the odds of discovering any unpleasant spring surprises, plumbing-wise – we simply do an about-face (of a sort) to open up the cottage, and re-

MAX'S AMAZING EASY PRIME

*Here's an easy solution to one of cottage country's less-cherished activities –
priming the pump. With the kitchen tap open, open the T-junction tap and pump
the priming pump. When water comes out the kitchen tap, turn the T-junction
tap off. Presto – the entire system is primed. Go make a cup of tea.*

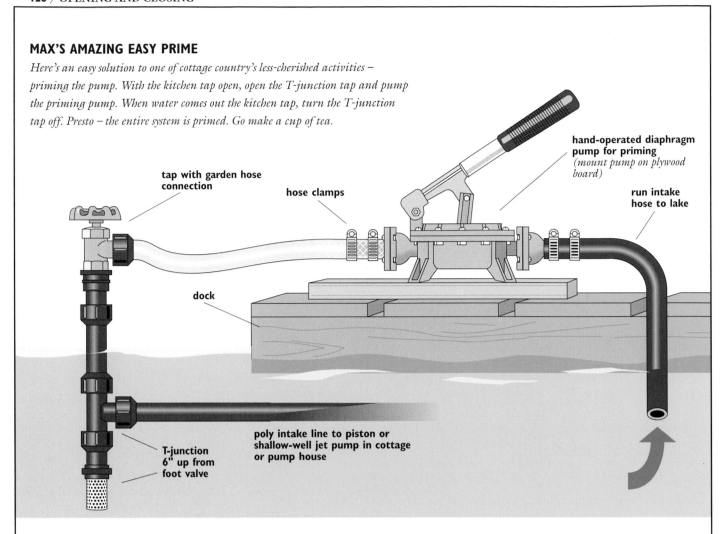

tap with garden hose
connection

hose clamps

hand-operated diaphragm
pump for priming
*(mount pump on plywood
board)*

run intake
hose to lake

dock

poly intake line to piston or
shallow-well jet pump in cottage
or pump house

T-junction
6" up from
foot valve

verse the whole procedure. Fortunately for cottagers not proficient at reading backwards, the opening-up tasks are set forth below.

GETTING THE INTAKE LINES BACK IN POSITION

If part of the cottage storage regimen included dealing with exposed intake lines, it follows that part of the opening-up experience includes such frivolities as unwinding those great coils of uncooperative poly pipe, forcing pipe onto couplings, taking it off because you forgot to put the joint clamps on first, forcing it back onto the couplings again, thawing your by now frozen fingers so the bandage will stick....

To ease some of the pain, lay the coiled pipe out in the sun for a while before attempting to make it lie straight and flat. You'll find plastic pipe a more agreeable substance to work with when it's warm. But those blasted barbed fittings are still a genuine hassle to force into the pipe. So spend the extra few dollars it takes to equip your intake lines with PolyGrip fittings. With a twist of the wrist and turn of a wrench, the joint is secure and leakproof.

Keep the ends of all lines capped until you're ready to make the connections. When it comes to sneaking into open pipe, sand and stones aren't particular about whether the line is being taken out or put back into the water.

Before tossing the end of the intake line down a well or into a lake, take a couple of minutes to verify that the foot valve and any check valves are indeed working. (See Chapter 4.) It could save hours of aggravation.

PRIME TIME: TRY "MAX'S AMAZING EASY PRIME"

Traditional priming methods are masochistic; running bucket brigades into crawl spaces or pump houses is not one of cottage country's cherished activities, nor is fiddling with stripped threads on priming plugs. For fast-acting relief from both, try "Max's Amazing Easy Prime" (patent pending).

With a piston or shallow-well jet pump drawing from surface-water sources, splice a T-junction into the intake line about 15 cm (6 in.) up from the foot valve. If that's not convenient, you can install the T-junction approximately where the line enters the water – though the first option is preferable, as it will allow you to prime the entire intake line before starting the pump. Install a section of pipe about 30 cm (1 ft.) long to the leg of the T, and then install a tap suitable for a garden-hose fitting at the end of this pipe.

Come time to prime, you will need two short sections of garden hose and a suitable portable priming pump. The preferred choice of priming pump is a hand-operated diaphragm pump (see Chapter 3), but a small drill-driven gear pump worth about $100, an electric drill (worth much less after you drop it into the lake), and a long extension cord will also suffice. First, open the kitchen tap. Back outside, lift the intake line up alongside the dock (or boat) to expose the T-junction tap, attach a hose between the tap and the priming pump's discharge (using suitable hose clamps), and run the other short hose between the priming pump's intake and the water. Open the T-junction tap, and start pumping. When water comes out the kitchen tap, turn the T-junction tap off and the entire system is fully primed. Disconnect the priming pump, drop the line back into the water, and go make yourself a cup of tea. And unless you own a piston pump and opted to take out the piston leather rather than fill the water box with antifreeze, notice that it wasn't necessary even to look at the cottage pump.

With shallow-well jet pumps or piston pumps, if a check valve is used on the intake line just before the pump instead of a foot valve at the submerged end, your choice of priming pump can be hooked directly to the end of the intake line for priming, with no T-junction or tap re-

MAX'S AMAZING EASY PRIME

Alternative configurations

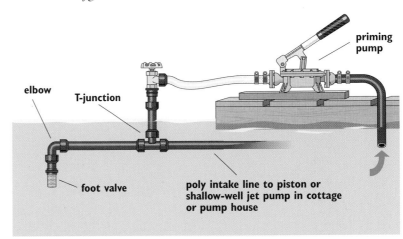

For a piston or shallow-well jet pump: *Although the configuration opposite is ideal, it may not be convenient. As an alternative, install the T-junction where the intake line enters the water, or at a similarly accessible location.*

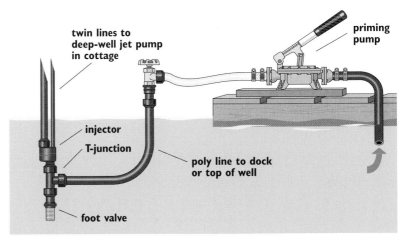

For a deep-well jet pump with a lift less than 40 ft: *Install a T-junction between the injector and the foot valve, and run the T-junction tap to the dock or the top of the well.*

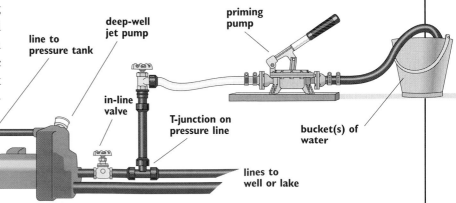

For a deep-well jet pump with a lift greater than 40 ft.: *Install an in-line valve (a valve without a tap) and then the T-junction along the pressure line. Have buckets of water ready by the priming pump.*

quired. Hold the end of the line under water when the priming pump is disconnected; otherwise, the water in the line may drain back out.

For deep-well jet pumps, the T-junction should go between the foot valve and the Y-fitting housing the injector. Delete the foot-long leg of the T if it's going into a well (for clearance), substituting a 90° elbow and sufficient pipe to run to the top of the well. The rest of the procedure applies as long as the lift is less than 12 m (40 ft.).

A little more work is involved for lifts greater than 12 m (40 ft.). First, install an in-line valve (a tap without a spout) on the pressure line (the smaller of the two) right where it leaves the pump, followed by the T-junction and tap. Run a hose between a hand-operated diaphragm pump's intake and a water source (the lake, buckets, rain barrels) and connect the discharge side to the T-junction tap. Open the kitchen tap (obviously, you could use any tap in the cottage, but I prefer the kitchen tap because it's closer to snack supplies), close the pressure-line in-line valve (which forces the water to flow down the pressure pipe rather than into the pump), open the T-junction tap, and start pumping. As it requires about 1 L of water to fill 3 m of 1-in. poly pipe (1 US gal. for 10 ft. of 1-in. poly), this could take a while if there is plenty of pipe between the cottage pump, water source, and kitchen tap. (Hence the need for snacks.) When the water comes out the kitchen tap, close the T-junction tap, open the in-line valve, and the system is primed, first time, every time. (This method can also be used for lifts less than 12 m or 40 ft.)

With a bit of ingenuity, a priming pipe can even be run down into shallow wells (check with local authorities to make sure this is legal in your cottage area), obviating the need to pull the line out for priming. Recently, on a well not equipped with a priming pipe, my Guzzler and I coaxed water *up* 76 m (250 ft.) of 1-in. line, having a 3-m (10-ft.) lift. With no prime. Now you know why I like hand-operated diaphragm pumps like the Guzzler.

Those blessed with submersible pumps need only open a tap and flick a switch for the pipes to fill with water.

OUT WITH THE ANTIFREEZE

Regardless of pumps or priming techniques, if any antifreeze was used during storage procedures, run the taps until it's flushed out of the system. Also, open the hot-water tank drain tap just enough to bleed the air and ensure that the tank fills with water before you turn it on. Without water in the tank, the heating element could quickly burn out. To reactivate any water-treatment devices, check the appropriate manual. It may be necessary to have the water tested to ensure that the devices are working correctly.

Once the little bit of plumbing required to make priming easy is completed, this annual rite of spring is pared down to a task that takes minutes (instead of weekends). Only a leak in the intake line can cause it to fail, the odds of which are also reduced if the above procedures are followed. The only downside of all this is that you may not be entitled to as many snacks, your fair fee for running between pump, foot valve, and kitchen tap. But then you could just reward yourself for being so clever in having done the job so quickly.

SPRING TURN-ONS: AN OPENING-UP QUICK LIST

- [ ] Connect the intake line, and test for the correct operation of the foot valve and any check valves before putting the line into the water (or connecting to a submersible pump).
- [ ] Prime the pump. (Cottagers with submersibles can skip this step.)
- [ ] Turn on the pump, and flush out any device that wintered with antifreeze.
- [ ] Bleed out any air in the hot-water tank before turning it on.
- [ ] Reactivate any water-treatment devices and ensure that they are all operating correctly before drinking the water.

12 GETTING WATER IN WINTER

Designing a system for use when the temperature plunges

A range of options:
You can simply chop a hole in the ice, or use the pump, same as you do in summer. But if you do, you'll need to take precautions to keep the intake lines from freezing.

SOLITUDE. NO PEOPLE. NO BUGS. ONLY THE snow-muted sounds of nature dare to intrude on the silence. This is a splendour experienced with all the senses. You see the reflected glow of the sun dancing across the snow, hear the silence broken by the cold crack of a tree cutting through the chill, smell and taste the cleanliness of untarnished air, and feel the temperature on your cheeks. Actually, it's damn cold, now that you mention it, which is why most people avoid visiting the cottage in winter.

Then there's the problem of water. Once frozen, water is not very good at flowing through pipes to cottage taps or toilet. But there are ways to sneak around nature's narrow-minded "closed for the season" approach to marketing.

How often you plan to visit plays a key role in your choice of the winter water system best suited to your cottage needs. Don't visit, and you don't need water. Visit for a week and you'll not only need a reliable source of drinking water, you might need a bath too.

BACK TO BASICS: THE HOLE IN THE ICE

You can melt snow or ice in a pot on the stove, but it's a slow process and doesn't produce a heap of water for the effort involved. It is, however, a convenient source for an afternoon stay, perhaps yielding enough water for hot drinks all around. For more water, you're better off poking a hole in the ice, then carting the water up to the cottage in buckets. If the ice isn't thick enough to walk on safely, take a bucket along so you can scoop some water up as you fall through. Of course, there's a good chance you'll drown doing this, so the smart move would be to wait until the ice is sufficiently thick to support your weight and then some (minimum 15 cm or 6 in.). Unfortunately, you will now have to engage in a little work to reach the water and you will need a suitable ice-chopping implement.

TOOLS FOR THE TASK: AXE VS. AUGER
Most neophytes reach for the axe. Long ago,

about the time I ruined two very fine elbows as a result of a day's worth of chop-'til-you-drop forest-management practices, I realized that an axe's role in cottage life is best restricted to horror stories told around late-night fires. The axe as an instrument of serious work is ideal for people who feel *obligated* to work, not for those who *enjoy* work. For instance, up our way, the ice is usually about 1 m (3 ft.) thick by midwinter. My buddy Paul, who has spent much of his life poking holes in ice in search of fish, says that with an axe it takes about a day to hack away a big enough gash in ice that thick to get a small bucket through. With an ice chisel – a 2-m (6-ft.) or so long metal rod about 3 cm–5 cm (1 in.–2 in.) in diameter and bevelled at the chopping end – Paul claims he can carve out a suitably sized hole in about two hours. A hand-operated auger will do the job in 10 minutes. A gas auger cuts through in about a minute. Those keen on preserving the tranquillity of their surroundings should opt for the hand-operated auger, while snowmobilers may prefer gas-powered versions.

Any hole in the ice should be fenced off or, if less than 30 cm (1 ft.) in diameter, marked with a 2-m (6-ft.) vertical stick to warn others of thin ice. A marker also helps to locate the hole later, saving you from having to bore through the thickest part of the ice every time you want a cup of water.

If the water required treating during the summer, chances are it will also need treating during the winter, although microorganisms, like people, aren't as likely to be mucking about when the temperature plummets towards the brass-monkey zone. Boiling or adding iodine tablets should take care of any bacteriological problems, but a batch distiller (see Chapter 6) is arguably the most effective way to treat small quantities of water.

Another option is to import water. It doesn't have to be carbonated or come from France – it can be local treated bottled water, or can even pour right out of your very own city tap. Importing water to the cottage is particularly well suited to day visits, or even the occasional weekend sleep-over, guaranteeing a reliable source of drinking water.

You'll also need a reliable place to dispose of excess bodily fluids. For this, nothing beats an outhouse, ready to serve in any weather. See Chapters 7 and 9 for indoor options.

FOR MORE WATER: WINTERIZING A PRESSURIZED SYSTEM

As in the warmer months, a pump remains the best method of getting larger quantities of water to the cottage. The traditional displacement hand pump can be used all winter if it is situated directly over a well or if the intake line runs at a steep enough slope (see below) to allow the water to self-drain back to its source. The pump must be drained after each use. (See Chapter 11.) The pump's flapper valves can freeze open or shut between uses, a problem solved by pouring a bucket of hot water over the top of the pump (so you might still have to melt some snow when you first get to the cottage).

We used a hand-operated diaphragm pump one winter, carrying the lightweight pump and buckets down to the water, pumping the water through a 1-in. hose into the buckets, and then carting the water and pump back up to the cottage. No worry about frozen lines or electrical power outages, and small holes are much easier to make in the ice than large ones. However, our supply of water was still limited to whatever we could carry.

For cottagers with greater water needs (or less enthusiasm for manual labour), it is possible to operate a pressurized water system during the winter months, just as we do back in the city. Of course, at the cottage the responsibility for keeping the system from freezing is all ours, even in our absence. The intake line, the pump, the pressure lines, the toilets, even the drains must not be allowed to freeze with water in them.

PROS AND CONS OF KEEPING THE HEAT ON
The simplest method of looking after the inside plumbing is to keep the heat on. This

Hole notes:
An auger makes getting through the ice easier. You can carve a suitably sized hole through 1-m (3-ft.) ice in about 10 minutes.

may sound like a decadent cop-out, but if you're visiting the cottage every weekend, it can make economic sense. Any structure possesses thermal inertia, and the more mass to the structure, the more inertia. When it's cold, the structure resists warming; conversely, when it's warm, it resists cooling. Therefore, if the structure is well insulated, maintaining heat in the building during short absences may consume less energy than what is required to reheat the structure left unheated. The key is to correctly install insulation and eliminate drafts while still allowing for ventilation. These topics are beyond the scope of this book, but there is no shortage of good information, much of it direct from government sources.

The problem with heat left on during your absence is that, in most of its permutations, it necessitates reliance on the electric company. This is undoubtedly a gamble – one lengthy power outage could burst pipes, pump, and fixtures, subsequently flooding the cottage when the heat comes back on. Power outages are more prevalent in outlying areas (like cottage country) than in major cities. If you don't feel comfortable with the gamble, have a trusted neighbour keep an eye on your cottage when you are away to minimize the risks.

Of course, you can eliminate those risks entirely by putting the cottage into storage each time you leave. This is not a difficult or time-consuming task if the plumbing has been installed to allow for easy self-draining. For periods of absence that extend beyond a couple of weeks, it's hard to justify heating the cottage, at least from an economic standpoint; and the longer you are away, the greater the risk of a power outage. Even if the heat remains on at a minimum setting to protect the structure, if you empty the pipes you'll never need to worry about whether the power is off or how you are going to repair any ice-damaged plumbing. Regardless, make sure that all outside taps are drained, or are of the "freeze-proof" type.

ARRANGE THE PLUMBING FOR HEATING EASE

A centralized plumbing layout works best for cottages doing wintertime duty. An arrangement where the kitchen, bathroom, and pump room are placed back to back to back saves money in supplies and facilitates easy draining. It also allows you the option of heating only those spaces housing the plumbing. And you can shrink the heated spaces even further, tucking the pump into a bathroom closet or similar cubbyhole. If this downsized pump room is extremely well insulated, heat loss and the transfer of pump noise are both reduced; a single 500W electric heater should be more than adequate to keep things warm, the insulation holding that heat in even during short power outages. However, the rest of the cottage water system will still have to be put into storage between visits.

WINTERIZING THE OUTSIDE LINES

Whether the water source is a lake, river, well, or reservoir, the greatest challenge to keeping the water flowing to the cottage is usually the line in. Often, it just sits exposed to whatever the climate, the snow gods, or humanity care to throw at it. A much better place for this pipe is underground, buried below the frost line – the depth below which the earth doesn't freeze. In most northern states and Canada, the frost line resides about 1 m–1.5 m (3 ft.–5 ft.) below the surface. It *is* possible, however, to artificially lower or raise the frost line.

CAPITALIZING ON NATURAL INSULATION

The earth above a pipe acts as an insulator. Insulation works by trapping millions of tiny air pockets within itself, making it difficult for the air to move around and swap heat for cold. This is true regardless of the insulating medium, whether it is fibreglass batts, expanded polystyrene, wood, snow, or dirt. If we compress any of these materials, the insulating properties are diminished. How do we compress dirt? Driving over it in the family wagon is a good method, although even the weight of our feet tramping over it is enough to "push" the frost line downward. Therefore water lines, both incoming lines and drain pipes, should not run under driveways or pathways. If there is no alternative, bury the line deep enough to compensate for the lost insulating factor above. Or avoid tramping over the area during winter months.

INCREASING THE INSULATION: BUILD A STYROFOAM BOX

Snow makes a pretty good insulator – hard to beat the price, but it's easily compressed. (See Chapter 7 for winter cautions related to septic beds.) One of the best insulators for underground applications is Styrofoam SM (a closed-cell extruded polystyrene manufactured by Dow Chemical). As a guide, 2.5 cm (1 in.) of SM is equivalent to about 30 cm (1 ft.) of earth. Because the heat of the earth can escape both upwards and sideways, it is necessary to insulate the top and sides of the pipe, building an upside-down U-shaped box around it. SM comes in 8-ft. lengths that are 2 ft. wide. Cut each piece into thirds lengthwise (creating three 8-in. x 8-ft. pieces), using two of the lengths for the sides of the box and the third for the top.

If the route of the pipe is subterranean, one layer of SM on the sides will usually suffice, but more can be added to the top, these additional layers being the full 2 ft. wide to increase protection. Our incoming water line passes over a chunk of bedrock that restricts burying the incoming line any deeper than 60 cm (2 ft.) at that point. Since the frost line in our area is 1.2 m (4 ft.) deep on average, 2 in. of SM would do the trick; however, we ran the pipe under a pathway (to avoid uprooting trees), so we added another 4 in. to the SM blanket. If the pipe runs close to the surface of a driveway, a U-shaped box of 2 x 10 wood nailed together around the SM box will protect it from compression.

Because water conducts heat faster than air does, if the soil is very moist you need to increase the insulation thickness still further.

I take advantage of another trick, permitted in most jurisdictions: I put the intake line in an outer sleeve of 4-in. corrugated drain pipe. (See Chapter 4 for application tips.) The sleeve prevents rocks or sand from caving in around the pipe, making it possible to remove it from its underground lair if repairs are necessary,

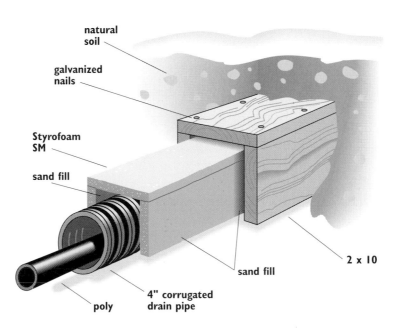

natural soil

galvanized nails

Styrofoam SM

sand fill

poly

4" corrugated drain pipe

sand fill

2 x 10

and then reinsert it without having to dig everything up. The surrounding air space also acts as an insulating buffer zone. Waste lines running to septic or grey water systems are usually of rigid ABS or PVC plastic pipe, and therefore cannot be pulled out of any sleeve for service, so sleeve these pipes only in U-boxed boards or culverts for protection under driveways and such.

Lay the pipes in place (sleeved or unsleeved), prop up the two side pieces of SM, dump in sand around both sides of the SM side walls (don't tamp it down; this only forces out the air pockets), level the sand to the top of the SM, place the upper layer (or layers) of SM over the SM side walls, and cover the whole mess up. (Alter this sequence if necessary to include any U-shaped wood protection.)

Pipe doesn't have to run underground to

Pipe protector:
Insulate your intake line by building a Styrofoam SM box around it, and then a wood box around the SM. If you run the intake line through corrugated drain pipe first, removing the intake line for repairs becomes much easier.

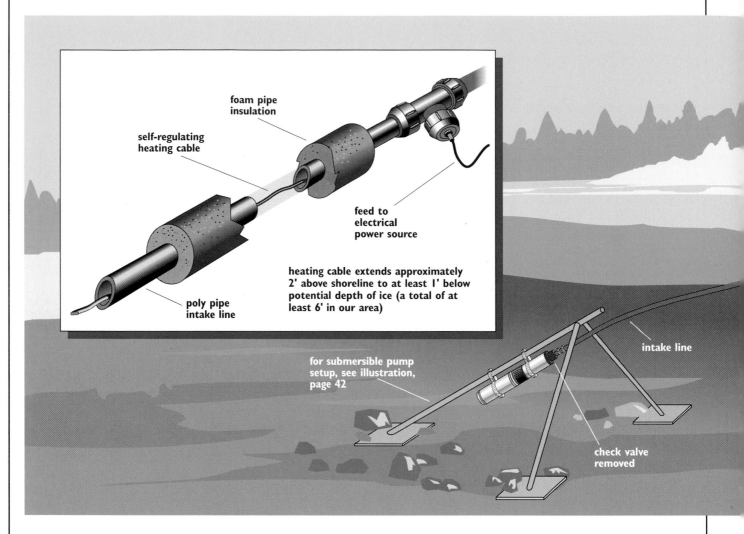

foam pipe
insulation

self-regulating
heating cable

feed to
electrical
power source

poly pipe
intake line

heating cable extends approximately
2' above shoreline to at least 1' below
potential depth of ice (a total of at
least 6' in our area)

for submersible pump
setup, see illustration,
page 42

intake line

check valve
removed

Heated discussion:
Since even a self-draining intake line will not drain past the level of the surface water, you need to heat the section of pipe where intake line meets water source. Your best bet is self-regulating heating cable, which can adjust to changes in temperature all along the pipe.

get this favoured treatment. A mound can be built up over surface-installed pipe. Keep the slopes gentle and plant something with a good root structure (grass, for instance) on top to prevent erosion. A couple of battlements built into the mound should discourage intruders.

Where ice conditions permit, an intake line can be left in a lake or river all winter. In some jurisdictions, however, it can't be buried into the shoreline. (Check with local authorities: Fines can range up to $300,000 for some lakeshore disruptions.) When the intake pipe has to enter the water above ground, use a section of rigid 4-in. ABS drainage pipe for a sleeve. This material is less likely to be crushed by ice than corrugated drain pipe. The problem with surface lines at water's edge is that any attempt to insulate them can easily be torn apart by winter's wrath. Depending on the size of the intake line and the size of the

sleeve, it may be possible to wrap the intake line in polyethylene foam pipe insulation before sliding it into the outer sleeve.

OTHER OPTIONS FOR ABOVE-GROUND LINES

Two other options for above-ground applications are self-draining intake lines and heated lines. The optimum solution often involves a combination of insulation, self-drainage, and electric heating cable.

SELF-DRAINING INTAKE LINES

A self-draining intake line allows water to flow to the cottage and fill the pressure tank before automatically draining back to the water source, leaving the intake line empty. This cycle repeats each time the pressure switch on the pressure tank signals the pump to start

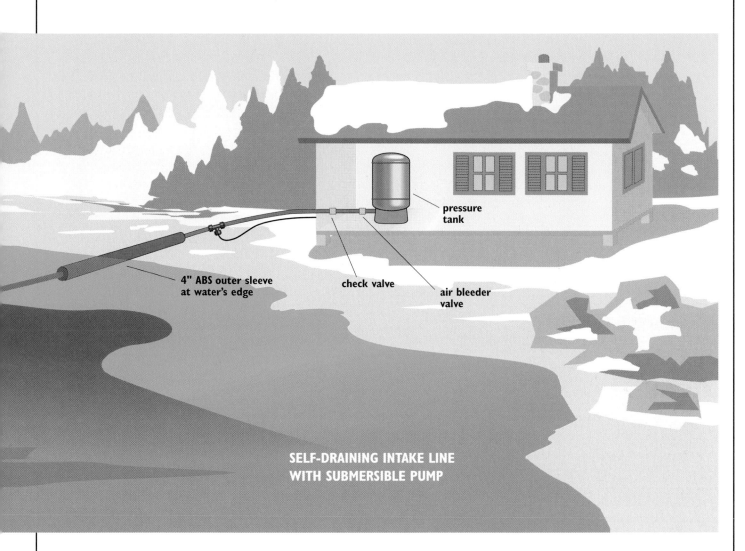

pressure tank

4" ABS outer sleeve at water's edge

check valve

air bleeder valve

SELF-DRAINING INTAKE LINE WITH SUBMERSIBLE PUMP

delivering water. The essential ingredient here is speed – the water must drain out fast enough so as not to freeze. For this to happen, the slope of the line must be increased from the normal minimum of 2 cm per 1 m (¼ in. per ft.) to a minimum slope of 1 in 13. In other words, whether you are measuring in metres, feet, chains, or shoelaces, for every 13 units of measure the line runs horizontally, it must drop a minimum of one unit vertically. If it drops two, so much the better. Because the empty intake line must be filled quickly every time the pressure switch kicks in, most pumps that draw water into the cottage, like piston pumps and jet pumps, won't work for this application. A submersible pump, however, will.

For the water to flow back down the intake line, the check valve usually mounted on the top of the submersible must be removed. This creates a problem: Most manufacturers strongly recommend that a check valve be installed either on the pump itself or in the line within 7.5 m (25 ft.) of the pump. Without this valve, the water will rush back down the line (which is what you want), spinning the submersible motor and impellers up to three times the designated operating speed. In reverse. Obviously, this isn't the best thing one can do for the motor, yet many plumbers are installing submersibles in this manner with no apparent problem. In fact, two of the pump manufacturers I contacted regarding this dilemma stated that while they didn't necessarily approve of the practice, they still lent advice on how to make it work.

First, use only a top-quality submersible pump. Lower-quality models are more likely to wear and break. At the top of the intake line, install a check valve immediately before the pressure tank to prevent water in the cottage system from draining back out the intake line. Just before the check valve, install a two-way air bleeder valve. This valve provides a means for the air to escape out of the line as water is being pushed up to the cottage, and lets air back into the line to hasten the draining of water back down to the source. Without this air bleeder valve, the pipe could burst. (I have yet to find such a valve that doesn't leak a bit, so install it in a heated area of the cottage with some means for collecting the seepage.)

The other crucial element of a self-draining system is the pressure tank. It must have sufficient drawdown (the amount of water drained out of the tank before the pressure switch activates the pump) to permit the water in the intake line to empty before the pump is asked to supply more. Should the signal be given for the pump to start while it is still spinning backwards, the odds are very good that the pump shaft will snap under the strain. How much drawdown is enough? That depends on the model of tank, the pressure your system is operating at (the more pressure, the less drawdown), and the length of the intake line. It takes about one minute for 30 m (100 ft.) of 1-in. intake line to empty on a 1-in-13 slope, so the pressure tank must have enough drawdown to supply the cottage for that period regardless of how many toilets are flushed, dishwashers started, and showers turned on. Your plumber or plumbing supplier should be able to help you choose a tank of the correct size based on your projected water consumption and the length of the intake line.

An alternative for cottagers reluctant to go against manufacturers' wishes is to drill a $\frac{1}{16}$-in. hole in the submersible pump's check-valve housing, between the valve itself and where the pipe gets connected to the valve housing. Although that hole seems very small, according to the plumbers I have consulted it is more than adequate to drain the water back down out of the pipe, and its diminutive size means no noticeable loss in pressure. However, that tiny hole can clog easily. If this should happen, you won't know about it until the line freezes. Boy, when it comes to gambling,

Las Vegas has nothing on cottage country.

The Achilles heel of the self-draining intake line is that the water will not drain past the level of the source water. If the source is anything but a deep well, the water in the pipe at the point where the intake line meets the source is subject to freezing, which kind of defeats the whole purpose of self-draining. Unless you heat that short section of pipe.

There are two basic types of electric heating cable: conventional heating cable and self-regulating cable, with each of these categories further divided into cable that is wrapped around the exterior of a pipe and cable that is inserted into a pipe.

CONVENTIONAL HEATING CABLE

Conventional heating cable works on the same principle that the majority of simple electric heating devices operate on: electricity is passed through a heating element, which provides a fixed amount of resistance to the flow of electrons, resulting in internal friction which in turn causes the element to heat up. By attaching a thermostat to the element's electrical feed, we can control how much electricity flows through the element over a given period of time; the thermostat turns the power feed off or on as the temperature rises or falls in order to maintain preset levels (an action called duty cycling).

The location of the thermostat's sensing unit is very important for accurate temperature control. As an illustration, if the sensing unit of an oven thermostat were placed in the refrigerator, the oven's heating elements would be instructed to work overtime to overcome the cold registered by the misplaced sensing unit. Obviously, the oven would get much hotter than what the setting on the thermostat called for. Goodbye, Sunday-night roast; hello, smoke detector.

Correct placement of an oven thermostat's sensing unit is an easy matter – stick it in, or next to, the oven. Unfortunately, life is not that simple with conventional heating cable. While the oven is a small, controlled environment, an outdoor pipe may have to cope with a variety of temperatures over its length. For instance, at water's edge, the temperature of an intake line can be close to the freezing mark; a few feet up from there, perhaps where the line runs out in the open over bedrock, the temperature will fluctuate with atmospheric conditions (which include ambient temperature, cooling from the wind, and heat from the sun). The section running under the cottage, meanwhile, could conceivably rise to well above freezing when the cottage is heated during visits. So where do you put the sensing unit? You compromise and put it somewhere between the fridge and the oven and hope for the best.

A pipe heated by conventional cable must always have water in it. Any loss of prime – the result of a foot valve failure, for instance – and the pipe could overheat to the point of meltdown. Granted, this may not rival Chernobyl, but it could result in a weekend disaster nonetheless. The problem is that the amount of heat generated by a conventional heating element, like this cable, is constant throughout the length of the element. It is unable to compensate for varying conditions, such as the sudden loss of water.

Conventional cable is also difficult to insulate without causing overheating. And it's an expensive way to heat too: Heat tends to migrate to the coldest regions, so much of the cable's heat is lost to the surrounding air, which is energy and dollars tossed to the wind. For all these reasons, if you decide that an electric heating cable is the route to go, pry open the wallet a little farther and install self-regulating cable.

SELF-REGULATING HEATING CABLE

Right up front, self-regulating cable will cost you about twice what conventional heating cable will. What do you get for the extra bucks? You get a cable that contains two wires separated by a thin layer of temperature-sensitive conductive material. As the temperature drops, resistance to the flow of electrons through this conductor increases, automatically

DEFROSTING FROZEN PIPES

Despite all your efforts, it's possible that water left in cottage pipes may freeze. Electricity gets cut off in a storm, no one is around to notice, the temperature drops, and quicker than you can read about repairing burst pipes, the water freezes.

With self-draining intake lines, the trouble spot lies at water's edge. Fortunately, when water freezes and expands at this point, the empty intake line above the water tends to encourage any ice forming to creep upward inside the pipe, rather than push outward. When the electric heating cable comes back on, it will melt the ice and water will once again flow through the line. At least most times. Plastic pipe, like poly, has some elasticity to it, allowing some outward expansion without *visible* damage. It is subject to fatigue over time, however, and hairline cracks may develop.

Speaking of repairs, avoid joints whenever possible and, in particular, near the water's edge. Joints are usually the weakest link in the system and, as a result, the spot most likely to be damaged in a freeze-up.

If a pipe without electric heating cable freezes, there are a few tricks for thawing it out (assuming it hasn't burst, in which case you must replace the damaged section). First, open any taps at both ends of the frozen section. This allows steam and air to escape without putting more pressure on the beleaguered pipe. Next, heat the pipe *slowly,* starting at the point closest to one of the taps, and working back as the ice thaws. If you start in the middle, steam pressure will build and, unable to get past the ice to the open tap, it could burst the pipe, ruining the pipe, your weekend, and possibly you.

Metal pipes can be heated with a propane torch, but be very careful with the flame in a confined area. With all your attention devoted to the job at hand, you may not notice that floor joist directly behind the pipe as the flame scorches it. Cold, wet rags placed over vulnerable areas (like the whole cottage?) will discourage the flame from heating up anything but the pipe. A hair dryer will also work on metal, and on plastic pipes too, but extra caution is advised in heating plastic. (Don't even *think* about heating plastic with a torch.) Hot, damp towels also work well for thawing plastic pipes, assuming you've got some place to heat wet towels.

Once you and the pipes are thawed, check the system for leaks and then, if possible, correct the problem that caused the pipes to freeze in the first place. Or, better yet, drain the system when you leave.

creating more friction and therefore more heat. Conversely, as the temperature rises, resistance decreases and less heat is generated. This happens over the entire length of cable, at each point along that cable. It's like having a million sensing units, each attached to its own tiny heating element.

Unlike conventional cable, a self-regulating cable will not overheat in an empty pipe. This makes it the best choice for heating self-draining intake lines at water's edge, where conditions inside the pipe can range from freezing at the water line, to above freezing below the water line, to extremely cold and devoid of water above the water line, all in the space of a few feet.

Regardless of which type of heating cable you choose, the water inside the pipe can still freeze. The power can go off, leaving the water to fend for itself. And if the pipe is situated in the open air and uninsulated, at about –25°C (–15°F) most heating cables are no longer able to create sufficient heat to offset the extreme cold. Then there's the wind. Wind cools off the water in a pipe the way it cools off the water in your car radiator. As the wind robs heat from the pipe, the heater's ability to cope is further reduced. Just getting the pipe out of the wind helps, but insulating it is what really makes a difference.

IT'S STILL A GOOD IDEA TO INSULATE

Because of its ability to adjust heat output based on a very localized demand, self-regulating cable allows you to insulate the pipe without fear of a meltdown. This is perhaps the greatest advantage of this type of cable. Such systems, out in the open with only ½ in. of polyethylene foam pipe wrap, are being used in the Northwest Territories in temperatures that regularly drop below –50°C (bloody cold F). As a bonus, when pipes are insulated, if a power failure should occur, freezing is delayed since the water retains heat for much longer periods. Insulation also keeps the water cooler in summer. And of particular appeal to my world-renowned parsimonious nature, insulating a heated water line results in serious savings on the electrical bill.

And it gets even better. A central thermostat can be hooked up to a self-regulating cable as a master control over those "million sensing units". According to one manufacturer, with this thermostat set to about 10°C (45°F), and its sensing unit tucked in between the outer pipe wall and the insulation, electrical consumption can be as little as 10% of the energy required to operate an uninsulated conventional heated line. Even if we factor in marketing braggadocio, and this setup only achieves half those savings, that's still worth bragging about. And while you may need a dedicated 240V circuit for conventional heating cable over 23 m (75 ft.) long, self-regulating cable gets by with the standard 120V circuit.

IN OR OUT: WHERE TO PUT THE CABLE

Heating cable can be wrapped around the exterior of a pipe or inserted through it. While exterior cable can be used for intake lines, it is more susceptible to damage by nature and humans. Therefore, interior cable is the better choice for intake duty. Also, even when the pipe isn't insulated, interior cable loses less heat to the world around it than exterior cable does.

Interior heating cable can be purchased pre-installed in poly pipe or separately, in a kit, to allow installation into an existing intake line.

In theory, a cable running inside the intake line can increase head loss, although in practice this concern appears to be unwarranted. Nonetheless, as a basic guide, 30 m (100 ft.) is considered the maximum for 1-in. line housing heating cable, while 1¼-in. line is good for about 90 m (300 ft.). Use only cable that has CSA, UL, or similar approval for use inside a water pipe. Cable not approved for this *specific* application has not been successfully tested by a recognized agency for off-gassing and toxicity levels, and should never see duty inside any pipe.

Interior cable should not be used for waste lines because it will restrict the flow of sewage. It also makes unplugging a plugged sewage line expensive, difficult, and a downright gucky job. (Picture having to withdraw from your waste pipe 100 ft. of cable dipped in … actually, it's too revolting to picture, so skip it.) If a sewage line needs to be heated – where it runs above ground from a raised cottage to a raised septic bed, for instance – use heating cable designed to be wrapped around the exterior of the pipe. Exterior cable can also be wrapped around the water box of a pump (but not the motor) if the pump is located in an unheated space. (This can be done with both water and sewage pumps.)

HEATED RECOMMENDATIONS: GO THE SELF-REGULATING ROUTE

For heating the cottage intake line, my personal preference leans towards self-regulating cable tied into a central thermostat, with the pipe well insulated. This system provides optimum protection and is economical to use. Heat-Line Corporation does a particularly nice job of putting together a cottager-friendly package that requires no special skills to install. Everything is designed to simply plug in – the cable into a standard electrical outlet (the plug has a built-in GFI), the company's thermostat into a standard outlet. Even the pipe, which you can purchase with cable and insulation pre-installed, essentially plugs into an existing pipe leading to the pump or pressure tank using a special PolyGrip (see Chapter 4) connector made especially for Heat-Line. The assembled cable with PolyGrip connector can be purchased separately for retrofitting, as can the company's pipe insulation, a ⅝-in. thick polyethylene foam that is manufactured *without* the use of chlorofluorocarbons (CFCs). Neat stuff.

As an aside, if you have a deep-well jet pump that needs protection from freezing, you've got two lines to heat, which doubles both your initial investment and your operating costs. Bury the line or sell the pump and get a submersible.

Cottaging in general is an escape from hectic lifestyles, but particularly so in winter when the tranquillity of a snoozing, snow-covered world surrounds all those adventurous enough to brave the cold. So why not try a few week-ends of winter roughing it? Whether you're hauling water from the lake or having it pour through heated lines, it's tough to beat the splendour.

13 BOOKS AND PRODUCTS

Where to go for more information

LISTED BELOW ARE THE MANUFACTURERS OF some of the products mentioned in this book. These are not the only manufacturers of such products by any means; this is simply a list of places to start your search. (The manufacturers of products more easily located in retail outlets are not included here.) Although I have no reason to doubt the integrity of any of these companies, from here on, it's buyer beware; you're on your own in the big and sometimes unforgiving world of business and commerce.

I have also included relevant organizations that you can contact for more information, and a recommended reading list.

ELECTRIC HEATING CABLE

Heat-Line Corp., 116 Fleetwood Rd., Lindsay, ON K9V 6G6, (705) 324-6781/800-584-4944, fax: (705) 324-9174
e-mail: info@heatline.com
website: www.heatline.com

BICC Pyrotenax Ltd.,(CAN) 250 West St., Trenton, ON K8V 5S2, (613) 392-6571/800-461-9583, fax: (613) 392-4555/800-410-8677
website: www.bicc-pyrotenax.com

(U.S.) 6507 Basile Rowe, East Syracuse, NY 13057, (315) 433-1166/800-839-5956, fax: (315) 433-2339

e-mail: info@bicc-pyrotenax.com
website: www.bicc-pyrotenax.com

FOOT VALVE INTAKE FILTERS

Precise Solutions, 100 Lancing Dr., Unit 10, Hamilton, ON L8W 3L6, (905) 575-9458/800-668-2183, fax: (905) 575-9458
e-mail: info@precisesolutions.com
website: www.precisesolutions.com

PIPE, FITTINGS, ETC

POLYGRIP

G.W.M. Industries Ltd., 12485 82nd Ave., Surrey, BC V3W 3E8 *(Also availible through Heat-Line, see Electric Heating Cable.)*, (604) 501-0258/800-993-2599, fax: (604) 501-0259
e-mail: johngwm@bc.sympatico.ca
website: www.gwmindustries.com

SOLDERLESS, NON-GLUE PLUMBING CONNECTIONS AND FITTINGS

Push 'N' Turn and Springo: Waterline Products Co. Ltd., 5159 Bradco Blvd., Mississauga, ON L4W 2A6, (905) 625-9440/800-361-3773 (CAN), fax: (905) 625-9481
e-mail: wpcli@sympatico.ca

BACK FLOW PREVENTORS, PRESSURE RELIEF VALVES

Watts Industries (Can) Inc., 5435 N. Service Rd., Burlington, ON L7L 5H7, (905) 332-4090/888-208-8927, fax: (905) 332-7068

e-mail: sales@wattscda.com
website: www.wattscda.com

Watts Industries (U.S.), 815 Chestnut St., North Andover, MA 01845-6098, (978) 688-1811, fax: (978) 975-8350
website: www.wattsind.com

PLASTIC SEPTIC TANKS AND WATER STORAGE CONTAINERS

Xactics Containers Ltd., 499 Calixa-Lavallee St., Joliette, QC J6E 7E2, (450) 756-0531/800-668-9228, fax: (450) 756-1127
e-mail: info@xactics.com
website: www.xactics.com

PRECAST CONCRETE SEPTIC TANKS, CISTERNS, WELL TILES

National Precast Concrete Association, 10333 North Meridian St., Suite 272, Indianapolis, IN 46290 (*List of member manufacturers in Canada and U.S.*), (317) 571-9500/800-366-7731, fax: (317) 571-0041
e-mail: npca@precast.org
website: www.precast.org

PUMPS

GOULDS

Canada: **ITT Industries**, Goulds Pumps, 55 Royal Rd., Guelph, ON N1H 1T1, (519) 826-0869/888-488-4033, fax: (519) 826-0874
e-mail: rbarg@goulds.com
website: www.goulds.com

US: **ITT Industries**, Goulds Pumps, 240 Fall St., Seneca Falls, NY 13148, (315) 568-2811, fax: (315) 568-2418
website: www.goulds.com

GUZZLER

Canada: **Rintoul's Hand Pumps**, 1225 Dorcas Bay Rd., RR 2, Tobermory, ON N0H 2R0, (519) 596-2612, fax: (519) 596-2612
e-mail: handpump@kanservu.ca
website: www.handpumps.com

US: **Bosworth Co.**, 930 Waterman Ave., East Providence, RI 02914, (401) 438-1110/888-438-1110, fax: (401) 438-2713

GRUNDFOS

Grundfos Canada Inc., 2941 Brighton Rd., Oakville, ON L6H 6C9, (905) 829-9533, fax: (905) 829-9512
e-mail: mhalter@grundfos.com
website: www.grundfos.com

Grundfos Pumps Corp., 3131 N. Business Park. Fresno, CA 93727, (209) 292-8000, fax: (209) 291-1357
e-mail: tkeierle@grundfos.com
website: www.us.grundfos.com

MCDONALD

A.Y. McDonald Mfg. Co., 4800 Chavenelle Rd., Dubuque, Iowa, 52004-0508, (319) 583-7311/800-292-2737, fax: (319) 588-0720
e-mail: sales@aymcdonaldmfg.com
website: www.aymcdonaldmfg.com

SEPTIC SYSTEMS

(information on alternative systems)

Centre for Research in Earth and Space Technology (CRESTech), University of Waterloo, Waterloo, ON N2L 3G1, (519) 885-5466, fax: (519) 888-4333
e-mail: lgeltho@admin.crestech.ca
website: www.crestech.ca

SOLAR INFORMATION

The American Solar Energy Society, 2400 Central Ave., Unit G-1, Boulder, CO 80301 (*Information on solar energy.*), (303) 443-3130, fax: (303) 443-3212
e-mail: ases@ases.org
website: www.ases.org/solar

Brace Research Institute, MacDonald College of McGill University, 21111 Lakeshore Rd., Ste. Anne de Bellevue, QC H9X 3V9 (*Information and plans for solar water heating, solar distillation, and home-made water pumps for irrigation.*), (514) 398-7833, fax: (514) 398-7767
e-mail: ae12000@musica.mcgill.ca
website: www.agrenv.mcgill.ca/facility/brace/brace.htm

Florida Solar Energy Center, 1679 Clearlake Rd., Cocoa, Florida, 32922 (*Information on solar water heating and solar water distillation.*), (407) 638-1000, fax: (407) 638-1010
website: www.fsec.ucf.edu

Solar Energy Industries Association, 122 C St. NW, 4th Floor, Washington, DC 20001-2109 (*List of member industries within U.S.*), (202) 383-2600, fax: (202) 383-2670
e-mail: info@seia.org
website: www.seia.org/main.htm

Solar Energy Society of Canada Inc., 116 Lisgar St., Suite 702, Ottawa, ON K2P 0C2 (*Information on solar energy. Publishes SOL, a renewable energy magazine; the Canadian Renewable Energy Guide 2nd Edition; and various renewable energy brochures.*), (613) 234-4151, fax: (613) 234-2988
e-mail: sesci@cyberus.ca
website: www.solarenergysociety.ca

SOLAR PRODUCTS

PASSIVE THERMOSYPHON SOLAR HOT WATER HEATERS

Copper Sunsation Systems, Radco Products, Inc., 2877 Industrial Parkway, Santa Maria, CA 93455, (805) 928-1881/800-927-2326, fax: (805) 928-5587
e-mail: radcoproducts@utech.net

PHOTOVOLTAIC SOLAR HOT WATER HEATERS

Thermo Dynamics Ltd, 44 Borden Ave., Dartmouth, NS B3B 1C8, (902) 468-1001, fax: (902) 468-1002
e-mail: solarinfo@thermo-dynamics.com
website: www.thermo-dynamics.com

TOILETS, COMPOSTING

BIOLET

Canada: **BioLet Toilets Ltd.**, 2255 Queen St. E., Suite 801, Toronto, ON M4E 1G3, (416) 693-7150/800-6BIOLET (800-624-6538), fax: (416) 693-0282

e-mail: biolet.ca@sympatico.ca
website: www.biolet.com

BioLet USA, 45 Newbury St., Boston, MA 02116, (617) 578-0435/800-5BIOLET (800-524-6538), fax: (617) 578-0465
e-mail: info@biolet.com
website: www.biolet.com

ENVIROLET

Sancor Industries Ltd., 140-30 Milner Ave., Scarborough, ON, M1S 3R3, (416) 299-4818/800-387-5245 (CAN)/800-387-5126 (US), fax: (416) 299-3124
e-mail: sancor@envirolet.com
website: www.envirolet.com

SUN-MAR

Canada: **Sun-Mar Corporation**, 5035 N. Service Rd., C9&10, Burlington, ON, L7L 5V2, (905) 332-1314/800-461-2461, fax: (905) 332-1315
e-mail: compost@sun-mar.com
website: www.sun-mar.com

US: **Sun-Mar Corporation**, 600 Main St., Tonawanda, NY, 14151, (800) 461-2461, fax: (905) 332-1315
e-mail: compost@sun-mar.com
website: www.sun-mar.com

TOILETS, INCINERATING

INCINOLET

Canada: **INCINOLET Products**, 2022 7th Ave. E., Owen Sound, ON N4K 6R9, (519) 372-1668/800-263-0379, fax: (519) 372-1642
e-mail: incinolet@bmts.com
website: www.bmts.com/~incinolet

US: **Research Products/Blankenship**, 2639 Andjon, Dallas, TX, 75220, (214) 358-4238/800-527-5551, fax: (214) 350-7919
e-mail: incinolet@incinolet.com
website: www.incinolet.com

STORBURN

Storburn International Inc., 47 Copernicus Blvd., Unit 3, Brantford, ON N3P 1N4, (519) 752-8521/800-876-2286, fax: (519) 752-5827
e-mail: storburn@sympatico.ca
website: www3.sympatico.ca/storburn

TOILETS, LOW VOLUME

(with self-contained sewage pump)

SANIPLUS

Canada: **Sanitary For All Ltd.**, 41-6535 Millcreek Dr., Mississauga, ON L5N 2M2, (905) 821-7731/800-36 FLUSH (800-363-5874), fax: (905) 821-4800
e-mail: sales@saniflo.com
website: www.saniflo.com

US: **Sanitary For All Inc.**, 5 Columbia Dr., Suite 472, Niagara Falls, NY 14305-1275, (800) 36 FLUSH (800-363-5874), fax: (905) 821-4800
e-mail: sales@saniflo.com
website: www.saniflo.com

WATER SAVERS

Brass Craft Canada Ltd., 35 Currah Rd., St. Thomas, ON N5P 3R2, (519) 633-0340/800-265-4322, fax: (519) 631-0777
website: www.brasscraft.com

Brass Craft Inc., 39600 Orchard Hill Place, Novi, MI 48375, (248) 305-6000, fax: (248) 305-6011
website: www.brasscraft.com

WATER TREATMENT INFO

Canadian Bottled Water Association, 70 East Beaver Creek Rd., Suite 203-1, Richmond Hill, ON L4B 3B2, (905) 886-6928, fax: (905) 886-9531
e-mail: ecgriswood@aol.com

International Bottled Water Association, 1700 Diagonal Rd., Suite 650, Alexandria, VA 22314, (703) 683-5213/800-WATER-11 (800-928-3711), fax: (703) 683-4074
website: www.bottledwater.org

Canadian Water Quality Association, 295 The West Mall, Suite 330, Toronto, ON M9C 4Z4, (416) 695-3068, fax: (416) 695-2945
e-mail: cwqa@ican.net
website: www.cwqa.com

Water Quality Association, 4151 Naperville Rd, Lisle, IL 60532, (630) 505-0160/800-749-0234, fax: (630) 505-9637
e-mail: info@mail.wqa.org
website: www.wqa.org

WATER TREATMENT: DEMAND-RELEASE IODINATED RESINS

Stuart and Miller Inc. Water Purification Products, 181 Big Bay Point Rd., Barrie, ON L4N 8M5, (705) 728-4599/800-309-9977, fax: (705) 728-8972

WATER TREATMENT: DISTILLERS

Polar Bear Water Distillers Mfg. Co. Ltd., PO Box 113, Pickardville, AB T0G 1W0, (403) 349-4872/800-363-7845, fax: (403) 349-5904

Waterwise Inc., 3608 Parkway Blvd., PO box 494000, Lessburg, FL 32749-4000, (352) 787-5008/800-874-9028, fax: (352) 787-8123
e-mail: questions@waterwise.com
website: www.waterwise.com

WATER TREATMENT: STANDARD FILTERS

Envirogard Products Ltd., PO Box 64, Richmond Hill, ON L4C 4X9, (905) 884-9388/800-667-8072, fax: (905) 884-3532

General Ecology Inc., 151 Sheree Blvd, Exton, PA 19341, (610) 636-7900/800-441-8166 (US), fax: (610) 363-0412
e-mail: gecology@ix.netcom.com
website: www.general-ecology.com

Keystone Filter, 2385 North Penn Rd., Hatfield, PA
19440, (800) 822-1963, fax: (215) 997-1839
e-mail: filters@keystone-filter.com
website: (2 sites) www.met-procom/keystone.html
www.keystonefilter.thomasregister.com/olc/keystone-
filter/home.htm

WATER TREATMENT: TANK FILTERS

Braswell Water Quality Systems, 415 East Washington,
Jackson, MO 63755, (573) 243-3660

Kinetico Canada Ltd., 7675 Baldwin St., Brooklyn, ON L0B
1C0, (905) 655-7777/800-463-3668, fax: (905) 655-8274
e-mail: kinetico@idirect.com
website: www.kinetico.com

Kinetico Inc., 10845 Kinsman, Newbury, OH 44064,
(440) 564-9111/800-944-9283, fax: (440) 564-9541
e-mail: custserv@kinetico.com
website: www.kinetico.com

RainSoft, Div of Aquior Partners LP (Water Treatment
Co.), 2080 E. Lunt Ave., Elk Grove Village, IL 60007,
(847) 437-9400/800-860-7638, fax: (847) 437-1594
e-mail: custserv@rainsoft.com
website: www.rainsoft.com

WATER TREATMENT: UV

Atlantic Ultraviolet Corp, 375 Marcus Blvd., Haup-
pauge, NY 11788, (516) 273-0500, fax: (516) 273-0771
e-mail: info@atlanticuv.com
website: www.atlanticuv.com

Trojan Technologies Inc, 3020 Gore Rd., London,
ON N5V 4T7, (519) 457-3400/800-265-5774, fax: (519)
457-3030
website: www.trojanuv.com

WELLS

(information, well drillers, pump manufacturers, etc.)

Canada: **Canadian Ground Water Association**, PO Box 60,
Lousana, AB T0M 1K0, (403) 749-2331, fax: (403) 749-2958
e-mail: cgwa@agt.net

US: **National Ground Water Association**, 601 Dempsey
Rd., Westerville, OH 43081, (614) 898-7791/800-551-
7379, fax: (614) 898-7786
e-mail: ngwa@ngwa.org
website: www.ngwa.org

WINDMILLS

Aermotor Windmill Co. Inc., 4277 Dan Hanks Lane,
PO Box 5110, San Angelo, TX, 76902, (915) 651-
4951/800-854-1656, fax: (915) 651-4958
e-mail: info@aermotorwindmill.com
website: www.aermotorwindmill.com

Koenders Windmills Inc., PO Box 126, 175 First St. E, En-
glefeld, SK S0K 1N0, (306) 287-3702, fax: (306) 287-3657
e-mail: koenders.wind@sk.sympatico.ca
website: www.humboldtsk.com/koenders/index.html

RECOMMENDED FURTHER READING AND HOW-TO BOOKS

Any jurisdictional building, electrical, and plumbing
codes. *(These can usually be borrowed from the local library
when needed.)*

New Complete Do-it-yourself Manual, Reader's Digest, ISBN 0895773783 *(Great reference for anyone who
has a hankering to take up a hammer and saw now and
then; good sections on basic plumbing and electrics.)* Cdn:
Reader's Digest Association (Canada) Ltd, Montreal, PQ
H3V 2V9 US: Reader's Digest Association Inc, Pleas-
antville, NY 10570.

Cottage Life Magazine, 54 St. Patrick St., Toronto, ON
M5T 1V1 *(Published six times a year, a must for anyone who
owns, or would like to own, a cottage.)*, 416-599-2000,
fax: 416-599-0500
e-mail: clmag@cottagelife.com

The Drinking Water Book, Colin Ingram, Ten Speed
Press, Berkeley, CA 1991. ISBN 0898154367 *(A little
doom and gloom, but some worthwhile information and
helpful product assessments.)*

Electrical Code Simplified, P.S. Knight, self-published,
9840 Seacote Rd, Richmond, BC V7A 4A5. ISBN
0920312179 *(Good book for basic wiring principles and
electrical codes. Unlike water and sewage regulations, most
electrical codes and wiring practices differ little between
jurisdictions in North America, however Canadians should
specify the province codes should to pertain to when ordering.)*

The Home Water Supply, Stu Campbell, Storey Books,
1991. ISBN 0882663240 *(Oriented towards Campbell's
own water problems, but some good information nonetheless.)*

Jacuzzi Pumps and Water Systems, Engineering Information. *(More for the professional, this still makes good
reading for those who thrive on mathematical computa-
tions and the theoretical side of bringing the water in.)*

The Specialist, Charles Sale, The Specialist Publishing
Co., 109 LA Mesa Dr., Burlingame, Calif., 94010. *(Turn-
of-the-century humour. Quaint, a good cottage read in between rain showers.)*

The Straight Poop! A Plumber's Tattler, P. Hemp,
Ten Speed Press, 1986. ISBN 0898151465 *(Good reference and how-to for basic plumbing repairs to fixtures and
such, with plenty of name-brand product assessments. Might
be hard to find.)*

The Vanishing American Outhouse, R Barlow, Windmill
Publishing, El Cajon, CA 92020. ISBN 0933846029 *(A
fun read, full of outhouse folklore and great pictures, but a
little weak on the technical side.)*

Water Systems Handbook, Water systems Council,
Chicago, 1977. ISBN 9995280043 *(Good technical reference for students of water systems.)*

14 INDEX

Numbers in bold type indicate illustrations on those pages

THE OBLIGATORY DEPRESSING ENVIRONMENTAL PLEA

Humans tend to be easily drawn into what are known as social traps. Social traps are similar in concept to animal traps, the victim (in this case, us) lured into the trap by some attractive bait. Like other species of animals, we do not notice or perhaps choose to ignore the trap surrounding the bait. For example, the bait may be a new boat that we can only afford to purchase if we don't fix the defective septic system that oozes effluent out onto our yard and from there into the lake. The trap is the destruction of the lake.

The trap is insidious by nature – few notice it has been sprung until it's too late. Yet each time one of us doesn't take the bait, chances improve that Mother Earth will still be a swell place to own a cottage next year, and in all the ensuing years.

Beware of the traps.